Sedated

James Davies is a reader in medical anthropology and mental health at the University of Roehampton, with a PhD in social and medical anthropology from the University of Oxford. He is a qualified psychotherapist (having previously worked in the NHS) and is the co-founder of the Council for Evidence-based Psychiatry (CEP), which is secretariat to the UK All Party Parliamentary Group for Prescribed Drug Dependence.

He has been an expert drug adviser for Public Health England and has appeared on *Today, PM, Newsnight,* Sky News, BBC World News and various national and local radio stations. He is the author of *Cracked: Why Psychiatry is Doing More Harm than Good.*

Sedated

How Modern Capitalism Created our Mental Health Crisis

James Davies

Atlantic Books
London

First published in hardback in Great Britain in 2021 by Atlantic Books, an imprint of Atlantic Books Ltd.

10 9 8 7 6 5 4 3 2

A CIP catalogue record for this book is available from the British Library.

Hardback ISBN: 978 1 78649 984 4
E-book ISBN: 978 1 78649 986 8

Design and typesetting benstudios.co.uk
Printed in Great Britain by Bell and Bain Ltd, Glasgow

Atlantic Books
An imprint of Atlantic Books Ltd
Ormond House
26–27 Boswell Street
London
WC1N 3JZ

www.atlantic-books.co.uk

CONTENTS

For my son, Oliver

INTRODUCTION

Medicine has progressed at an astonishing rate over the last forty years. Just consider the treatment of childhood leukaemia as an example. If in the late 1970s a child had contracted this heartbreaking disease, their chances of survival would have been around 20 per cent. But if a child contracts leukaemia today, their chances of survival are around 80 per cent. This means that outcomes in this area of medicine have improved by a full 300 per cent in the last four decades alone.[1] And this wonderful feat is not only reserved for paediatric oncology, since impressive rates of improvement can also be found in almost every other area of medicine. I say *almost* every other area, as regrettably, there is one exception: the area of psychiatry and mental health.

In fact, in this area not only have clinical outcomes broadly flatlined over the last thirty years, but according to some measures they have actually got worse.[2] And this outlier exists despite tens of billions of pounds having being spent on psychiatric research in the last two decades;[3] despite £18 billion being spent on mental health services annually in the NHS; and despite nearly 25 per cent of the entire UK adult population now being prescribed a psychiatric drug each year.[4] Despite all this spending and wide coverage, the mental health of the country has not been improving over the last two decades. In fact, things appear to have gone from bad to worse. So why are successive governments consistently failing to act? Is this really all down to poor investment and sparse resources, or is there something more ominous about our whole approach to mental health that our politicians have been simply unwilling to confront?

In this book I will provide an answer, by revealing how, since the 1980s, successive governments and big business have worked to promote a new vision of mental health; one that puts at its centre a new kind of person: resilient, optimistic, individualistic and above all, economically productive – the kind of person the new economy needs and wants. As a result of this shift, our entire approach to mental health has radically altered to meet these market demands. We define 'return to health' as a 'return to work'. We blame suffering on faulty minds and brains rather than on harmful social, political and work environments. We promote highly profitable drug interventions, which, if great news for big pharmaceutical corporations, are in the long term holding millions of people back.

I will show how this marketised vision of mental health has stripped our suffering of its deeper meaning and purpose. Consequently, our distress is no longer seen as a vital call to change or as anything potentially transformative or instructive. It has rather become, over the last few decades, an occasion for yet more buying and selling. Whole industries have thrived on the basis of this logic, offering self-interested explanations and solutions for the many pains of living. The cosmetics industry locates our misery in our ageing, the diet industry in our bodily imperfections, the fashion industry in our being passé, and the pharmaceutical industry in our so-called faulty brain chemicals. While each industry offers its own profitable elixir for emotional success, they all share and promote the same consumerist philosophy of suffering: your central problem is not that you've been mis-taught how to understand and engage with your difficulties (your ageing, your trauma, your sadness, your anxiety or grief), but the fact that you experience suffering at all – something that targeted consumption can address. Suffering is the new bad, and failing to consume the right 'remedies' is the new injustice.

This book tells the story of how, since the 1980s, this pro-market agenda has begun to harm both the UK and the West in general, turning our entire approach to mental health into something preoccupied with sedating us, depoliticising our discontent and keeping us productive and subservient to the economic status quo. By putting economic servitude before real individual health and flourishing, our priorities have become dramatically and dangerously misplaced, and more suffering, paradoxically, has been the unhappy result.

I have written this book to do my part in helping to correct this dominant yet misguided approach, and to discuss how we might put things right by understanding and solving the real roots of our mental and emotional distress. To do so, I have travelled widely to speak with leaders in the mental health and associated professions: senior politicians, public officials, civil servants and key academic thought leaders. I have become immersed in the relevant literature and archives, and have spent much time trawling the corridors of power in an attempt to help reform mental health from the inside. From these activities, I've gained invaluable insight into the socio-economic causes of our current mental health crisis, the revelations of which, often strange and disconcerting, litter the pages of this book.

As you follow me through the coming chapters, you will encounter an array of harms caused by the very professions that purport to help us: from the perils of over-medicalisation to excessive psychiatric drug prescribing, growing stigma, rising disability, the overvaluation of ineffective therapies, and poor clinical results. Yet, most crucially, you will also see that these problems did not emerge in a vacuum, but have thrived under the new style of capitalism that has governed us since the 1980s, one favouring a particular type of thinking about mental health and intervention; one that has put the needs of the economy before our own, while anaesthetising us to the often psychosocial roots of our despair. As a result, we are rapidly becoming a nation sedated by mental health interventions that greatly overplay the help they bring; that subtly teach us to accept and endure, rather than to stand up and challenge, the social and relational conditions harming us and holding us back.

In November 2013, in a small, tatty apartment on the Upper West Side of Manhattan, I sat searching the sales figures for perhaps the most influential book in the history of mental health: the *Diagnostic and Statistical Manual of Mental Disorders*, otherwise known simply as the DSM. The DSM, now in its fifth edition, is a weighty 947-page blue and silver tome. It is the book that lists and defines all the mental disorders that psychiatry believes to exist, and with which tens of millions of people across the globe are diagnosed each year.[5]

I was searching for the DSM's sales figures that November evening because the following day, at Columbia University, I was set to deliver a two-hour lecture on the making of the manual. Between 2009 and 2012, with a grant from my university, I'd undertaken research into the DSM's development, trawling its archives in Washington DC and interviewing its leading architects and writers. The data I had gathered appeared to support the growing international criticism of the DSM then playing out internationally in leading newspapers and medical journals.[6]

A central criticism of this sprawling 'book of woe' is that since the 1980s it has unjustifiably expanded the definition of mental illness to encompass more and more domains of human experience. It achieved this by rapidly increasing the number of mental disorders believed to exist (from 106 in the early 1970s to around 370 today), and by progressively lowering the bar for what constitutes a psychiatric disorder (making it easier for any of us to be classed as 'mentally ill').[7] These processes resulted in much of our everyday human distress being wrongly medicalised, pathologised and eventually medicated. Grief at a significant loss, struggling to reach orgasm, experiencing lack of concentration at school, undergoing trauma, feeling anxious about public events or simply underperforming at work are just some of the manifold painful human experiences that the DSM has medically rebranded as symptoms of psychiatric illness.

What strengthened the international critique was that this expansion occurred without any real biological justification. Unlike for most physical illnesses in general medicine (e.g. heart disease, cancer and infectious diseases), no biological causes have been found for the vast majority of mental disorders in the DSM. This explains why there are still no blood or urine tests, no scans, X-rays or other objective assessments that can verify any psychiatric diagnosis. There are simply no discovered biological abnormalities for which to test. Psychiatric labels, in other words, do not correspond to known biological pathologies that treatments can then target and 'cure'. They are rather socially constructed labels ascribed to collections of feelings and behaviours deemed disordered or pathological by the psychiatric committees who compiled the DSM.

Given that the manual's expansion was therefore not driven by advancements in neurobiological research (DSM disorders were not first discovered in our biology and then later added to the book), on what basis did it so rapidly expand? Well, that was the question I set out to discuss in my seminar the very next day, and I did so by first citing research showing that its expansion largely occurred by way of committee consensus[8] – that is, through small teams of psychiatrists coming together and reaching agreements among themselves about whether new disorders should be devised and included, how they should be defined and what symptom thresholds people must meet to receive a diagnosis. The fact that these agreements were mostly made in the face of weak and contradictory evidence has long been a bone of contention in the mental health community. As one of the most important figures in the seminal edition of the DSM (DSM-III) summarised rather well: 'There was very little systematic research [guiding the creation of the DSM], and much of the research that existed was really a hodgepodge – scattered, inconsistent, and ambiguous. I think the majority of us recognised that the amount of good, solid science upon which we were making our decisions was pretty modest.'[9]

Given that the evidence base was scattered and ambiguous, how was DSM committee agreement eventually reached? According to the archival and interview data regarding the most important modern edition,[10] it was mostly done by way of committee vote. One leading member of the DSM-III committee described to me a typical voting process: 'Some things were discussed over a number of different meetings, [which would sometimes be] followed by an exchange of memoranda about it, and then there would simply be a vote ... people would raise hands, there weren't that many people.' Another said: 'We had very little in the way of data, so we were forced to rely on clinical consensus, which, admittedly, is a very poor way to do things. But it was better than anything else we had ... If people were divided, the matter would be eventually decided by a vote.'[11]

The DSM's categorisation of diverse human experiences into approximately 370 separate psychiatric disorders was not, then, the outcome of solid neurobiological research. It was mostly based on vote-based judgements reached by small, select groups of DSM psychiatrists – judgements then ratified and seemingly scientifically legitimised by their inclusion in the manual.

The fact that the majority of these psychiatrists (including the DSM's three previous chairs) also had financial ties to the pharmaceutical industry is of course hardly inconsequential, given that the industry has profited immensely from the vast expansion of DSM that such financially conflicted psychiatrists have engineered.[12]

As I sat in that Manhattan apartment, searching for the DSM's sales figures, I soon stumbled upon a webpage that made me sit bolt upright: DSM-5, its most recent edition, had somehow managed to reach *number one* on Amazon's bestseller list. Odder still, it turned out that it had been in the Amazon top ten for six months since its publication earlier that year. To give you a sense of scale: the most recent Harry Potter book came in at number six, while *Fifty Shades of Grey* was listed at number nine. But what bemused me more was that DSM-5 cost a whopping $88 a copy (in paperback). So who on earth was buying this vast and pricey dictionary of distress?

The following day, I put that question to a professor working in the Department of Psychology at New York University. While undertaking research in the New York State primary care sector, she had discovered why DSM sales were so high: 'The bottom line is that the pharmaceutical industry has been buying DSM in bulk and then distributing copies for free to clinicians up and down the country,' she said. 'That's why the figures are soaring.' For her, it was obvious why the pharmaceutical industry would do this: 'As almost any kind of suffering is caught by the DSM, disseminating it is just good business: it drives up diagnosis rates and with this, prescriptions.' Indeed, as the most important chairperson in the history of the DSM, Robert Spitzer, later acknowledged: 'the pharmaceuticals were delighted' with the manual's widespread medicalisation of distress, as it created a vast and highly profitable market for their products.[13]

The above claim about pharma's distribution of DSM[14] is perfectly consistent with what we have come to learn about the tactics drugs companies have deployed over the last thirty years to aggressively promote psychiatric drugs, on both sides of the Atlantic. The truth is, since the 1990s, the pharmaceutical industry has been a major financial sponsor of UK and US academic psychiatry, significantly shaping psychiatric research, training and practice within the field.[15] It has also opaquely funded many influential mental health charities, patient groups, heads of psychiatry departments,[16] as well as leading professional psychiatric organisations – including, naturally, the publisher of the DSM.[17]

Furthermore, the industry has paid for, commissioned, designed and conducted nearly all the clinical trials into psychiatric drugs (antidepressants, antipsychotics, tranquillisers).[18] This has enabled companies to literally create an evidence base in their favour, often by way of dubious research practices designed to legitimise their products.[19] These include burying negative data; ghost-writing academic articles; manipulating outcomes to boost the appearance of effectiveness; hiding inconvenient harms; enticing journals and editors with financial incentives, and concealing bad science behind slick and deceptive medical marketing campaigns.[20] We also know, through countless academic studies, how most leading psychiatric drug researchers have received industry money (i.e. funding, consultancy fees, speaker's fees or other honoraria), and how such financial entanglements exert demonstrable biasing effects.[21] This is to say that clinicians, researchers, organisations and DSM committee members who receive industry money are far more likely to promote and advocate drug company products in their research, clinical practices, teaching and public statements than those without such financial links. Given that these links have literally littered the profession over the last thirty years, it is little wonder that the over-medicalisation and medicating of emotional distress has similarly proliferated.[22]

But this book is not about the unholy alliance between drug companies and establishment psychiatry, which I covered more extensively in my previous book, *Cracked*. It is about how the wider social and economic climate of late capitalism has allowed this highly medicalised, marketised and depoliticised way of managing our emotional distress to flourish unimpeded, despite its clear failings on a whole host of the most important outcome metrics.

According to the NHS's own Independent Mental Health Taskforce, mental health outcomes have actually worsened in recent years, as have rates of suicide.[23] In fact, since 2006, there has been an 11 per cent increase in suicides in people who use mental health services,[24] and, despite widening access to services,[25] no reduction at all in the prevalence of mental disorders since the 1980s.[26] Additionally, while as a society we have made some extraordinary gains in life expectancy over the last fifty years (largely due to biomedical advances in general medicine), for people diagnosed with severe mental health problems, the gap between their life expectancy and everyone else's has doubled since the 1980s.[27] In fact, in the UK, the mortality of those suffering from severe and sustained emotional distress is now 3.6 times higher than in the general population, with people so diagnosed dying approximately twenty years earlier than the average person.[28]

There are many reasons given for these dire statistics. Those diagnosed with mental health conditions often have to contend with discrimination, social isolation and exclusion, poorly funded social and mental health support, as well as more intangible factors like 'diagnostic overshadowing', where physical complaints are often wrongly attributed to the mental health problem, making it more likely that these complaints will go unexplored and untreated.[29] But while such factors certainly play a role in bad outcomes and lower mortality, they clearly do not provide the whole picture. They exclude, in particular, growing concerns regarding the harmful effects of psychiatric drugs themselves, like antipsychotics, anxiolytics and antidepressants.

For instance, in precisely those nations where antidepressant prescriptions have doubled in the last twenty years (e.g. the US, the UK, Australia, Iceland, Canada), we have also witnessed the doubling of mental health disability during the same time period. This means that rising prescriptions, in country after country, has presided over rising mental health disability, which is the opposite of what you would expect if the drugs were working. This worrying correlation suggests, as I will explore in Chapter Two, that our drug-heavy approach may partly explain why mental health outcomes are falling far behind other areas of health care, especially since the long-term use of psychiatric drugs is associated with an increase in a whole host of problems: dependence on medical help,[30] weight gain,[31] relapse rates,[32] risk of neurodegenerative diseases such as dementia,[33] likelihood of severe and protracted withdrawal,[34] sexual dysfunction,[35] worse functional outcomes, mortality,[36] and so on.

While the data show that our over-reliance on drug interventions may be doing more harm than good over the long term, another critical driver of poor mental health outcomes has been the effect of over-medicalisation itself, something widely promoted by diagnostic manuals like the DSM. While some people report feeling validated by receiving a psychiatric diagnosis, building their identity around it, research shows that having our emotional distress reframed as mental 'disorder', 'illness' or 'dysfunction' (which, incidentally, is now a precondition for accessing NHS services in the UK) may adversely impact our recovery. This is especially true if people are led to believe that their problems are rooted in biological abnormalities, which calling these problems 'medical' or 'mental illness' encourages.[37] For example, people who come to believe their problems are due to chemical imbalances experience worse pessimism about their recovery, increased self-stigma, more negative expectations and self-blame[38] as well as more depressive symptoms after the close of their treatment,[39] compared to people who reject this hypothesis. Similar results have been found for those who embrace biogenetic explanations for their distress,[40] which regularly increases stigmatising attitudes among patients and mental health professionals[41] as well as hopelessness in those believing their conditions to be chronic (i.e. lifelong).[42]

One of the probable reasons why medicalising our distress can cause such harm is that once people identify with being 'mentally ill', it may become harder for them to think of themselves as healthy participants in normal life, or as being in control of their own fate. They now have a psychiatric illness that has set them apart and rendered them dependent long term on psychiatric authority. As a result, they are subtly requested to rethink, or even downgrade, their prospects and ambitions for the future, as well as to relinquish part of their agency. While all this can exacerbate self-stigma, self-blame and pessimism for many people, being medicalised can also negatively influence how others treat and perceive those who have been diagnosed. We know, for example, that framing emotional problems in terms of an illness or disorder is more likely to kindle fear, suspicion and hostility in other people than if we articulate those very same problems in non-medical, psychological terms.[43] When a research team at Auburn University asked volunteers to administer mild or strong electric shocks to two groups of patients – if these patients failed at a given test, for example – it turned out that those believed to suffer from a biochemical disease rooted in their brains were shocked at a faster and harder rate than those believed to be suffering from problems caused by psychosocial events in their past.[44] Framing emotional distress in brain-based, medical terms appeared to exert a subliminal effect on the volunteers, leading them to treat those who had been medicalised less humanely.

Similar forms of stigma even exist when people are ascribed the least stigmatising labels, such as depression. For example, recipients so labelled are still more likely than non-recipients to be viewed by others as having frail wills or character flaws, as being afflicted by personal weakness, or as being lazy and unpredictable.[45] And when people are ascribed with more serious labels, like schizophrenia, they are more likely to be perceived as highly unpredictable and potentially dangerous, which can compound their sense of isolation through social rejection.[46] In fact, even when people are given false diagnoses by researchers, members of the public will still stigmatise the behaviour of these patients, despite such patients behaving completely normally. The labels, in other words, have powerful cultural effects that shape public perceptions of those being diagnosed, even if these negative perceptions bear no relation to the person at all. It is perhaps for these reasons that the largest ever meta-study into how medicalisation impacts outcomes simply concluded that 'Medicalisation is no cure for stigma and may create barriers to recovery.'[47] If we want to reduce stigma and its various harms, the research implied, we should start by reducing the medicalisation that drives it up.[48]

Compared to even twenty years ago, public conversations around mental health have hugely proliferated. We are perhaps more able and willing than ever before to open up about our private woes. This of course is a good thing. But it is clearly insufficient in making things better. What matters more is how a person's actual distress is understood and managed once it has been courageously disclosed, and whether this is done in humane and effective ways. And with respect to honouring this part of the deal, we certainly have a very long way to go. Despite the various ways in which we're told it's 'good to talk', the responses awaiting most people when they do are fairly homogenous and predictable. Whether we encounter these messages at school, at work, at home or on social media, most are still laden with an underpinning medicalised philosophy that subtly pathologises and depoliticises our distress. And in the post-COVID world, where we are all being asked to open up ever more readily, the effects of this are only set to spread further, as rising distress is reframed as rising mental illness, and as psychiatric prescriptions further vault in response.

Given this culture's continued expansion, it is absolutely vital that we question why it thrives year on year despite its presiding over the very worst outcomes in our health sector. To answer this, I believe we must move beyond the expansive power and ambition of Big Pharma and the mental health professions themselves, and look at the wider political and economic arrangements that have enabled a particular ideology of suffering to dominate our lives over the last thirty years. Only by doing this will we be able to glimpse the various hidden mechanisms that keep our failing system operational at considerable human and economic expense.

PART ONE

THE NEW OPIUM

1

AN ECONOMIC PRELUDE

In October 2017, a parliamentary assistant walked me down the central hallway of the Houses of Parliament. As we turned into a narrow corridor, she suddenly halted, before ushering me into a small enclave. 'Wait here, please,' she said briskly, pointing to some green leather benches lining the wall. She then slipped through a large wood-panelled door, before appearing again a few moments later. 'This way,' she said with a smile. 'He's ready to see you now. You only have thirty minutes – he'd give you more but it's been a long day.'

As I entered the bustling Peers' Common Room in the House of Lords, I immediately began scouring the room for my interviewee. I soon spotted him nestled in a quiet corner, framed by a stately Gothic window that looked out onto the Thames. As I approached, he slowly rose, one hand extended, with the other clutching the armrest for support. 'Welcome, James,' he said kindly. 'Please sit down and join me for coffee.' As I settled in the plush seat opposite him, it seemed suddenly surreal to be interviewing one of the most influential politicians of the modern age, the man who masterminded the historic economic reforms of Thatcher's Britain and the new style of capitalism under which we now all live.

I was meeting Lord Nigel Lawson, the former Chancellor of the Exchequer, in order to explore an event that had fascinated me for many years. It concerned an encounter that had taken place over thirty-five years earlier, in a room at Number 10 Downing Street, between Prime Minister Margaret Thatcher and the eminent journalist Ronald Butt. In that meeting, Butt wanted to know whether Thatcher was pleased with her government's performance since being elected two years earlier. Over the course of an hour, little was said that would surprise any informed listener, until something unexpected happened – perhaps something that shouldn't have happened.

Butt asked Thatcher what her priorities were for her remaining term as prime minister. She responded by declaring that politics over the past thirty years had become far too socialist; that people had come to rely too much on the state rather than on themselves and each other. 'That approach is wrong,' she stated flatly. 'We have to change the approach.'

She then explained how she would do it: 'It isn't that I set out on economic policies,' she said earnestly, 'it's that I set out to change the approach, and changing the economics is the means of changing that approach. If you change the approach, you really are after the heart and soul of the nation. *Economics are the method, the object is to change the heart and soul.*'[1]

This confession had long captivated me, because it unmistakably exposed a core principle of Thatcher's political philosophy: that economic reform was not an end in itself, but a means to what she believed to be a far greater social good – to transform the hearts and minds of an entire population; to shape people into better versions of themselves.

'Thatcher's aim to bring about human change through economic reform raises a critical question,' I said to Lord Lawson. 'What changes in the national psyche did her new economics aspire to achieve? In what direction do you think she wanted our collective hearts and souls to strive?'

"Well, James,' answered Lawson slowly, 'I think that by talking about the heart and soul, Margaret Thatcher felt very strongly that there were certain important virtues – self-reliance, independence and self-responsibility – that economic reform could nurture and develop.'

He then elaborated by referring to the founding text of modern capitalism: Adam Smith's *The Wealth of*

Nations. 'You see, there is a widespread view out there that for Adam Smith, the wealth of nations consisted of actual gold. But actual gold had absolutely nothing to do with it. The true wealth of any nation exists in people working to better their own and their children's lives. For Smith, the *true* gold was not found in vaults, but rather in who people *were* and what they *did*.'

For Lawson and Thatcher, the 1970s economy they'd inherited from their predecessors simply did not encourage these golden virtues: hard work, competitiveness and personal initiative. Rather it fostered baser metals: dependency, complacency and entitlement to state support. 'For us, big government was a critical problem in the 1970s,' Lord Lawson continued, 'something even demeaning to human nature itself. Being a creature of the state created dependency. We believed, and still believe, that a high degree of self-reliance is what makes a good society. So in that sense, yes, Margaret was right: our objective to reform the economy went far beyond economics.'

As I sat listening to Lord Lawson, a childhood memory flashed through my mind of eating with my family by candlelight. No lights in the house were working that evening, and it all felt a little ominous. I remember my sister asking my mother why it was so dark. Her response suggested that something serious was happening in ways that we just wouldn't understand.

'It's dark because we have to save energy – most people in the country have no lights tonight.'

The scene I describe occurred in the mid 1970s, a period of acute economic volatility and widespread industrial unrest. A key problem was spiralling inflation, which was triggered by the oil crisis earlier that decade. This led the Labour government of the day to reject union demands for higher wages. As the government dug in, the unions fought back, and widespread strikes and blackouts were the result for many households across the country.

For Thatcher, the strikes were yet another symptom of a deeper national malaise rooted in the economic policies of the 1970s. In her view, the growing power of the unions was encouraging feelings of selfish entitlement in the working population, while the expansion of the welfare state was rewarding dependency on the state and economic lethargy. Additionally, the tight regulation of business was discouraging innovation, while the nationalisation of key sectors was stifling the competitive spirit. In the end, too many individuals had come to view the state as a kind of benevolent father, something Thatcher believed was corroding individual initiative, independence and responsibility. If Britain were to thrive, these state-created flaws in the national character needed to be excised. Economic reform would be the surgical procedure, and moral and economic health the national reward.

While the perceived corrosion of the national character was a central target of Thatcher's reforms, by rejecting the 1970s social order, she was also rejecting an entire economic worldview that had dominated in the UK and most other developed Western nations since the end of World War II. 'For us,' as Lord Lawson confirmed to me, 'there was a very strong sense [in our 1980s administration] that social democracy had been tried and failed. The question for us was now what to put in its place.'

What Thatcher's government saw as tried and failed in the 1970s was the very same economic worldview that had, during the 1950s and 1960s, created widespread economic prosperity and growth. Whatever names have been given to this previous paradigm ('social democracy', 'regulated capitalism', 'the post-war consensus', 'Keynesian capitalism'), they all point to a style of capitalism in which the state played a more central role in the economy than it does today (discounting the emergency measures during COVID, of course). In essence, this period of post-war 'regulated capitalism' embraced the idea that the state could create a prosperous and equal society by playing a central role in regulating the economy, developing national institutions and infrastructure, investing heavily in public services, and restraining market forces.

During the 1950s and 1960s wherever this model was

embraced – from Western Europe to east Asia and the United States – positive economic and social development followed.[2] This was the period of expanding social security and health coverage, and of historically low levels of unemployment across many developed nations. Steady economic growth soon became the norm too, reaching an annual average of 4–5 per cent in those areas where the paradigm dominated. For these reasons, this period is now regularly referred to as the Golden Age of Capitalism – a period when personal debt was low, inequality went down, wages went up, social liberalism and civil rights expanded, social mobility grew, unemployment almost disappeared, industrial, scientific and technological innovation unfolded at a steady and productive pace, and sustained international peace (between Western nations at least) was broadly secured.[3]

By rejecting the 1970s, then, Thatcher was also rejecting an entire economic and social model that had brought high and sustained levels of economic prosperity throughout the 1950s, 1960s and part of the 1970s. From now on, that old paradigm – regulated capitalism – would be superseded by a new economic order: a new capitalism, a neo-liberalism, increasing the role of market forces in society and encouraging the kinds of personal qualities – competitiveness, self-reliance, entrepreneurialism and productivity – esteemed by Thatcher's political elite.

Thatcher set about unleashing the market to do its work. From now on the state would reduce its role in the economy, while corporations would be given far greater freedoms to expand, state-run industries would be privatised and many labour, welfare and social protections would be cut. Standing before the US Congress in 1985, Thatcher praised the effect such reforms had already exerted in America under Ronald Reagan, and described how Britain was, by copying the US, rapidly catching up:

> Now the sun is rising in the West [*Congress applauds*]. For many years our vitality in Britain was blunted by excessive reliance on the state. Our industries were nationalised, controlled and subsidised in a way that yours never were. We are having to recover the spirit of enterprise which you never lost. Many of the policies you are following are the policies we are following. You have brought inflation down, so have we. You have declared war on regulations and controls, so have we ... But above all, we are carrying out the largest programme of denationalisation in our history [*large applause*]. Just a few years ago in Britain, privatisation was thought to be a pipe dream. Now it is a reality, and a popular one ... Members of Congress, that

is what capitalism is. A system which brings
wealth to the many, and not just to the few
[*standing ovation*].[4]

To understand how these sweeping economic changes
would soon transform not just the deeper structures of
society, but the internal structures of our psychological,
personal and moral lives, we must first take a detour to a
time and place far removed from late-twentieth-century
Britain; to a time when capitalism was undergoing its
first major industrial expansion; to a place where some of
our most radical economic ideas were first being forged.

———————

In August 1844, two intellectuals in their mid twenties
met at the Café de la Régence on the Place du Palais in
Paris. The conversation that ensued was so engrossing
for both of them that it would continue each day for
a further ten days. What captivated both men was a
radical conclusion that each had reached independently
of the other: that the industrial revolution then sweeping
across Europe was crippling the many while enriching
the few. This was due to the relationship between
the owners of industry and those working in their
factories, a relationship that had become one of essential
exploitation. The two men had grown convinced that if
balance were to be restored, employees must learn that

their economic interest lay in fighting for a new set of working relations – one forbidding their exploitation and more evenly distributing profits while at the same time honouring employees' basic dignity and rights.

The first man in that Parisian café had come to this conclusion by observing the desperate plight of factory workers in the mills of Manchester. His moral shock at the conditions under which they worked had been exacerbated by his meeting and falling in love with one of these very workers – a twenty-year-old woman called Mary Burns, who would later become his wife. A potent brew of moral outrage and heady passion led him to begin writing political pamphlets criticising the industrialism of the age; these soon fell into the hands of the man who sat opposite him in the café: a man whose journey to the same conclusion had followed a course only slightly less romantic. It involved his mixing with other young radical thinkers in Parisian salons and reading widely in philosophy and political economy. As the conversations unfurled over the next ten days, the two men finally committed to collaborating on a new writing project together. Six months later, that commitment materialised in a book entitled *The Holy Family*. Its authors were, of course, Friedrich Engels and Karl Marx.

Both men believed that the exploitation of factory workers could only succeed if the workers themselves accepted their own oppression to be both natural and inevitable. What concerned them was the extent to which this acceptance had become deeply engrained in the workers they observed, keeping them in a state of servitude (which compounded their oppression) and a state of isolation from each other (which inhibited their working together for constructive change). Oppressive working conditions had dehumanised people to the extent that they had become detached or alienated from their essential human rights and needs, leaving them in a state of moral and political limbo. And in this demoralised and politically apathetic state, all that remained for them were soothing illusions and anaesthetics – sedatives to compensate them for the painful oppression they endured. Before Marx and Engels met in that café, Marx had already set about identifying one such powerful sedative: organised religion.

Marx felt that religion, unknown to itself, was helping to support the exploitation of factory workers by sedating them to the very suffering that, if fully experienced, would lead them to unite to fight for reform. His view was based on the idea that suffering had always been a powerful driver of social reform: once people experienced the full force of their own despair, they would be compelled to identify and overthrow its causes. Religion, he believed, was interfering with this natural process by recasting the suffering of workers not as a legitimate response to their oppressed situation, but as a 'hallmark of the pious life'; a godly experience that, if simply endured in this life, would be handsomely rewarded in the next.

Marx believed that by making a religious virtue of suffering, Christianity was indirectly teaching people to accept and endure rather than fight and reform the oppressive conditions harming them.[5] Just like any other sedative, religion could offer temporary respite from harsh social and economic realities. But in the long run it would end up causing greater harm, suppressing the human instinct for social reform and allowing harmful circumstances and institutions to live on. It was in this sense that Marx characterised religion as the real opium of the masses, as it sedated the drive for necessary social transformation.

While any student of economics or sociology will be familiar with this aspect of Marx's critique, we forget how radical it was at the time. In fact, what his early writings on religion helped establish was an entirely new and enduring style of enquiry in the social sciences, one that focused on how the main institutions of society (religion, education, law, media and medicine) always evolved to serve the aims of the particular economic system in which they were rooted.[6] While Marx's early analysis was specific to how religion served industrial capitalism of the mid 1800s, the fundamental idea that all institutions of society would gradually conform to the main economic aims of the day would have a huge impact on twentieth-century social science, whether those deploying this idea sat on the economic left or right – whether they sympathised more with Karl Marx or Fredrick Hayek.

Over the course of the century, this type of social science would have enormous impact on social and political thought, whether those using it identified as Marxists, centrists or neo-liberal capitalists. Studies would proliferate identifying the many ways in which a given style of economy reshaped its various social institutions as these institutions literally bent themselves to satisfy the economy's will.[7] This was particularly true for those institutions, like religion, that directly explained and managed human suffering. After all, once a sufficient proportion of the population came to suffer under a given set of economic arrangements, those arrangements would not survive for long. People would challenge them either through the democratic process, through organised opposition or, when such processes failed, through civil unrest.

What Marx had in effect discovered through his analysis of religion was that those social institutions responsible for understanding and managing suffering were critically important to the aims of an economy.

They had the power to defuse politically dangerous emotions by sedating people to the true origins of their distress (cutting off the route to finding the right social solutions). As this understanding unhitched itself from Marxism, and became part of mainstream social science, it started to be applied to the domain of mental health, with many new insights emerging from the 1980s onwards. These revealed the precise ways in which our distress was being misread, exploited and depoliticised for clear economic ends. If I were to draw up a list of how this works, it would look something like this:

- Conceptualise human suffering in ways that protect the current economy from criticism. That is, reframe suffering as being rooted in individual rather than social causes, leading individuals to think that it is them rather than the economic and social system in which they live that is at fault and in need of reform.

- Redefine individual well-being in terms consistent with the goals of the economy. Well-being should be characterised as comprising those feelings, values and behaviours (e.g. personal ambition, competition and industrious endeavour) that serve economic growth and increased productivity, irrespective of whether they are actually good for the individual and the community.

- Turn behaviours and emotions that might negatively impact the economy into a call for more medical intervention. Behaviours and feelings that perturb or disrupt the established order (e.g. low worker satisfaction) should be medicalised and treated, as these can frustrate the economic interests of powerful financial institutions and elites.

- Turn suffering into a vibrant market opportunity for more consumption. Suffering should become highly lucrative to big business as it begins to manufacture and market its so-called solutions – solutions from which increased tax revenues, profits and higher share value can be extracted.

Now, while it is tempting to dismiss the above devices on the grounds that they all sound a little too conspiratorial, it is important to understand that those who exposed them never claimed that they were deliberately concocted in small smoky rooms with calculated intent.[8] Their point was far subtler than that: if any institution is to thrive, it must broadly adapt to what its society wants. And so, in the case of mental health, these strategies arose spontaneously as the sector struggled to endure under a new set of economic arrangements. The embracing of a mental health ideology favourable to the wider economy would not just reconfigure the entire mental health enterprise, but would increasingly help alter the psychological outlook of a whole generation. In this sense, Margaret Thatcher was correct when she said that if you wanted to change the heart and soul of a nation, you must change the whole economic approach, as this is the surest mechanism for influencing in powerful ways the direction in which people and institutions ultimately strive.

To begin the process of understanding how the grand economic shift towards new capitalism began to reshape our hearts and souls via the rise of a new mental health ideology, I think it is fitting to look first at the most administered mental health treatment over the last thirty-five years: the blockbuster bestselling class of psychiatric drug we all know as the antidepressant.

2

THE NEW CULTURE OF PROLIFERATING DEBT AND DRUGS

In April 2020, the UK economy was experiencing its most significant recession in the history of modern capitalism. As COVID-19 infections soared, the entire country was eventually confined to lockdown, with the wheels of commerce and community life juddering to a sudden halt. Offices, shops, restaurants, gyms, schools, hotels and tourist sites all lay empty, with hundreds of billions in revenue being consequently lost within a few weeks, forcing the economy to roll and pitch from one disastrous economic metric to another. The stats were unprecedented. In one month alone in the UK, GDP dropped by 20 per cent; the service sector contracted by a quarter; unemployment rose by 1.5 million, and government borrowing topped an extra £100 billion.[1]

As the bleak outcomes continued to pile up, however, one economic variable defied the gloomy statistics. As people's access to goods and services was curtailed, they had fewer things to spend their money on. By default, millions of people began saving, with millions more soon paying down their personal debts. The frugality that lockdown unexpectedly foisted upon us saw consumer debt in the UK fall by £7.4 billion in April 2020 alone, the largest ever fall recorded by the Bank of England.[2]

The reason why this economic metric is so noteworthy is because it bucks a trend that has unfurled almost uninterruptedly since the 1980s – the decade when levels of household debt began their rapid ascent to the unprecedented levels of recent years. This growth in debt began with the deregulation of the credit card market back in the mid 1980s, which made it far easier for people to borrow without undergoing proper checks. This was the decade when our TV screens were littered with jabbering Visa cards informing us that they were our 'flexible friend' – sating our desire to consume things hitherto far beyond our financial reach.

Initially the left-leaning Labour government criticised these credit reforms. But the fact is, by the 1990s, there was little to distinguish the two parties when it came to making cheap credit widely available, and almost nothing to distinguish them by the early 2000s. This was because both parties had come to understand that easy credit was an essential cog in the new capitalist economy, upon which the entire machine's workings ultimately depended.

The history of why consumer debt became such a crucial cog in the modern economic machine is an interesting one. Very briefly put, we can trace it to the idea that rising inflation in the 1970s was mostly due to unions demanding excessive wages for workers. This belief led Thatcher's government to dismantle union power, which saw employers reap the dividends, as they were able to pay their workers less. This fall in wages was further compounded by the importation of new machine technologies that replaced much human labour, and by the outsourcing of local jobs to cheaper workforces abroad. As these changes rendered many previous jobs redundant, competition in the employment market rose rapidly, which naturally depressed wages even further.

While all these changes helped bring wages and inflation down, they also introduced deeper structural problems into the economy. Lower wages meant that people had less disposable income in their pockets to spend on goods and services, which of course would adversely impact consumption and profits. This in turn would threaten investment, potentially creating a cycle of further job losses, lower consumption and yet more contractions in the economy. Fear of this spiral downwards explains why successive governments made credit so accessible throughout the 1980s, 1990s and onwards: debt enabled consumer spending to remain active even when wages were flatlining. In this sense, debt became the sticking plaster covering a deeper structural infection. (See Figure 1.)

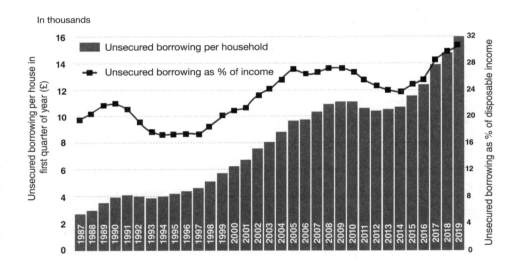

Figure 1 Rising UK household debt[3]

The use of personal debt as a kind of economic Band-Aid to shield us from deeper structural problems in the economy did not only generate significant societal effects, it was also responsible for shaping the dynamics of our individual selves, or, as Margaret Thatcher put it, the very 'hearts and souls' of those becoming increasingly indebted. Up until the 1970s, having personal debt beyond a mortgage held a certain stigma. If you took on any debt at all, it had to be for investment purposes. Other forms of debt (to consume, to 'keep up with the Joneses' or to 'make ends meet') were largely considered off-limits. A combination of tight cultural mores and credit regulations therefore kept household debt low throughout the 1950s, 1960s and 1970s.

But owing to the deregulatory and structural changes to the economy outlined above, public attitudes soon liberalised, making the adoption of debt almost essential to modern living. From the 1980s onwards, as borrowing became more ubiquitous, young adults in their twenties and thirties were 50 per cent more likely to take on debt than their equivalents living in the three previous decades.[4] Being indebted was quickly being normalised. And with this, the very psychological outlook of those indebted began changing too. Owning increasing amounts of debt was altering the complexion of how people envisaged themselves and their future, creating mass shifts in attitude and behaviour not seen before.

To understand this, consider for a moment what happens – psychologically speaking – when we take on debt. When we use that money to satisfy a particular current need, we immediately become shackled to its repayment, and this will impact our choices regarding the future. This is what led the social critic Noam

Chomsky to argue that student debt was ultimately detrimental. Taking on excessive debts at a young age limits students' horizons at a time when they should be at their most expansive. As the reality of borrowing large amounts of money looms, more students are forced to think pragmatically, fiscally, electing to study safe subjects they feel will lead to the highest-paid jobs. This explains why as student fees go up, applications for creative and humanities subjects go down.[5] It also explains why modern students are more likely to become fiscally conservative early on, as they've been socialised by debt into deferring to a life of repayment. For Chomsky, debt renders students conformists in the economy, forcing them to accept rather than oppose the economic realities of the system they are entering. Debt, in other words, is a potent form of socialisation into neo-liberalism – forcing young people to submit, early on, to the economic status quo.

Underpinning critiques like the above is the view that indebtedness not only alters how we think and act, but impinges upon our freedom. Having to repay debt reduces our options, trapping us in future obligations and activities we never directly sought. From this standpoint, the common phrase 'to borrow against my future self' actually means 'to borrow against my future freedom'. What I borrow today frees me now, but ensnares me tomorrow. This is why assuming debt feels easier than it should. In the short term, only its benefits are felt, while entrapment is deferred for another day. Beyond debt for rational investment (and student debt, admittedly, can potentially take this form), most types of debt are not about investment at all, but about operating rationally in a consumerist economy, trying to make ends meet or in some cases trying to survive.

While the effect of indebtedness, both societal and personal, has received extensive coverage since the 2008 recession, the plain truth is that debt is just one example of how many deeper problems in the economy have been managed with sticking-plaster solutions. Soon other economic Band-Aids would surface from the 1980s onwards, and not all in the realm of wages, taxation, debt and consumption. We would see economic sticking plasters being deployed throughout our public services: in education, in local authorities, in the NHS and, of course, in the domain of mental health. Here sticking plasters analogous to the usage of consumer debt would rapidly proliferate in unexpected ways, often in the name of spreading safe, effective and useful treatments. And this is, you may have guessed, where antidepressants come in.

In 2007, the Pulitzer Prize finalist and former fellow at Harvard University's Safra Center, Robert Whitaker, encountered a newly published research paper that would alter the course of his professional life. Although the paper had generated little attention at the time, Whitaker believed that its findings threatened to turn conventional clinical wisdom on its head. In essence, it showed that many psychiatric drugs, when consumed long term, were harmful to a large number of the people they purported to help.[6]

The research was undertaken by Professor Martin Harrow at the University of Illinois, and published in the *Journal of Nervous and Mental Disease*. Harrow's research constituted the most comprehensive study of long-term psychiatric drug use so far conducted. It followed a large cohort of patients diagnosed with schizophrenia, asking how well they were doing five years, ten years and fifteen years after their first diagnosis and course of antipsychotic treatment. The results were contrary to what was expected. While all patients started out with the same diagnosis, the patients who improved most were not those who had remained on their medication over the years, but those who had stopped earlier on. For example, after 4.5 years, around 39 per cent of those who had stopped their medication had entered full recovery, compared to only 6 per cent of those who had continued taking their meds. And after ten years, that gap had widened further, with 44 per cent of the non-medicated now in complete recovery compared to just 6 per cent still taking their medication. Furthermore, a remarkable 77 per cent of those who had stopped their medication were now also free from any psychotic symptoms, compared to a lowly 21 per cent of those still taking the drugs. In fact, whichever symptoms or functional outcomes were assessed (levels of anxiety, cognitive function, capacity to work, etc.), the non-medication group greatly excelled. The longer people remained on the drugs, the results showed, the worse their outcomes on every measure.

Now an obvious response to this study is as follows: surely those with milder symptoms simply self-selected to stop their medication, whereas those with more severe problems elected to stay on the drugs. Perhaps this can explain why those who remained on medication ended up doing far worse in the long term: they were more severely distressed in the first place. And indeed this critique would have been fatal for Harrow's work had his data not also revealed something alarming: that on aggregate, the more severely ill people who stopped the drugs did better than the less severely ill who stayed on them.[7] In other words, his results starkly contradicted the widespread belief in psychiatry that most people with major mental disorder should stay on these drugs for life.

While many in the psychiatric community oddly bypassed this highly significant finding, Whitaker's reaction was decidedly different. Some years earlier, after working as director of publications at Harvard Medical School, he had written an award-winning critical history of psychiatry entitled *Mad in America*. The book was published in 2002 and documented the rise and fall of psychiatric treatments over the twentieth century. It showed how, time and again, treatments that had once been celebrated as highly effective by psychiatry (lobotomies, insulin-coma and fever therapies) ultimately proved very harmful to patients. He then questioned whether the hype surrounding newer psychiatric drugs was also now following a similar course: as the pharmaceutical industry and those psychiatrists it had funded had been shown to have dramatically exaggerated the value of these drugs, often manipulating, burying or simply ignoring negative data, would we someday look back upon our dramatic over-prescribing of them as yet another costly mistake – as hype that ultimately harmed?

While Whitaker left that question hanging in his 2002 book, Harrow's 2007 research now appeared to provide a compelling answer, by showing that the long-term consumption of psychiatric drugs for severe problems was making life worse for many patients. When I interviewed Whitaker from my office in London, I asked him how Harrow's work had inspired his future research. 'Harrow's paper appeared to confirm not just something I'd hypothesised in *Mad in America*,' he replied, 'but what so many patients had told me since: that during their long-term treatment their conditions got worse, not better. And if this were true for patients diagnosed with schizophrenia, was this also happening to other patients diagnosed with things like depression, bipolar disorder and so on? I had to find out.'

The starting point for Whitaker's new research was novel. He began by sifting through reams of governmental data on national rates of mental health disability, assessing the number of people receiving disability payments for psychiatric conditions. He did this to gain a perspective on how the arrival of new psychiatric drugs had affected national mental health trends. And this was when he noticed something bemusing. Whichever country he assessed – the UK, US, Sweden, Iceland, Finland, Australia, Canada – rates of mental health disability had uniformly vaulted upwards since the 1980s. The number of people receiving disability payments for mental disorders (anxiety, depression, schizophrenia, bipolar) had risen rapidly across the developed world – tripling over the last thirty-five years in most Western countries.[8]

But this was not all. Alongside this surge in mental health disability sat a different yet related escalating trend. 'Wherever you observe mental health disability rates vaulting,' said Whitaker, 'you also observe huge rises in the number of psychiatric drugs being prescribed

– antidepressants, antipsychotics, sedatives and so on.' In country after country, in other words, prescriptions and mental health disability were escalating side by side. If you look at Whitaker's graphs (Figure 2) you will see what he means.

'When I first saw this data,' Whitaker told me, 'I needed to know whether this was more than mere correlation. Was there some way in which rising drugs and disability are causally linked?' This question became particularly consuming for him, given another crucial trend he'd noticed: that wherever you witness the use of antidepressants going up, you also witness a rise in the kinds of disability caused by the very disorders they are prescribed to treat: anxiety, depression, bipolar disorder and so on. Could our drug-based paradigm of care in some unforeseen way be fuelling this modern-day mental disability epidemic?

To answer this, Whitaker began the arduous task of gathering every study he could find, conducted since the 1950s, on how drugs affect the long-term prospects of those diagnosed with major mental disorders. 'While the conventional view was that disorders like schizophrenia, bipolar and major depression were lifelong conditions requiring lifelong medication, when you actually look at the research since the 1950s, you find something else entirely being indicated.' In fact, as Whitaker started digging, the story that gradually emerged appeared to

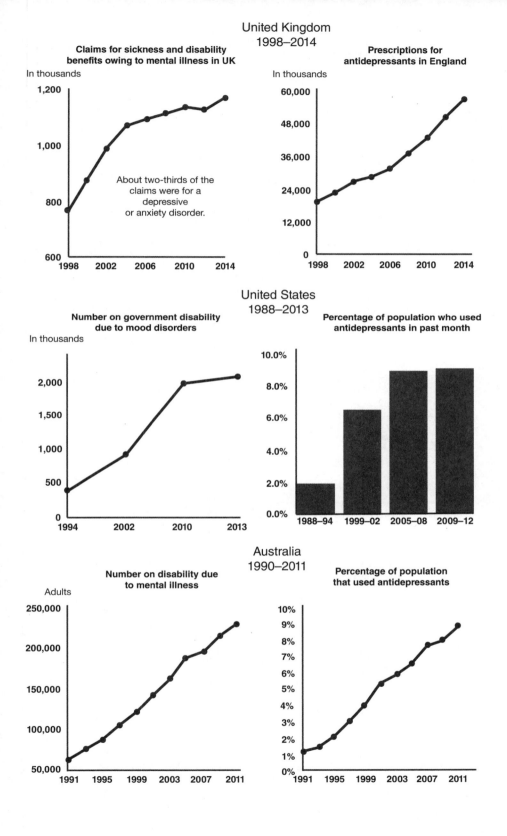

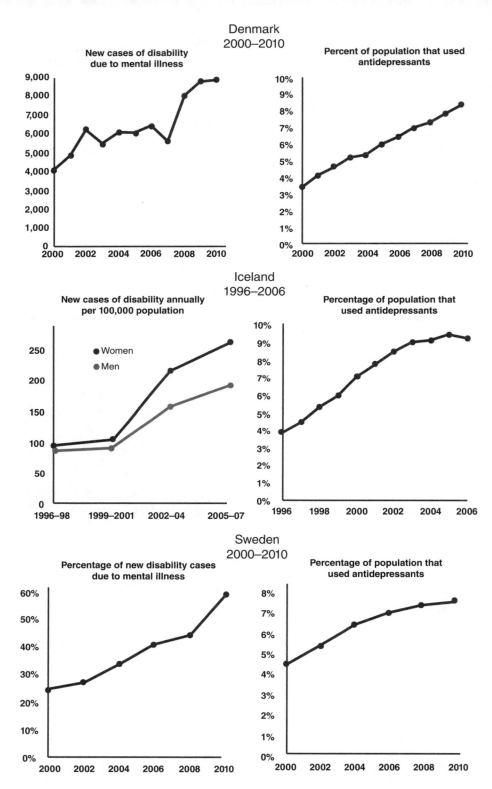

Figure 2. Antidepressant usage and disability due to mental illness across several countries.[9]

reinforce Harrow's 2007 findings: in the aggregate, people who continue to take psychiatric medications do much worse over the long term than those who stop the drugs.

One critical piece of evidence that Whitaker encountered was based on data obtained in the 1950s by Vermont State Hospital in the United States.[10] At that time Vermont Hospital had discharged 269 middle-aged patients into the community, all with the diagnosis of schizophrenia. Twenty years later, researchers managed to track down all the patients from that cohort who were still alive (168) to see how their lives had turned out. The good news was that, in total, a full 34 per cent had entirely recovered. They were symptom-free and living independently in the community – they had close relationships, were employed or were otherwise productive citizens with full lives. But what the researchers found next was unexpected: what this 34 per cent had in common was that they had all 'long since stopped taking medications'. Moreover, being medication-free was a central factor distinguishing them from those who had not recovered. This led the researchers to conclude that it was a 'myth' to say that people diagnosed with schizophrenia 'must be on medications all their lives'.[11] After all, their research clearly revealed a large proportion of people living and thriving without medication.

As unforeseen as this research was, it wasn't an outlier; it was consistent with the general thrust of the data Whitaker was unearthing. He found early studies showing that people on psychiatric drugs like Thorazine ended up staying in hospital longer than non-medicated patients with the same diagnosis.[12] He encountered research indicating that long-term antidepressant use increased the risk that a person would become depressed for life, and other research showing that a person with standard depression was more likely to convert to a more severe bipolar diagnosis the longer he or she took the drugs.[13] He discovered studies revealing that long-term exposure to antidepressants appeared to be 'shortening the intervals' between depressive episodes – in effect, extending the periods during which patients were depressed. As the volume of research he found is far too great to cover here, what follows is just a small sample of some of his other findings:

- Research published in the *British Journal of General Practice* separated depressed patients into groups, with only one group receiving antidepressants. The antidepressant patients stopped getting better after three months, while the non-drug group continued to improve. As the authors wrote, by the end of the study at twelve months, 'Those patients not receiving drugs did better [in terms of symptoms lost and their diagnostic status] … even after adjustment for initial scores on each instrument' – a result different from what you'd expect to find if antidepressants yielded better results over the long term.[14]

- A team of researchers at Zurich University of Applied Sciences found that in the long term, antidepressants might impair recovery and increase the risk of rehospitalisation in patients diagnosed with both depression and bipolar disorders. They concluded that the higher rates of rehospitalisation in antidepressant users could be due to adverse reactions to long-term antidepressant use. As they stated: 'Our findings, therefore, challenge the alleged long-term benefit of antidepressants and raise the possibility, that, in the long run, antidepressants may possibly do more harm than good.'[15]

- Research published in the *American Journal of Psychiatry* by the former director of the National Institute for Mental Health showed that long-term drug administration caused 'substantial and long-lasting alterations in neural function'. After a few weeks, the patient's brain would function in a manner that was 'qualitatively as well as quantitatively different from the normal state'.[16] These alterations (or neural adaptations to the drugs) might be responsible for the brain's susceptibility to future episodes of depression after cessation of the drugs. For instance, a team of researchers, publishing in *Frontiers in Psychology*, showed that the 'risk of relapse (back into depression) after antidepressants' discontinuation was higher than the risk of relapse after remission on placebo'.[17] This finding has been supported by research showing that after two years, antidepressant users are more likely to relapse than antidepressant non-users;[18] and other research revealing that, over the long term, antidepressant users are much more likely to have recurrent depressive episodes and to become disabled by the disorder, compared to non-users. The authors of the original research therefore conclude, 'there is an emerging need to address the lack of epidemiological evidence confirming the population-health benefits of increased antidepressant treatment'.[19]

- The largest comparative study of its kind, conducted by the World Health Organization, found that long-term outcomes for schizophrenia were worse in countries where more patients received antipsychotics. For instance, it revealed that after five years, the best symptomatic and functional outcomes were found not in developed countries where 90 per cent of patients were taking antipsychotics, but in countries such Nigeria, Colombia and India, where on average only about 15 per cent of the patients were taking antipsychotics. The authors stated: 'A major part of the difference in the prognosis of schizophrenia in the two kinds of setting may be reduced to the failure of many patients in the developed countries to attain or maintain a complete remission of symptoms.'[20] This is somewhat ironic given that that is precisely what the drugs purport to do.

- Research published in the *American Journal of Psychiatry* showed that after six years, antidepressant users were three times more likely than non-users to have suffered a cessation of their principal social role, and nearly seven times more likely to become incapacitated. Users saw their economic status markedly decline during this period, while 59 per cent of non-users saw their incomes rise.[21]

In all, the picture emerging did not look good. 'Even with my initial scepticism about the medications,' said Whitaker, 'I was still surprised at the coherence of the story unfolding. Again and again, studies of very different types led to the same result: psychiatric drugs – whatever the diagnosis you look at – worsen long-term outcomes.'

But this was not all. The story that Whitaker was uncovering now appeared consistent with one of the most significant pieces of psycho-pharmacological research published in the last thirty years. It was conducted by researchers at Harvard University, and reviewed all the outcome data internationally since 1895 for the treatment of 'major mental disorder'. What the analysis revealed was chilling: unlike in all other domains of medicine, where patient outcomes dramatically improved over the course of the twentieth century (envisage a line moving diagonally upwards as the decades unfold), psychiatry's outcomes did nothing of the kind; rather they peaked and troughed (the line starts low, moves upwards a little, and then falls back down again). From 1895 to 1955, the number of patients with major mental disorders who improved was around 35.4 per cent. This improvement rate then travelled upwards to 48.5 per cent by the 1970s. But after the 1970s, strangely enough, it started to decline rapidly again, falling to pre-1950s levels (around 36.4 per cent).[22] This led the Harvard researchers to conclude that the prospect of getting a good outcome in modern-day psychiatry 'has diminished to a level that is statistically indistinguishable from that found in the first half of the century'.

'The only ray of hope in that powerful study,' said Whitaker, 'is that you do see a moderate improvement in patients during the 1960s.' And what happened during the 1960s to enable that moderate yet temporary improvement? 'According to the official interpretation, new drug treatments were released that revolutionised patient care – effective drugs led to better outcomes. But that interpretation doesn't stack up, because as more drugs are prescribed in the 1970s, 1980s and 1990s, outcomes don't stay up, but actually start going down again, which is the opposite of what you'd expect if the drugs were working.'

So is there a more plausible explanation for the moderate improvements of the 1960s? According to Whitaker, 'This was the time when the old eugenics theories of mental illness were dying out, when lobotomies started to fall out of favour, when the asylums began to close, when less distressed people started being diagnosed with schizophrenia (so more recovered), and when social attitudes towards those defined as mentally ill became more benevolent. All these factors help explain the small improvements you see in the 1960s. The reason why outcomes fall after that is because we then enter the modern period, when drug prescriptions really accelerate. And wherever you start seeing this acceleration, you also see clinical outcomes dropping and mental illness disability escalating.'

On the eve of his book's publication in 2010, Robert Whitaker was nervous. 'There were two things in particular that caused me some anxiety,' he said. 'I feared that maybe I had missed something – the research literature is so vast. Had some bias led me to find only what I wanted to find? But on the other hand, I knew my review was thorough, covering all the available studies on long-term use to prevent any bias. My second anxiety was that, with a lot of the research I had encountered, the investigators (in the abstract and the discussion parts of their studies) were often trying to explain difficult data away, trying to fit them within a conventional narrative. As a result, I had focused on presenting the data from these studies, without their spin, but this left me in a potentially awkward position: would the investigators say I had mis-cited their research, even though I had been scrupulous in presenting their data accurately?'

The response to *Anatomy of an Epidemic* was immediate and vigorous. 'The counter-attack was brilliantly orchestrated,' said Whitaker, with some of America's most eminent psychiatrists lining up to write scathing reviews.[23] But as the criticisms started rolling in, he wasn't prepared for what happened next. 'Despite being in the middle of this onslaught,' he said, 'I started to experience my anxiety going down and my confidence going up. And this was for the simple reason that in review after review and debate after debate, no investigator was claiming that I had mis-cited their data, and no one was presenting counter-evidence to the book's central argument.' And when you look at the main criticisms launched against the work, you'll see what he means.

The first common criticism was this: as the number of diagnostic categories had dramatically increased since the 1980s, more people were being classed as mentally ill, which may have led to more people seeking disability payments. Whitaker responded: 'Imagine there is an infectious disease in a population and then you develop an effective drug for that disease. Imagine you also get better at recognising that disease and so more people now get effective treatment. If this were to happen, the toll that disease takes on the population should drop, not rise. So if psychiatric medications were effective long-term treatments, then an increase in diagnosis and treatment shouldn't lead to a rise in disability – but that is precisely what you find.'

The next common criticism was stronger: reforms to welfare in the 1990s in the US and UK made it much more difficult for the poor to collect benefits. This may have led many people to seek disability welfare as a replacement source of income. While Whitaker agreed that this was possible to some extent, the data also showed that disability payments for mental disorders were rising uniformly across many different countries

(Sweden, Denmark, Iceland, the US and the UK), despite their having dissimilar welfare/health systems and policies, with varying degrees of welfare ease of access and generosity. 'What united all these different welfare systems,' Whitaker pointed out, 'were uniform rising psychiatric prescriptions, irrespective of the individual welfare policies.'

The final criticism that Whitaker commonly heard was the age-old 'correlation is not causation' – if prescriptions and disability simultaneously rise, this does not prove the former caused the latter. Perhaps increased recognition of mental illness caused both to rise. However, Whitaker emphasised that this interpretation doesn't fit with the big picture. The correlation must be viewed in the context of other data that clearly show that the drugs lead to worsening long-term outcomes in the aggregate, and can transform milder 'illnesses' into more serious ones. 'When you view all the data together,' he said, 'the causal link becomes overwhelming.'

But it wasn't only the weakness of the counter-arguments that strengthened Whitaker's position – it was the research that began to emerge after his book was published. Three years after *Anatomy of an Epidemic* was released, the *Journal of the American Medical Association* published the first randomised clinical trial into how patients diagnosed with a major mental disorder fared on long-term antipsychotic medication.[24] Its results again clearly supported Whitaker's position. After randomly dividing patients into two groups, one group staying on meds, the other gradually stopping, the trial showed that as time went on, those who stopped medications did much better than those who continued: after seven years, their functional recovery rate had doubled (40.4 per cent) compared to those who had remained on the drugs (17.6 per cent) – an outcome that Whitaker's work of course predicted. The troubling implications of this research led to a significant amount of global coverage, with the former director of the National Institute of Mental Health, Thomas Insel, finally conceding that: 'Antipsychotic medication, which seemed so important in the early phase of psychosis, appeared to worsen prospects for recovery over the long-term.' He continued: 'For some people, remaining on medication long-term might impede a full return to wellness ... we need to ask whether in the long-term, some individuals with a history of psychosis may do better off medication.'[25]

In 2017, yet more support for Whitaker came in. A large study into long-term antidepressant use, published in *Psychotherapy and Psychosomatics*, assessed the progress of around 3,300 patients over nine years.[26] The results were again consistent with Whitaker's argument: medicated patients had significantly more severe symptoms at nine years than those who had stopped treatment. In fact, even people who received no treatment at all did better than those who received medication over the long term. The study concluded that even if antidepressants might have short-term benefits, long-term use appeared to be detrimental.

While these and other data continued to support Whitaker's position, an authoritative piece of neuro-biological research soon added a somewhat more unnerving dimension. One of America's foremost neuroscientists, Professor Nancy Andreasen, led a team exploring how long-term drug use affected the brain. What the MRI scans revealed was that long-term use of certain antipsychotics was 'associated with smaller brain tissue volumes' (with decreases in both white and grey matter). Crucially, this degeneration was not a symptom of the 'disease', as previously thought, but rather an outcome of long-term psychiatric drug use. While these degenerating effects had long been shown in animal studies, this was the first time brain shrinkage was shown in humans as a result of medications.[27] As Andreasen said when interviewed about her research in the *New York Times*: apart from the other well-known effects of these drugs, they 'also cause the prefrontal cortex to slowly atrophy'.[28] This atrophy was further confirmed in 2020, when a large randomised control trial published in the prestigious *Journal of the American Medical Association* showed that antipsychotics damage the brain in multiple areas, including atrophying its cortical thickness. As the authors concluded in slightly understated fashion: 'Given that reductions in cortical thickness are typically interpreted in psychiatric and neurologic disorders as non-desirable, our findings could support a reconsideration of the risks and benefits of antipsychotics.'[29]

When all such findings are placed side by side, it is little wonder that many of the foremost international researchers are now demanding that we radically change our prescribing practices. Taking articles published in the *British Medical Journal* in 2020 alone, we hear statements such as: 'Widespread prescribing has not reduced mental disability or suicide, raising questions about the assessment of evidence on effectiveness and safety of antidepressants ... Given limited efficacy and long-term safety concerns, the current level of UK prescribing is a major public health concern.'[30] And, in another *BMJ* article: 'The benefits of antidepressants seem to be minimal and possibly without any importance to the average patient with major depressive disorder. Antidepressants should not be used for adults with major depressive disorder before valid evidence has shown that the potential beneficial effects outweigh the harmful effects.'[31]

While research over the last fifteen years has therefore brought down with a crash the antidepressant optimism of the late 1990s and 2000s, there have nevertheless been some periodic attempts to resuscitate the flagging reputation of psychiatry's bestselling drug. One of the more recent high-profile efforts followed the publication of a large meta-analysis in February 2018 that captured headlines across the globe. This was undertaken by Andrea Cipriani and colleagues and was published in the prestigious medical journal *The Lancet*.[32] This study assessed the largest number of antidepressant clinical trials yet assembled to try to settle the debate, once and for all, as to whether antidepressants worked better than placebos (sugar pills). While we already knew that for mild to moderate depression they worked, on average, no better than placebos (despite millions of mildly and moderately depressed people being prescribed them each year),[33] Cipriani's study concluded that, for the minority of patients classed as severely depressed, they did in fact work a little better than placebos. This led many senior psychiatrists, in the study's press release, to hype the results in the most positive way, which shaped the global media coverage. The press release comments that drove the headlines included: 'This meta-analysis finally puts to bed the controversy on antidepressants'; 'Antidepressants do work and, for most people, the side-effects are worth it'; and 'For the millions of individuals with depression who are taking antidepressants at present … it confirms that these drugs are safe and effective.'

What most people reading these statements almost

certainly did not know was that, firstly, they were all issued by psychiatrists with strong financial ties to the pharmaceutical industry, and, secondly, these comments entirely glossed over the serious limitations of Cipriani's work. As myself and colleagues pointed out in our *Lancet* response to the study,[34] the differences found by Cipriani between placebo and antidepressant were so minor that they actually did not pass the threshold for 'clinical significance' – meaning that the clinical benefits of taking an antidepressant rather than a placebo would hardly register in a person's actual experience.[35] Moreover, as Cipriani's study only looked at trials on people who had been taking antidepressants for 8–12 weeks, his findings were irrelevant to most users today, as the vast majority of people on antidepressants take them for many months or years. Finally, when you assess people who have been taking antidepressants over the long term, not only are the effects even lower than those found by Cipriani,[36] but the drugs actually worsen the course of depression for many, as Robert Whitaker's work above clearly illustrates.

In 2016, the Norwegian health ministry ordered four regional health authorities to introduce 'medication-free treatment' in selected psychiatric hospitals. This order defied the objections of mainstream Norwegian psychiatry, which had long placed prescribing drugs as the heart of what psychiatrists do, and which now felt threatened by the initiative. Instead of heeding the many protests and warnings by senior psychiatrists, however, the Norwegian government instead put the voices of patients first. It listened to what patient groups were demanding: a chance to manage their difficulties without forced medication; a chance to be helped in more holistic and relational ways.

That the government would do what is rarely done (listen to patients who defy the establishment consensus) was consistent with a principle set deep in Norwegian culture: allow grassroots concerns to inform social policy and let neglected voices be heard. This principle had led, in the past, to many progressive social reforms in the areas of gender equality and gay and abortion rights. And now the government, by applying this principle to the realm of mental health, had begun heeding patients' protests too: there was too much institutional denial of the failure of drugs, too much closed-mindedness to the idea that better alternatives existed, and too much abuse on psychiatric wards (being restrained and overly medicated but rarely heard). These patient protests, the Norwegian government soon learnt, were not without evidence. In fact, the patient groups had meticulously gathered the corroborating evidence, and when this was finally handed over to the health ministry, that tipped the balance. As the health minister, Bent Høies, commented to me at the time: 'For me, it was the clearly expressed need from the patients that triggered my decision ... Medication-free treatment is an important step in changing and modernising mental health services.'

Central to the evidence presented to the Norwegian government was Robert Whitaker's work and the extensive reviews he had compiled. In fact, the service-user groups that lobbied the Norwegian health ministry largely celebrated Whitaker as a champion of their rights, regarding him an independent and honest broker of the research. Such groups also gained further inspiration from a growing number of professional and patient-led movements that were succeeding in helping severely distressed people recover with minimal or no drug use at all. In the northern reaches of Lapland, for example, an initiative called Open Dialogue had long been under way, achieving at the very least comparable levels of recovery by way of offering community and inter-personal support with a clear emphasis on reducing medication early on. The same could be found in other international service-user movements and centres, like the Hearing Voices network and Soteria House, both of which were also achieving good outcomes, high satisfaction scores[37] and, in some cases, superior outcomes when compared to traditional treatments.[38] They were achieving this by articulating suffering in non-medical ways, offering support within communities while supporting people's withdrawal from medication to aid their recovery.

When we leave Norway and travel back to the United Kingdom, we encounter a less open-minded climate. For despite some pockets of progressive practice[39] and mounting dissatisfaction among many UK service-user groups with our medicalised approaches to distress, our national attachment to psychiatric drugs appears stronger than ever before. While the dominant psychiatric approach has always been to keep people diagnosed with major mental disorders on psychiatric drugs long-term or for life, we are now witnessing long-term prescribing becoming the norm for the milder and moderate problems too – for the kinds of mental health issues managed by GPs in their surgeries. In fact, a key reason for antidepressant prescriptions doubling in the last ten years is that longer-term use is soaring across the UK, with more people starting antidepressants each year than there are people stopping them.

Today, around 4.4 million people in England have been taking antidepressants for longer than two years, even though we now know that a large proportion of these long-term users have overcome their difficulties and should be actively withdrawing.[40] Not only is this unnecessary long-term prescribing at huge public expense, but it is also at huge human cost, as more people are rendered disabled needlessly by the damaging effects long-term use can cause, as we have seen.

A recent article in the *British Journal of General Practice* has shed some light on why people seem unable to come off medications like antidepressants when they should be withdrawing from them. It discusses how patients (and, surprisingly, also their GPs) are often deeply apprehensive about what effects stopping will have. This fear is due to certain misleading myths about antidepressants and depression that have been exported from psychiatry to primary care over the last three decades. These myths include the false and unsubstantiated idea that major depression is often a chronic (lifelong) condition requiring continuous treatment, and that any improvement while on the drugs is mostly due to the drugs themselves rather than to other factors (such as situational change, placebo effects, or the natural course of depression coming to an end). For those subscribing to these myths, stopping antidepressants is often advised against, because, as the doctors put it, 'Why disturb the patient's equilibrium'?[41]

If the above myths help propel unnecessary long-term antidepressant consumption, they nevertheless pale in comparison to the next driving factor. This is the dominant myth that any withdrawal effects that accompany stopping antidepressants are invariably mild and short-lived (usually lasting for only 1–2 weeks). The origins of this myth can be traced to a symposium held in 1996, which was funded by the drug company Eli Lilly, the maker of the antidepressant Prozac. Here a committee of company-funded psychiatrists reached the consensus that antidepressant withdrawal was largely a minor affair, resolving over about a week. From here, this myth eventually made its way into clinical guidelines internationally, despite it enjoying no real corroborating research. As it took root in clinical practice, doctors who then encountered severe or protracted withdrawal reactions would often deny these reactions, rather believing that their patients were relapsing into their original problems. As a consequence, drugs would often be reinstated and longer-term use would ensue. This dynamic may partly explain why, since the guidelines were issued in 2004, the length of time the average person in the UK spends on an antidepressant has doubled.

Two years ago, this myth was finally debunked when research emerged that showed antidepressant withdrawal to be, on aggregate, more severe, protracted and common than clinical guidelines acknowledged.[42] It revealed that around 50 per cent of antidepressant users experienced withdrawal, with up to half of those reporting their withdrawal as severe, and that a significant proportion experienced withdrawal for many weeks, months or beyond. In 2019, these findings finally led to the UK's national clinical antidepressant guidelines being revised, a revision later adopted, in a major U-turn, by the Royal College of Psychiatrists. Now that severe and protracted withdrawal is formally recognised, the hope is that long-term prescribing will consequently reduce, as withdrawal is less regularly misread as relapse and drugs are less unnecessarily reinstated.

False myths are not the only factors fuelling our long-term prescribing epidemic. Despite the misdiagnosis of withdrawal problems and people's fear about stopping the drugs, many people take or continue to take them simply because there are so few alternatives on offer. In England last year, 7.4 million adults were prescribed an antidepressant in the NHS, compared to only 1 million who were referred for a psychological therapy. And this is not because people prefer the drugs; the majority of people consulting a GP for help would prefer a talking therapy[43] or some form of social support. It is rather because our services are bereft of psychosocial alternatives, leaving 1 in 10 people having to wait over a year to access NHS therapy (and the rest often waiting for many weeks or months).[44] Thus drugs have become the overwhelmingly prevalent mental health intervention not because of their high safety, efficacy and desirability, but due to decades of chronic underfunding of services, the dominance of powerful pharmaceutical/psychiatric interests, and a drug-first approach that has neatly aligned with the preferences of late capitalism (as we will later explore). In this sense, they have thrived not because they have improved the emotional life of the nation (the opposite, in fact, is more likely to be true), but because they have served as a sticking plaster for deeper maladies caused by structural problems afflicting our mental health sector and wider economy.

———————

I began this chapter with a discussion of household debt. Perhaps you may now begin to understand why. There is something oddly analogous about how debt and drugs have operated socially since the 1980s. While the use of both was modest in the 1970s, their consumption has exploded in the decades since. And although there are obviously rational uses for both (debt for sensible investment, and some drug use for short-term stabilisation of the most severe forms of distress), the vast proportion of both household debt and drug consumption appears harmful in the long run. The reason why the consumption of both is at an all-time high, therefore, has nothing to do with improving people's lives, at least not in any deep and sustainable sense. It is rather a response to profound structural problems in our society that debt and drugs have sought to mask. In this sense, both have become definitive sedatives of our times, which, as work like Robert Whitaker's reminds us, may ultimately create more problems than they solve.

But this is not where their similarities end. Aside from pouring vast wealth into the hands of large corporations, debt and drugs have also both acted ideologically, by reclassifying social problems as individual/internal handicaps that their products can purportedly remedy. Psychiatric interventions are framed as targeting biological irregularities supposedly sitting at the base of our ailing mental health, while debt interventions are framed as targeting the economic inadequacies supposedly driving our ailing financial health. Each debt or drug intervention, by claiming to remedy so-called individual deficits, also subtly acquits new capitalist ideas, institutions and policies of any causal responsibility.

In the coming chapters we will see how this depoliticising dynamic is now playing itself out in other settings where mental health interventions are deployed, such as workplaces, schools, therapy clinics and unemployment centres. All such interventions now readily recast the problems arising from new capitalist social predicaments as personal maladies, problems or threats. In what follows, I want to explore the ways in which such interventions have become ideologically pervasive, being, as they are, supportive of new capitalist modes of thought and action. The starting place for this discussion will be the social institution in which most of us spend the vast majority of our waking lives: the world of daily work. For perhaps it is there, more than anywhere else, where it is believed the effective management of emotional distress will yield the most significant financial benefits, not just for individuals, but for the wider political economy.

3

THE NEW DISSATISFACTIONS OF MODERN WORK

From the 1980s onwards, working life in the West underwent a seismic shift. As the manufacturing sector that had dominated the British economy during the era of regulated capitalism was gradually dismantled (shrinking from 40 per cent of the economy in the 1970s to a mere 10 per cent today), there was an explosion under new capitalism in the service sector, that part of the economy whose primary aim is not to *make* things, but rather to *sell* things; the things we consume daily: goods, services, health care, leisure, tourism, education and financial services. As the manufacturing sector dried up, the service sector gradually boomed, until by 2018 it was consuming a remarkable 80 per cent of the British entire economy.[1]

The national lurch towards the service sector brought profound changes to the working lives of the UK population, placing on it new and unique demands. Some of these demands were obvious from the start, as they could be easily measured. Firstly, from the 2000s, the average number of hours people worked began to rise considerably, as overtime became almost obligatory in the new twenty-four-hour services economy.[2] Secondly, as the service sector demanded more flexible workers, who could move jobs with ease, the average length of time spent in any given job dropped by around a half[3] – with the average employee now changing jobs once every six years.[4] Since 2015, such required flexibility has also fuelled the rise of the 'gig economy', where nearly five million people in the UK now work on temporary or day-by-day contracts, enjoying no secure employment.[5] Finally, as the service economy largely operated in urban centres, where property prices had grown most steeply, more of us began seeking cheaper homes in suburban settings, increasing the average time we spend commuting each week to nearly five hours (or closer to seven hours for Londoners).[6] In short, these changes mean we now work much longer, commute much further and move jobs much more frequently than we did in the previous four decades.

While these changes have had significant knock-on effects for community cohesion, our personal and family lives, our sense of job security and our emotional health, there were other changes to our working lives whose consequences were more profound still. These changes concern the demands now being placed on employees from within the workplace itself – demands that go to the very core of the kind of people we are. Today, in very particular ways, the modern worker looks, feels and behaves very differently to the average worker of the past, and this has had, as we will see, profound implications for the mental and emotional health of our current working population.

In the mid 1980s, as the service sector expanded, a problem arose that soon began costing businesses millions of pounds a year: too many people, after being hired, turned out to lack the personal qualities required to get the job done. This meant that employers could either try and dismiss newly hired staff (and, if successful, initiate costly rehiring processes) or invest heavily in employee training, in the hope of instilling the qualities workers lacked.

As companies from London to Boston, Manchester to New York grappled with this problem, a simple yet revolutionary idea soon emerged: why not just ask all candidates to sit a personality test as part of their initial job interview? This way companies could better protect against making costly mistakes, by testing for the character traits they most desired in prospective employees and weaning out those who failed to fit the desired psychological profile. These personality tests, first deployed by a handful of companies in the 1980s, rapidly caught on, until by 2014, 80 per cent of all Fortune 500 companies were using them,[7] while between 13 and 65 per cent of all new job applicants in the UK and US were being required to undertake them, depending on the sector.[8]

In 2017, I met one such applicant in a busy café in London's Sloane Square after a mental health seminar I'd run for a group of young playwrights at the Royal Court Theatre. Natalie, a talented twenty-four-year-old writer, was keen to tell me about the struggles of getting her writing career off the ground. Having little money, status or job security, she'd taken on temporary work in the City of London, writing her plays late into the night as her partner slept. As we spoke about her work in the City, I returned to the topic of personality tests, something I'd briefly touched upon in the seminar. 'The damn thing about those tests,' shot back Natalie, 'is that I was rubbish at taking them. I would sit there and try to answer the questions very honestly – as a writer I can be introverted, wild, creative, unpredictable, rebellious. So I'd put it all down. But then I never got the job – what the hell! It was all very demoralising.'

She soon became savvy to the art of personality testing after doing a bit of online research. 'There are literally hundreds of websites telling you how to cheat the tests, telling you what boxes to tick depending on the job you're going for. They claim that if you want a job you *have* to fake it – imitate the person your employers probably want. I learnt very quickly that earning a bit of money depended on being a very good impostor.'

Natalie recounted all this cheerfully, but behind the facade she felt guilty about duping the system; about feigning a particular personality to get a job. The plain truth is that she is not alone in faking assessments to gain an edge in the employment market. As the largest and most recent study on personality testing revealed, over half of all participants game the tests, emphasising traits they believe are desirable while hiding those they fear could jeopardise their job chances.[9] In other words, Natalie belongs to a vast pool of people embroiled in an elaborate personality game, where winning relies upon your capacity to identify and perform the persona your prospective employers may most desire.

When I raised the topic of personality tests with Dr David Frayne, a leading authority on work psychology and a fellow at New York University's prestigious Global Institute for Advanced Study, he was clear about the growing obsession with personality in the modern workplace: 'In the more industrial economy of the pre-1980s, it was relatively easy to spot the productive employees in your workforce,' he told me. 'You just measured how many units or items they made per hour of their labour, and worked back from there. But as making things became less common in the new services economy, output became more immaterial, less easy to pin down, making the actual productivity of workers far more difficult to assess.'

So from the 1980s onwards, big business began devising new ways of gauging the precise kinds of employees most likely to thrive in the new services economy: 'They soon realised that making profit was now directly connected to the actual *conduct* of their workers – their capacity to deliver a service with a smile, so to speak,' continued Frayne. 'So they focused more on our personal characteristics, on our character, our professionalism and displays of commitment to the company, which led to a deeper regulation and monitoring of our conduct: of how we look, relate and act.'

While different jobs demand slightly different worker qualities, the 'good worker' is broadly someone who demonstrates, as Frayne wrote, 'mastery over the social norms of professionalism, displaying commitment, enthusiasm and an alignment with the goals of the organisation'.[10] In essence, companies are after those deemed to be team players, optimistic, friendly, aspirational, extrovert if possible, and not too intransigent.

Such people are considered good for a company's image, profits and *esprit de corps*. As the culture of work changed over the 1980s and 1990s, our concept of the good worker changed too; a concept putting greater emphasis on who you are or who you appear to be, rather than on what you do or produce.

———————

On 5 January 2015, commuters on the London Underground encountered a curious sight in the curved ad spaces located above their seats. On train after train these spaces were filled with bright yellow posters, each containing one of the three following sentences, all written in bold Helvetica script:

It's as if someone were out there making up pointless jobs for the sake of keeping us all working.

Huge swathes of people spend their days performing tasks they secretly believe do not really need to be performed.

How can one even begin to speak of dignity in work when one secretly feels one's job should not exist?

While you'd expect most people to smile wryly at yet another oddity on the Tube, that's not quite how things played out. The posters rather set off a Twitter storm, as thousands of people began posting and vigorously discussing the statements online. The anonymously distributed posters, it soon became clear, had hit a deep chord on the morning commute.

Around the same time as the posters were issued, I was involved in a research initiative at the University of Exeter exploring the relationship between mental health and work/life balance. As part of my contribution, I'd started focusing on the sentiments expressed in the posters – a proliferating sense of deep worker dissatisfaction and meaninglessness. As I began exploring the academic literature, in particular, on how such dissatisfaction was being interpreted and managed in our workplaces, the Tube messages seemed uncannily prescient.

Despite the different measures and definitions used in the studies I consulted, they all consistently showed that the highest numbers of employees (around two-thirds) were located in the 'not engaged' or 'dissatisfied' categories.[11] This meant that the majority of UK workers experienced no positive emotional engagement in the work they did (it left them emotionally cold, so to speak) and/or they simply disliked their jobs (they were dissatisfied, bored or unhappy at work). This was also consistent with more recent research from 2018 revealing that around 55 per cent of Brits feel under excessive pressure, exhausted or regularly miserable at work,[12] and that nearly 40 per cent feel their jobs make no meaningful contribution to the world. More startling, 46 per cent of men say they believe their jobs to be entirely meaningless.[13] In short, and to amend slightly one of the Tube posters, not only do huge swathes of us spend our days performing tasks we secretly believe do not really need to be performed, but a significant proportion of us also find our work meaningless, dissatisfying and/or emotionally disengaging.

Levels of worker dissatisfaction and disengagement show some striking changes over time. For example, since the 1970s, these figures have continued to rise – by between 8 per cent and 19 per cent depending on the study consulted.[14] So while levels of dissatisfaction weren't ideal in the 1970s, they have become much worse. But more than this, such rising worker dissatisfaction and meaninglessness is now also closely related to another problem that has persistently vexed the UK economy – a problem the personality tests were originally designed to address: ailing worker productivity. As worker discontent gradually went up nationally, growth in output or productivity gradually went down.[15] See-saw-like, the two trends, the research shows, are inversely related.

As companies were busy trying to recruit the right types of people, the wrong kinds of workplace emotions were now creeping in – dissatisfaction, disengagement, meaninglessness and futility – emotions that were hurting balance sheets far and wide. If personality tests could not protect against these costly workplace emotions, then perhaps other interventions needed to be embraced that targeted these emotions directly. Growing worker distress was therefore opening up a potentially vast new market, one that would be highly profitable for any industry that could claim to reduce these growing levels of worker dissatisfaction.

By the mid 2000s, numerous mental health consultancies had begun developing, packaging and selling their well-being programmes to offices and workplaces far and wide, to a diverse range of employers in both the private and public sectors. Mental health and other initiatives would gradually spring up across our working environment, until what was initially a scatter of outlier courses and schemes would, over the next ten years, spread to every crevice of Britain's working landscape. Indeed, there are now more than eighty different well-being providers in England alone,[16] all suggesting that their services will deliver greater workplace happiness and (of course) productivity.

Today, once we have passed the personality tests that guard the gates to employment, the well-being movement awaits us on the other side, teaching us how to understand, frame and manage any difficult workplace emotions in ways that are having, as we will see, significant and far-reaching effects.

On 19 February 2018, a university lecturer called Malcolm Anderson woke at 4.40 a.m. as usual, and made the 56-mile trip to his office at the University of Cardiff. Before the early rush of students began, he climbed the empty stairway that wound languidly to the top of the university's library. Once there, he opened a large window, climbed precariously onto the ledge and threw himself a hundred feet to the ground below. Moments later, a horrified cleaner noticed the crumpled heap and dashed to his aid. 'Help me, help me,' Malcolm managed to groan before finally losing consciousness. He died later that morning in hospital, leaving behind his wife and three children.

Some weeks after his death, his suicide note, found in a locked drawer in his office, was finally made public. Malcolm had said that he could no longer cope with his crushing workload; the pressure had become too much and he could find no other way out. For weeks and months he had been suffering in private agony, having far more work than anyone could handle, yet no one seemed able to intervene in the way he needed. He had complained to management on a number of occasions about his work allocation, but said he had always received the same unhelpful response.

When I spoke to a lecturer at the university about Malcolm's suicide, he was clearly emotional: 'The whole event illustrates some very serious problems. I mean, the tragic irony of the suicide note was that it was published just as the university was in the middle of its "well-being fortnight", a programme designed to improve the mental health of staff and students and safeguard against these kinds of dreadful events. But the well-being fortnight didn't encourage people to discuss workload or any more substantial matters, neither to come up with meaningful solutions. It was all about, you know, come on a free excursion! Or go on a bike ride, because cycling is good for your health and well-being! There were no substantial or structural changes being offered as viable solutions – the kind of changes obviously Malcolm needed.'

Had Malcolm Anderson come into contact with this expanding well-being movement, what precisely would he have learnt? And would what he learnt have prevented the events leading to his death?

To address this question, allow me to introduce you to one of the largest and most successful workplace well-being providers of them all: Mental Health First Aid – or MHFA for short.[17] It was first launched in England in 2007 under the auspices of the UK Department of Health, and now operates in 24 countries worldwide.

In essence, MHFA's global mission is to create an international army of what it calls 'mental health first-aiders'. Essentially, these are the go-to colleagues in your office who have been trained by MHFA, over a one- or two-day course, to 'identify, understand and help a person who may be developing a mental health issue' in the workplace.[18]

Since 2007, MHFA has trained nearly half a million 'first-aiders' in England (with over 70,000 being trained in 2019 alone). These now operate in a diverse array of workplaces right across the country. This rocketing uptake in MHFA's services has been helped by its claim to address worsening mental health at work and the billions it costs employers each year.[19] By successfully marketing itself as a service that will increase employee productivity and loyalty, while reducing absenteeism and costly sick leave, MHFA relies upon a very simple logic designed to be attractive to the modern employer: any purchase of its services will be far outweighed by the well-being benefits (financial and otherwise) those services will promote.

In June 2019, with this marketing rhetoric in hand, I had little difficulty convincing my university HR department to fork out the £200 one-day training fee required to allow me to join the growing army of mental health first-aiders being trained across the UK. After some initial email exchanges with MHFA, a week later

I was sitting with twelve other attendees in a small conference room in west London, where over the next seven hours we would learn the rudiments of what being a mental health first-aider was all about. Over a steady stream of PowerPoint slides, Morgan, our designated MHFA trainer, would inform us what mental illness actually was, how to spot its emergence in colleagues, when and how to step in to help, and to whom to refer fellow workers when we believed they had become ill. If this all felt like a little bit too much to master in a mere seven hours, well, never fear, we could always rely on the free MHFA manual that was included in the fee, where every pertinent concern and FAQ would be clearly addressed.

During one of our breakout discussions, I quietly slipped away from my group of chatty, coffee-sipping attendees and approached our instructor to ask a few questions in private. 'Thanks very much for this morning's presentation, Morgan, but something does kind of worry me,' I said after a few opening pleasantries. 'It seems that MHFA is using the medical language of "illness" and "disorder" in a very loose fashion, since many of the problems your slides describe as illnesses might be better read in non-clinical ways.'

To illustrate, I then recalled to him the case study our group had just discussed, concerning a middle-aged woman called Louise. Louise had worked for a company for eight years and had always performed well during that time. But in a recent appraisal she had said she was sleeping poorly, was finding it hard to concentrate at work and was feeling low and tearful. Despite our group learning that her workload had recently increased, they appeared unconcerned by the relevance of this, or anything else going on at work. Instead they agreed that Louise was displaying the classic signs of depression and might therefore need some professional help.

This emphasis on veering away from discussing *what had happened to* Louise by instead considering *what was wrong with* her (with a view to recommending what support she should seek) is very much at the heart of MHFA's approach. For example, while it does recognise that for some people in distress 'some reasonable workplace adjustments may be necessary', it is clear that first-aiders are not being trained to think about how to facilitate such adjustments. Rather, they are being asked to direct the people they have identified as suffering towards seeking 'appropriate professional help' such as 'medication, counselling or psychological therapy' – help that will enable them to recover more quickly and so return to their working demands. If people do not respond positively to these suggestions, first-aiders are asked to 'identify any barriers and reluctance a person may experience about accessing treatment' so that such barriers can be removed.

'What concerns me about all this,' I noted to Morgan, 'is that the general thrust of MHFA training is not about encouraging or empowering us to challenge managers and the organisational culture of our workplaces, but is rather about asking us to manoeuvre people towards mental health services that generally don't explore these things, and that invariably end up medicalising our distress and treating it accordingly – as a problem rooted in self rather than environment.'

Morgan appeared a little taken aback, before responding curtly: 'We don't make up the rules. We just outline the known symptoms of mental illness and teach you how to recognise them so you can refer people for professional support if needed.' To be fair, he was indeed correct. MHFA doesn't make up the rules: it simply teaches first-aiders how to play by them. But it is also true that the organisation doesn't question these rules either. You could even say that it advocates them, despite the fact that if we start uncritically advocating medical understandings of employee distress, other serious questions must follow: what happens to the idea that our environment, social circumstances or our jobs may be responsible for our misery? And what about the fact that more and more people find their work dissatisfying or meaningless; would this not affect their mental health? By not even mentioning these things, is MHFA not simply colluding with – or even worse, becoming an ambassador for – the uncritical medicalisation, and thus depoliticisation, of widespread worker distress?

Morgan and I continued talking until the end of the break, at which point we agreed to resume later. While I did not get to talk to him privately again (he now seemed to be avoiding me), I did manage to corral a couple of fellow first-aiders during lunch and asked whether they shared any of my concerns. David, head of human relations at a mid-sized London firm, was buoyant: 'It's great that courses like these exist – when I started working, it was all stiff upper lip in the office. This helps to change that, I think.' I agreed that the stiff-upper-lip culture was silly and harmful, but asked what happened to people once they did open up. Were they being asked to frame their problems in useful ways? Should first-aiders like us really be advising people to consult their GPs?

'What's wrong with that?' asked David. 'Surely that's where they'll get the help they need?'

'Well, not if their problems are situational or social or caused by work itself,' I answered. 'How can a GP possibly resolve issues like that, especially in a mere five-minute consultation? The fact is that they can't, and what's more, they are not trained to do so – and so instead, you are likely to be given a prescription, which shifts the emphasis towards something within *you* that is now being corrected rather than something within the workplace.' David and I enjoyed going back and forth a few more times, until his phone started buzzing, at which point I approached Jayne.

Jayne, it turned out, was the only other researcher on the course. She worked as a statistician at the University of Southampton, crunching demographical data for primary care services. 'I am here because there were quite a lot of mental health crises at work last year. As I showed interest in some of these issues, the department nominated me to come along.'

I asked her for her impressions of the course so far. 'Well, some of the research patter is a little bit questionable,' she responded, 'especially the stuff on outcomes – whether what MHFA offers has any positive effect on the workplace. I couldn't help notice,' she continued, 'that there was nothing at all on whether mental health first-aiders actually benefit co-workers or the company itself.'

She was right. The research on this matter was entirely absent. The MHFA website only cites four pieces of research, none of which address whether MHFA services actually improve employees' mental health and deliver the raised productivity and cost savings their marketing suggests. Instead, the research merely assesses whether first-aiders feel more knowledgeable and confident about managing mental health issues once their training is complete. So, despite hundreds of thousands of people in England training in MHFA, and hundreds of millions of pounds being spent on these courses globally, there is actually no evidence whatsoever that MHFA services benefit anyone other than the first-aiders themselves.

This absence of supportive evidence is not just true for MHFA, but for a burgeoning number of other well-being providers operating across the country today. When the UK government's Public Health England commissioned the first major review of these well-being programmes, not one was able to provide evidence showing that they directly improved worker productivity, lessened absenteeism or raised staff well-being. In fact, where organisations provided evidence on mental health outcomes, only one, a mindfulness-based online resource, could prove that it reduced stress and anxiety. The fact that this mindfulness resource was not actually a workplace programme, however, left me bemused as to why it had been included in the review at all.

Given that the research into these well-being programmes does not appear to support their implied claims, you'd expect this government-commissioned study to offer some strong words of caution about them. But that is not what we get. Rather, we hear words of praise and optimism: 'This study provides insight into a complex landscape with many levels of objectives and stakeholders. The workplace wellbeing sector appears vibrant but is still maturing in its ability to provide strong evidence for health and wellbeing outcomes.'[20]

Would the study have been so generous (and would the services have been so popular with employers) if these workplace programmes encouraged employees to reflect critically on the conditions of their working life? Imagine asking a line manager to pay for a well-being course that tries to raise awareness of the various ways in which modern work can make you feel miserable and hopeless. Imagine their paying for a course that teaches that the growing crisis of worker distress has less to do with an epidemic of mental illness than with an epidemic of worker dissatisfaction and disengagement brought about by a host of factors, from flatlining wages to rising wage inequality; from the increase of short-termism in the employment market to longer working hours; from the growing pressure for dual-working households to the erosion of unionised working protections; from lower job security to the rapid expansion of the service sector.

The fact that well-being programmes such as MHFA completely veer away from any of these thorny social concerns is perfectly understandable from the standpoint of their own market ambitions. To sell their wares effectively they have to be attractive to their customers: the companies and organisations that pay for them. And what is more attractive than services that relocate responsibility for employee distress away from the organisational and social conditions of work itself and towards the more private structures of self. The whole business model of workplace mental health consultancies, in other words, fundamentally rests on a message that organisations will happily pay for: one that favours back-to-work policies and exonerates working conditions, while at the same time enabling organisations (and the government that helps fund these programmes) to declare sanctimoniously that they are tackling poor mental health.

———————

In 2011, the Canadian Mental Health Association posted a short animation on its website that quickly went viral. A six-year-old girl narrates the film, which relays a procession of pictures that she has drawn. The first picture is of her and her father smiling and hugging as they play ball in the garden – the sun shines brightly in the background and a big pink flower is in bloom. Over the picture the little girl narrates: 'My daddy is the bestest daddy in the world. We play, laugh and have lots of fun, before he goes to work.'[21]

As soon as the girl says the word 'work', a gloom descends. The next picture shows her father, now very sad, leaving for work in his car, with dark clouds brooding overhead and a red tear rolling down his cheek.

There then follows a picture of her with a very sad face, holding a drooping teddy. She narrates in a downcast voice: 'When my daddy comes home, he looks very tired and sad. I wish my bear could make my daddy feel happy again.' Her final picture shows her father sitting at his desk, head in hands, alone at the end of the day.

While this film is indeed very touching, that alone cannot account for why it enjoyed such wide impact. Along with packing a powerful emotional punch, it does something else extremely well: it leaves the nature and causes of her father's unhappiness at work purposely vague, which makes it easier for almost anyone who feels miserable at work to project their own experiences onto the film. This way, the narrative becomes very personal, speaking to anyone experiencing discontent at work for whatever reason. Once the film has built this personal connection with the widest possible audience, its webpage then invites you to consider the solutions for your own work distress. The first arrives in the form of an online survey devised to help you identify 'where your level of mental fitness could be improved to help you cope with all of life's up and downs'. Its thirty questions assess your levels of individual resilience, flexibility, ability to enjoy life and self-actualisation. Once filled in, the survey's algorithms set about calculating what personal qualities you should aspire to develop or improve in order to acquire such mental fitness. The next test – a work/life balance quiz – claims to be able to tell you accurately whether you are dedicating sufficient time to friends, family, hobbies and outside interests. If not, some rebalancing will be necessary to bring life back into happy accord again.[22]

While both tests seem harmless enough, their surreptitious message is far less innocent: your distress, they imply, is due to something gone awry within you or your own life that you have the freedom to put right. Perhaps you need to reboot your work/life balance, or to become more flexible, resilient or better at self-actualising. Without explicitly saying so, the central message is basically that you need to change, and change is in your own hands. Questions about the external causes of and solutions for your distress simply don't arise; nor do questions as to whether people actually have the time or financial freedom to change.

While most of us would like to spend more time with family and friends, surely reducing our working hours is a luxury that only few can afford. And while self-actualisation also sounds appealing enough, how viable is it for the 60 per cent whose leisure time will be largely spent recovering from jobs that leave them empty and exhausted? Sure, while developing more flexibility and resilience sounds compelling on the page, are these developments really going to improve your well-being or will they simply better adapt you to the kind of work that goes against your fundamental human desires and needs? The real world does not allow us to easily embrace the idealistic self-improvement strategies that these campaigns simplistically advocate; strategies that, despite any good intentions, are mostly impractical distractions from realities often best unseen.

This dominant theme of changing our selves rather than our relationship to the contexts in which we operate can be seen in a final example. It concerns a recent national initiative undertaken by the UK Advisory, Conciliation and Arbitration Service (ACAS) and largely funded by the government's Department for Business Innovation and Skills.[23] Since its launch in 2015, a central focus of ACAS's Promote Positive Mental Health at Work campaign has been teaching managers across the country how to identify and manage mental distress or 'illness' in their employees. Like the ongoing MHFA campaign, ACAS agrees that if you can spot mental health problems in your workforce early on, you will spare yourself costly losses to employee productivity down the line. So how are managers advised to intervene in worker distress?

Firstly they are told not to think too much about wider social causes of distress in the workplace. After all, mental illnesses have 'many possible causes'. And while 'some of these causes may be related to workplace issues ... more often than not these [workplace issues] will compound existing medical or personal problems'. In other words, while workplace issues may be implicated in worker distress, they are rarely to blame, because there is some existing fault within you making these issues more impactful than they otherwise would be.

Managers are then told to be vigilant when trying to spot mental illness, as it is 'less conspicuous than physical illness' and also because employees 'may work very hard to disguise their symptoms'. Despite these barriers to detecting the mentally unwell, managers are informed that they should still be able to identify them if they work hard to 'take note of what you see as you walk around or in team meetings'; if they familiarise themselves with the signs of illness, so to speak. So what *are* the classic signs of 'mental illness' that managers should try to identify in their colleagues? Well, fortunately, ACAS provides a list:

- Uncommunicative or moody behaviour

- Poor performance

- Poor timekeeping

- Poor decision-making

- Lack of energy

- An increase in unexplained absences or sick leave

Given the countless understandable reasons why someone could manifest any of these issues at work, it is odd that ACAS provides no rationale for why these signs should be reframed as so-called symptoms of illness. This is all the more surprising since none of the signs actually map onto any official diagnostic criteria for depression or anxiety (as problematic as these criteria can be),[24] and all of them could be interpreted in manifold non-medical ways – as classic signs of worker dissatisfaction and disengagement, for starters.

After managers are taught how to medicalise normal human behaviours, they are then asked to 'engage with the problem'. This involves 'developing a rapport with the employee' to get at a 'deeper understanding of their problem', which will enable them to identify 'the best coping strategies' for that particular person. While such strategies may include superficially tweaking the immediate working environment (helping with desk swaps, advising walks in the park and the use of to-do lists), if these tweaks don't work, you are advised to refer your colleagues for counselling, employee assistance or specialist clinical services such as the kind of psychological therapies we will consider in the next chapter – therapies, as we will see, that are designed to serve the task of getting people back to work with minimum fuss or expense.[25]

In short, when we inspect the expanding raft of

workplace well-being interventions, we learn that MHFA is no outlier in the burgeoning mental health consultancy world. It is rather one typical example of a rapidly expanding social movement that is busy medicalising and reframing how we should understand and manage the pains of work in modern life.

Six months after Malcolm Anderson took his own life, academics at the University of Cardiff had had quite enough. Over five hundred of them now took direct action, highlighting their workplace grievances in a joint public statement. The university, by failing to tackle the deeper institutional and social roots of workplace distress, was purposely 'sticking its head in the sand', and the new mental health programme being championed as a solution was 'just an inadequate sticking plaster'.[26] As one Cardiff academic put it to me: 'These workplace programmes are simply a distraction – they are about depoliticising the problems of work, which have structural and organisational roots. In fact, you could even say it is more insidious than that – they are really about trying to control the way we are allowed to talk about our distress, shaping it in a way that always tries to exonerate the organisation.'

Of course, many advocates for these programmes would counter that they perform a vital public service by emphasising the links between work and emotional health, by suggesting that working too hard for too long can be harmful and by insisting employers and managers should be sympathetic to employees in emotional need. When and where their messages help people in distress, these advocates do have an important point. But what many Cardiff academics were now realising was the extent to which such programmes are also political tools that subtly redirect our discourse away from challenging the major problems afflicting working life (especially with regard to how it has evolved over the last thirty years) and towards thinking of ourselves as somehow at fault, and in need of services that may remedy our afflictions (at a cost).

While many academics therefore see things critically, the growing popularity of these programmes suggests that most of us probably do not. And perhaps we do not for understandable reasons. Such programmes, after all, target managers and employees, who are often struggling, tired and overworked; who often lack the time, job security and in some cases the critical resources needed to challenge the status quo. They also overlook the widespread meaninglessness of much modern work, while evading critical reflection on the economics that shape the employment market. By subtly accepting that increased worker output and productivity, rather than the nurturance of wider human potential, should be the primary goal of their interventions, these programmes give simple and attractive solutions to problems that have far deeper and more complicated roots, and provide moral cover to both corporations and politicians who claim, in good faith, that they take mental health seriously via the services and funding they offer.[27]

Given the evident benefits such consultancies bring to organisations, it is little wonder that they continue to thrive despite there being no evidence for their effectiveness – no research showing they make people less distressed and more productive at work. But perhaps, from the standpoint of company and organisational interests, being effective is not really the point. After all, when push comes to shove, these programmes still deliver significant value for money, by largely helping to control the narrative about what causes workplace distress. By removing difficult work experiences from the domain of public discussion, and placing them into the private domain of the consultancy room, the negative effects of modern work can be medicalised, individualised and depoliticised and thus more safely, quietly and confidentially diffused.

In October 2019, after attending a meeting in London at the Royal College of Psychiatrists, I noticed a large placard bolted to the wall behind the main reception desk as I left the building. Across the placard, emblazoned in bright green letters, were the words: *Mental Health First Aid.* MHFA had somehow managed to manoeuvre its way into the heart of the British psychiatric establishment. The placard's prominent positioning in the main lobby symbolised the college's seal of approval and the fact that certain allegiances had already crystallised. After all, the medicalisation of common forms of emotional distress is central to what both organisations do, with both promoting drugs like antidepressants for evidently social and psychological problems (even if this only happens by implication with MHFA). Whatever your view on the spread of these consultancies, the placard illustrates that they are winning mainstream support and have ideologically aligned with the biomedical thrust of our mental health system as it has developed over the last few decades – a system to which they send dissatisfied and disengaged workers for medical and psychological interventions. As to how these interventions operate, well, that will be the topic of the next chapter.

4

THE NEW
BACK-TO-WORK
PSYCHOLOGICAL
THERAPIES

In January 2005, two men entered a room in the UK government's Cabinet Office to address the prime minister's strategy unit. The room was crammed with public officials, MPs and senior advisers, all hoping to hear a solution to a problem vexing the government: how to fix a mental health system in crisis. While millions of people were being prescribed psychiatric drugs each year, the latest evidence was now revealing that these drugs were far less safe and effective than originally supposed. What was more, patients were complaining in their thousands of being offered no alternative to medication, a situation that was quickly turning political after it emerged that less than 1 per cent of the entire NHS budget was being spent on psychological therapies. This meant that the average waiting time for receiving talking therapy was 8–12 months. Even the government's independent body for clinical effectiveness, the National Institute for Clinical Excellence (NICE), was declaring the situation unsustainable. And so crucial questions were now reverberating through Whitehall. How could therapy provision be increased across the country in a safe, economical and effective way? Was there a form of national provision that, while addressing the needs of a nation, could also fit neatly within the government's budget constraints?

The two men who entered that Cabinet Office meeting believed that they possessed the answer. The first was Lord Layard, an economist by profession, who had made a career at the London School of Economics studying the economic burden of unemployment, and who had now turned his hand to addressing the costs incurred to the economy as a result of poor mental health. The second was an academic called David Clark, a professor of psychology who had spent years championing a form of therapy known as cognitive behavioural therapy (CBT), which had apparently shown superior results in the things that mattered to public officials: treating people quickly and cheaply – getting them well and back to work.

The pair had fifty minutes to sell their vision of how a national psychotherapy programme could operate across the country. Their argument had to be as succinct as it was powerful. Layard opened by presenting the economic case: depression and anxiety cost the British economy around £12 billion each year in incapacity benefits, lost productivity and lost tax receipts. If the government were able to spend around £0.6 billion annually on a national therapy service, this service would not only pay for itself but could actually save the economy around £1.5 billion a year by keeping people productive, in work and off benefits.[1] He now had the room's attention.

Then up stood David Clark, a self-assured Cambridge academic, perhaps quietly confident that his audience would soon be wooed. He began by championing the virtues of CBT, a relatively new therapy that was largely about changing people's perspectives; helping them better adapt to the circumstances in which they found themselves. The theory went that people continued to be depressed or anxious because they were thinking and/or behaving in irrational or distorted ways, so if you simply changed their style of thought and behaviour, you would change how they felt. From this perspective, suffering resulted from a kind of thought disorder that had to be dredged up, challenged and revised. By way of such cognitive restructuring, sufferers would be guided towards a more optimistic outlook. 'The aim of CBT,' as NHS Choices later put it, 'is to help you think more positively about life and free yourself from unhelpful patterns of behaviour.' To achieve this, therapists would get you to set new goals and try to uproot negative thought patterns. CBT is therefore primarily about changing people (their attitudes, beliefs and behaviours) rather than situations. It's about helping people better adapt to their work, social and domestic pursuits.

Layard and Clark's joint presentation was a palpable success. The vision they offered promised recovery to potentially millions of people and assured a dramatic reduction in the economic burden of poor mental health. It was also politically non-threatening, as it located the cause of people's problems squarely within themselves, within their psychopathology, and not within their circumstances or situations. This perspective was further affirmed by the fact that the new therapy service would only admit people whose distress had first been medicalised – reframed in terms of a depressive, anxiety or more serious internal mental disorder; as a dysfunctional reaction to an apparently sane social world. In other words, the service would ensure that the medicalisation (and so depoliticisation) of distress was a precondition for receiving therapy. 'No diagnostic assessment, no access', or so the mantra went.

The Labour government was so impressed with this vision, it pledged in its next election manifesto a vast increase in psychological therapy, precisely along the lines advocated by Layard and Clark. Within six months, the two men were asked to design, lead and implement this new national therapy programme, which would be called Improving Access to Psychological Therapies – or IAPT for short.

By 2006, the national rollout of IAPT had begun, starting with two treatment centres, which expanded to ten within a year. By 2008, a full 32 IAPT therapy centres had been opened, a figure that has now reached around 220. In short, the IAPT programme was soon being heralded as one of the most ambitious and swiftly implemented state-run therapy initiatives anywhere in the world. Its success was being marketed by reference to the number of people being treated (nearly ten million since its inception in 2005) and the solid results it was apparently achieving. Alongside the growing reputation of IAPT, the programme catapulted its two masterminds, Clark and Layard, almost to celebrity status within the UK's mental health arena, and the media responded accordingly, with article after article rooting the salvation of our nation's ailing mental health in the continued expansion of the initiative. By 2011, the new coalition government had been persuaded too; surprisingly, in a time of austerity, it pledged a further half a billion pounds to the service over the next few years.

———————

In 2010, Dr Michael Scott, an urbane clinical psychologist in his mid sixties, based at the University of Manchester, began to notice something odd when assessing IAPT patients. Alongside his job working as an academic and clinician, Scott had acted for twenty years as an expert witness for the courts, reviewing hundreds of compensation cases for people who had been involved in accidents of varying kinds. As part of these assessments, he was made privy to their medical records, including the records of those who had accessed IAPT treatment either before or after their accident.

'What I heard time and again,' he told me as we discussed his research, 'was people saying that their IAPT treatment had simply not helped them, irrespective of what they were suffering from. People were either dropping out of IAPT therapy because it felt just irrelevant, or, if continuing the therapy (usually of around six sessions), telling me they were unimpressed by what it had achieved. In some cases, I even found people pretending to their therapists that they were better, in the hope that this would bring their course of treatment to a quicker end.'

As Scott encountered more and more of these negative

accounts, by 2012 he was growing sceptical about the accuracy of the results being reported by IAPT. Why did they paint a picture far more glowing than the negative reports he was encountering through his work in the courts? He decided to investigate this by looking more closely at how the effectiveness of IAPT therapy was being assessed.

The first matter that intrigued him was that IAPT was responsible for gathering data on its own performance. There were no independent assessments being conducted – no Trading Standards Authority or any other organisation holding IAPT to independent account. 'And so I began to wonder to what extent the impressive results could be, at least in part, a product of IAPT simply marking its own homework.' It was at this point that Scott realised that he was in a unique position to address this question more systematically, by undertaking an independent assessment of IAPT's true effectiveness.

He started by reviewing just 65 cases of people who had passed through IAPT services. His method was to follow a standard yet robust litigation procedure for evaluating claimants' mental health, which included undertaking in-depth, open-ended interviews, carrying out standard diagnostic assessments and reviewing all therapy and medical records. Once the data were analysed, he found that whatever the condition being treated, only around 16 per cent of people could be said to be actually recovering as a result of their IAPT therapy – an outcome that was seriously at odds with the results being publicly reported by IAPT. 'If you look at the official IAPT results,' Scott told me, 'apparently half of people [46 per cent] recover as part of their IAPT treatment. But here I was finding only a small fraction of that reporting any positive experience at all.'

When you delve into Scott's research, you do encounter some shortcomings. The sample was small – 65 people in total. Also, as everyone in the sample was seeking accident compensation, perhaps they were downplaying their recovery to increase their chances of receiving a payout. This would have been fatal for the research were it not for the fact that around 20 per cent of the sample had actually undergone IAPT therapy before their accidents, making their therapeutic outcomes entirely irrelevant to any claims they were seeking. What's more, this 20 per cent reported the same recovery rates as everyone else in the sample, further suggesting that rates were not being downplayed to increase a perceived chance of compensation.

While Scott's research therefore had some limitations, these weren't sufficient to invalidate his findings, which raises the question as to why the recovery rates he unearthed (16 per cent) were so much lower than those being reported by IAPT (46 per cent). I put this question to him.

'Well, you have to look at how IAPT's official stats are actually gathered,' he replied, 'because what initially looks like a positive finding is nothing of the kind.'

Here is what he means. There are three types of patient in IAPT: those who are referred for treatment but never turn up; those who access treatment but soon drop out; and those who complete a course of treatment, usually between two and six sessions. 'The reason IAPT claims 46 per cent of patients recover through therapy,' says Scott, 'is because it only assesses the people in the final category; only those patients who have actually completed treatment.' This means that a full half of all IAPT patients, the half that actually drop out of treatment, are simply not factored into the final results.[2]

The reason critics have seized upon this omission is because the correct way to conduct research on recovery is to include all those who drop out of treatment in your final results, because by not doing so you will artificially inflate the recovery rates in a positive direction. After all, we know that a large proportion of people drop out because they feel the treatment is just not working, is not meeting their needs or is simply harming them. 'And this is why,' said Scott animatedly, 'I would go as far as saying IAPT is fiddling the books, by assessing and reporting the data in such a way as to make their service look as successful as possible.'

So what happens if you do what IAPT is not doing and include all those who drop out of treatment in your final recovery result? Well, this is precisely what the University of Chester's Centre for Psychological Therapies did, only to discover that the number of patients recovering through IAPT suddenly plummets from 46 per cent to around 23 per cent; a figure that is, incidentally, far closer to the 16 per cent recovery rate originally found in Scott's research. When the results are analysed in the correct and standard way, in other words, it turns out that only around 2 in 10 people actually recover as a result of IAPT treatment, which is woefully below the nearly 5 in 10 people being officially reported by IAPT itself.[3]

But if 2 in 10 seems a very poor outcome indeed, then just consider what happens when you question how recovery is defined by IAPT. Does it mean that a person's mental health problems have disappeared, or that they have experienced an obvious and meaningful change in how they feel, or that their friends and family notice they're back to their usual self again? Well, it means nothing of the sort, and the following thought experiment helps explain why.

Imagine for a moment that you have been referred for IAPT therapy because you are feeling low. At the beginning of your treatment you are asked to complete two questionnaires that assess on a scale from 1 to 20 how depressed or anxious you are. The higher you score the worse your condition is thought to be. After each therapy session you will fill in these questionnaires, until the therapy has run its course. If at the end of your therapy your score is lower than it was at the start, this means you have improved. So how much lower does your end score have to be for you to be classed as recovered? This is what IAPT has to say: 'Someone who initially scored just above the clinical threshold for depression at the start of treatment [as the clinical threshold is 10, let's say they scored 11 at the start], and just below this threshold at the end of treatment [let's say they scored 9 at the end], will have "recovered" in the sense of no longer having clinically significant symptoms.' To translate: IAPT can officially class you as recovered even if you have only improved by a mere two points on the scale, which is an improvement so minor that it will invariably represent almost no change at all in your actual experience. This is to say, you can be classed as recovered even though, oddly enough, you may not feel you have recovered at all.

This situation seems so peculiar that I decided to contact the Health and Social Care Information Centre, the organisation that collates IAPT's data, to enquire as to how many of the 23 per cent classed as recovered improved by only 2 or 3 points on the scale. They responded that their analysis had not looked into this matter. All they could tell me was how far, on average, IAPT patients generally improve. Of the small numbers recovering from anxiety, that average improvement is around 5 points, and for those with depression around 7 points. To put this in perspective, given that a person can move 5–7 points on the scale if they are merely sleeping and concentrating a little better, even these improvements do not herald any kind of resounding clinical success.

To put all this in its barest terms, then: the 2 out of 10 people who recover as a result of IAPT therapy are improving, on average, in small and often clinically inconsequential ways. 'And this is where things become more concerning,' said Scott, 'because even these very minor improvements may actually have nothing to do with the therapy itself.' This is what he means. IAPT does not compare the patients who recover through its service with what is known as a 'control group' – a group of patients suffering from the same problems but who were given either an alternative treatment (such as a placebo) or no treatment at all. 'Without doing such a control group comparison,' continued Scott, 'you do not know whether the 2 in 10 people who recover through IAPT would have actually recovered without the treatment.'

The reason why this is so serious is because we know that people almost inevitably present at mental health services when they are feeling at their worst – perhaps when things are bad at work or in their relationships. But with the passage of time, they often make some minor adjustments, leading to improvements that have nothing to do with the treatment they are undertaking. For example, people may improve due to a small change in their diet, or an increase in their exercise levels, or through making tweaks at home or at work, or due to the effects (placebo or otherwise) of the medication they are taking (the majority of IAPT patients, by the way, are also taking antidepressants). 'And this is why control group studies are essential,' said Scott. 'You have to know whether patients are improving because of the therapy, or because of something else entirely. If you don't have that information, it is impossible to know for sure what is responsible for any positive clinical change.'

What makes his point all the more prescient is that the largest and most recent meta-analysis conducted on recovery from depression showed that a full 23 per cent of people spontaneously overcame their symptoms of depression within three months without receiving any treatment at all[4] – a figure that exactly matches IAPT's 23 per cent recovery rate when you analyse their data correctly. In other words, administering IAPT to a patient may be, on average, no more effective than administering no treatment at all.[5]

Whatever way you look at it, the story of IAPT does not instil confidence that its results approach anything near acceptable. But even this, unfortunately, is not where the story ends, because there is increasing evidence that it is not only failing hundreds of thousands of patients annually, but is now, in certain quarters, inflicting significant harm – and on the very people you'd least expect.

———————

In 2015, the British Psychological Society surveyed the emotional state of over 1,300 psychological therapists working mainly in IAPT services.[6] The figures that emerged were more alarming than anticipated. They revealed that being employed as an IAPT therapist is now far worse for your mental health than working in almost any other UK job or industry. Nearly half of all therapists surveyed reported suffering from depression, two-thirds reported finding their job highly stressful, and one-third reported having developed a long-term chronic condition. Finally, and perhaps understandably given IAPT's poor success rate, half of all therapists reported feeling a failure in the work they do. As the British Psychological Society concluded: 'The overall picture is one of burnout, low morale and worrying levels of stress and depression.'[7] The report then quoted some typical declarations of unhappiness reported by IAPT staff:

> Being target-driven is the bane of our lives
>
> I am so disappointed, I have just resigned
>
> I carry my resignation letter in my diary now, as I feel that I'm on the verge of giving up the battle
>
> IAPT is a politically driven monster which does not cater for staff feedback/input in any way. All we are told is TARGETS!!! And work harder

When you delve into this and other reports on the experience of working in IAPT services, a pattern begins to emerge regarding what is truly ailing its employees. We hear complaints about a working culture obsessed with form-filling, hitting targets and scoring high on outcome measures. We hear of staff under great pressure to get results in as few sessions as possible, and of distressed patients being discharged before the therapy is done. We hear of recovery being often poor or superficial, of staff having to manage cases beyond their expertise. We hear about a large proportion of IAPT therapists feeling demoralised and overwhelmed by the pressures of having to deliver far more than their resources allow. But more than this, we hear about how this target-driven culture is leading to endemic data manipulation within IAPT services, with figures massaged to hit government targets and to keep the service, and jobs, afloat. This theme also regularly surfaced during my interviews with IAPT staff:

> While we were trying to do good things behind the scenes, data was manipulated to hit targets and not get into trouble ... This is bad for your professional integrity – helping prop up something that is a bit of a lie (Dr Emma Russell, ex-director of an IAPT service)

> In our service if patients did not want to complete their questionnaires [by which services are rated], we are told by our managers to fill them in ourselves ... The subtext is 'be generous' (ex-IAPT worker, west London)

> To hit the waiting list targets we'd offer people some minor intervention but it was not what they really needed – it was what we could offer to get higher results (ex-IAPT lead)

> If you have two sessions where certain clinical measures are taken, the IAPT computer system will assume the client has begun treatment, even

though no proper treatment has been delivered. This blatant example of fudging the statistics, in order to help you hit wait time targets, is used in many IAPT services (Dr James Binnie, ex-clinical lead, IAPT)

We know if our results are low the service is put under threat – and the only help people have will be taken away; this has an effect on how we count things (current IAPT worker)

I have heard from IAPT staff that they are told on workshops to only take 'IAPT patients' – i.e. those who are likely to get better recovery scores (IAPT researcher)

There is no need to pile up more examples, even though I could. What these and other confessions illustrate is how a pervasive surveillance and audit culture is reconfiguring the behaviour and experience of staff on the ground, since 'hitting your targets' is essential to ensuring that your service (and your job) remains intact.

Professor Rosie Rizq left IAPT out of a profound sense of disillusionment and subsequently became one of the UK's most prominent IAPT researchers, looking in particular at staff experience. 'What the designers of IAPT failed to understand,' she told me when I interviewed her at her home in west London, 'is the extent to which therapists experience the work of therapy as a deep vocation. This commitment to what they do may be why they are able to endure poor pay and long hours. But in IAPT that commitment is being exploited. This sense of vocation is being twisted to serve a very different agenda, which has put hitting outcome and efficiency targets over the deeper psychological needs of the people the therapists see. So many of them now find themselves being literally forced, in every detail of their work, into doing something they no longer believe in. When this happens, a terrible strain is generated, which is why we are seeing vaulting levels of psychological distress, anger, futility and a deep, deep sense of disillusionment among IAPT staff.'

Rizq was indicating that such widespread burnout and distress can actually be traced to a particular public sector ideology that consecutive UK governments have implemented since the 1980s. This ideology rests on the belief that if left alone, publicly funded institutions (schools, hospitals and universities) will inevitably tend towards inefficiency. This is because, as the philosophy goes, they operate outside the competitive sphere of the market. By trying to replicate the pressures, demands and productivity of the market within our public services, then, governments have introduced a barrage of targets that services must hit, and consequent penalties should they fail. It was Margaret Thatcher's government that first made moves in this direction by introducing the internal market into the NHS (where trusts have to compete with each other for resources), and then by introducing new styles of business management that punished employee and institutional underperformance.

New Labour took up the baton with their reforms. These introduced the concept of payment by results (payment being linked to performance), and the idea that NHS services should compete with private providers to win government contracts, something that has continued apace during the Cameron, May and Johnson governments. In other words, while consecutive governments have been busy since the 1980s deregulating the private sector, they have done the opposite in the public sector, heaping up regulation after regulation by introducing new targets, incentives and competitive measures with the aim of making services apparently more efficient and businesslike. As the eminent political economist Raymond Plant put it: rather than creating a 'small state', consecutive governments over the last thirty years have actually created a larger 'market state'.[8] This market state, in the absence of governments being able to privatise services, uses government interference to try and refashion public institutions in the image of the market.

In the case of IAPT, such reforms have not only created a target-driven compulsion in services and employees to demonstrate and raise efficiency, but have now turned the services themselves into tools for raising wider productivity – in the form of getting distressed people to return to work. Dr Emma Russell, a former director of one of the UK's largest IAPT services, put it to me this way when I interviewed her about her many years working on the front line: 'Everything about IAPT, from the very beginning, was about putting a price on depression – it was all about getting people back to work; whether reducing their sick leave or getting those out of work in work. This is why IAPT therapists are now being put in unemployment centres.' It is also why workplace consultancies like Mental Health First Aid, as we saw in the last chapter, now widely refer dissatisfied workers to IAPT's therapy programmes. 'The thinking is all joined up,' said Russell. 'It's part of the same old political rationale, despite the fact that most people don't enter therapy to hit back-to-work targets.'

Using IAPT as a mechanism to keep work engagement rates high, and disability and unemployment payments low, is perhaps an even more powerful driver of burnout and depression among staff. After all, one of the dilemmas leading Russell to resign as the clinical lead in a comparatively successful IAPT service was the clash of aims experienced by her staff: for therapists, what matters most is helping people overcome their distress, developing insight into their situation, goals and relationships, and facilitating changes that their patients – not government – define as positive. What seems to matter most to IAPT is proving its own efficiency and cost-effectiveness by treating as many people as possible as swiftly as possible and returning them to productivity – a goal reflected in the work assessments patients are asked to fill out after each session, which religiously monitor how successfully the back-to-work policy is operating.

'While we all know that satisfying work is good for our well-being,' said Russell, 'what the back-to-work agenda does not consider is that there aren't always good jobs for people to go to or return to – jobs that are conducive to mental health or to raising people's self-esteem. If IAPT were less driven by work outcomes, it would be far more sensitive to this.' In the cool calculus of IAPT's target-driven utopia, critical nuances between meaningful and meaningless work – work that inspires and work that depresses – are entirely overlooked. Whatever the nature of the work – zero-hours, part-time, low-paid, insecure – any return is chalked up as serving the wider statistical good, despite clear evidence that the effects of work on your well-being are dependent on the kind of work you do.

Studies have shown, for instance, that moving from good work to bad work has a detrimental effect on our mental health, and that it is only work that people find meaningful, interesting and secure that supports their emotional health.[9] But as the IAPT researcher and therapist Paul Atkinson reminds us: 'Everyone knows that such jobs are increasingly rare [in our economy], and are unlikely to be on offer to anyone bearing the stigma of a mental health label.' Despite this, the IAPT programme rests unashamedly on the principle that 'work is good for you', without any honest acknowledgement of this principle's evident nuances and limitations.[10] In short, while we all acknowledge that helping people back to work is a vital social endeavour – especially if the work is fulfilling – it is clear that if a therapeutic service is designed with that endpoint as a primary target (instead of viewing it as a useful side effect of people recovering), problems are bound to ensue.

–––––––––

When we look at the effects the IAPT programme exerts on both patients and therapists, questions arise as to what the case of IAPT really illustrates. It speaks to many critical themes – such as how data can be manipulated to present the illusion of efficiency, how a culture of target-hitting can drown individual care needs, and how, if wrongly implemented, a reasonably effective therapy can become ineffectual at great cost. All such issues are doubtless important, but for me they still fail to capture the essence of what the IAPT story teaches. For me, this lesson goes beyond the revelation that services are not always what they seem, to informing a debate that sits at the heart of our political life about how and why certain public services fail.

On the one hand, the failure of a state-run service like IAPT might be read as supporting the idea that the state, by its very nature, will always be less effective than the private sector in providing services, no matter how draconian the targets you set. After all, if a private organisation were to fail on the scale of IAPT, it would need to self-correct or it would otherwise fold. The market, in other words, is where inefficiency is best corrected. The problem with this reading, however, is that private industry is replete with examples of failure being buried or bailed out (rather than self-correcting), while there are countless instances of state-run initiatives undergoing swift and effective reform. For these reasons, it is a mistake to see privatisation as *always* the best solution for service failure. So within the NHS, for now at least, the debate has moved on: from whether we should entirely privatise our health service, to what kinds of state (or mixed state/private) provision should be preferred.

The failure of IAPT has therefore nothing to do with its being a state-run initiative, but rather with its being a particular type of state initiative. Built into IAPT's philosophical DNA are political and economic aspirations that are irrelevant to the core needs of the people involved in the service: such as a patient's need to overcome their distress in a meaningful way, or a professional's sense of vocation for their work. Rather, IAPT aims to satisfy broader economic ambitions, such as those advanced by David Clark and Lord Layard when they marketed their vision to the British government in 2005, promising to save the economy billions of pounds each year.

From this standpoint, the service is failing, not because the therapy itself is ineffective (there is ample evidence that the therapies IAPT uses work effectively when deployed outside of the IAPT system), but rather because it has appropriated and distorted the values and practices of psychotherapy to serve its fiscal and pragmatic agenda. In this sense, IAPT was never really about healing people in the way that most therapists understand, but about using therapy to serve abstract economic aims. When you speak to IAPT staff and patients, this indeed seems to be the explanation of its failure that best matches their experience – either those being short-changed by ineffective treatments, or those being demoralised by targets in which they don't believe.

In 2015, the then Chancellor of the Exchequer, George Osborne, announced in his spring budget that IAPT workers would be placed in 350 job centres across the UK. At the same time, there would be employment advisers in every IAPT service. Therefore, in a pro-work quid pro quo, IAPT patients now receive back-to-work encouragement and job advice, while the unemployed can receive back-to-work therapy. Whatever your route into the IAPT system – via workplace consultancies like MHFA, your GP or your local job centre – you can expect your recovery to be measured in terms of what supports your employer and the needs of the wider economy; forms of support that, as we will see in the next chapter, are now being used to manage some of society's most vulnerable members – that is, the ever-growing pool, particularly since COVID, of the unemployed.

5

THE NEW CAUSES OF UNEMPLOYMENT

I met Zabar Kahlil on a wet and windy Thursday evening, at a drive-through coffee shop on the outskirts of Slough. We both ordered hot chocolate to ward off the cold spray gushing in each time the café door blew open. Once sitting down, Zabar told me he was married with four young children and was in his late forties. He had kind, bright eyes, and a soft and gentle manner, which betrayed an almost childlike vulnerability. His parents had emigrated from Pakistan to Slough before he was born, and Zabar had never wanted to move out of the area. Everyone locally knew him as a popular and caring member of the community; a family man it was always good to have around. He did not drink or smoke. He never took days off from work. And at the weekends he enjoyed managing his son's local football team. I immediately warmed to him.

The reason I'd travelled to meet Zabar was because he had a powerful story to tell. Six years earlier, on a nondescript weekday, there was a loud knock at his front door at 5 a.m. He'd opened it to see two policemen on the porch. Zabar's immediate response was to feel relieved. 'Ah, you have found our TV then,' he declared. Two months earlier, someone had broken into their family home; oddly, the TV was the only thing they had taken. The police looked at each other in bemusement before saying they weren't here about his TV. Rather they'd come to arrest Zabar on numerous accounts of committing fraud.

Over the following six months, Zabar's life degenerated into a living nightmare. His wife had just given birth to their third child, but the terrible shock of being arrested and subjected to a lengthy court case made him disengage from his new domestic situation. The national press began widely reporting events, making him constantly terrified he'd lose his job, his only means of keeping his family financially afloat. People in his local community also began to talk – had Zabar really committed a serious crime? Soon many people he loved gradually turned away, and his children also begin asking questions. During the harrowing three-month court case, he would take the train to Reading daily.

'Why do you go into town every day, Daddy?' his kids would ask. He let them believe he had taken a job at the railway station. When the case was in its most fraught stages, he would stay up late when his wife and children had gone to bed, sometimes crying alone.

So what had happened to plunge Zabar into this terrible situation?

I asked his barrister, Bartholomew O'Toole, just that. 'Zabar worked for an employment recruitment agency,' he told me, 'whose job was to find work for unemployed people, in particular for those with disabilities or with a history of finding work difficult. It provided training and skills to help these people get work.' The agency was funded by the government's Department of Work and Pensions (DWP), and it operated on commission: the more people it got into work, the more money it would make.

Zabar had been working at the agency for a few years when irregularities started occurring. Key members of staff felt under immense pressure from senior management to get more people into work more quickly. 'If an employee got more than four people into jobs each week, they'd get a bonus,' said Zabar. 'If they didn't hit these targets, though, the suggestion was you might lose your job.' This was the context where things started to go wrong for Zabar. Under pressure, some recruiters began making up fictitious people they had apparently found jobs for. 'During the court case, I learnt that the recruiters would go into places like this coffee shop we are in now and find out who had been recently hired,' he told me. 'They'd then persuade them to sign up as having passed through our scheme, in return for a small handout.'

Zabar was oblivious to these activities. Unlike the recruiters, his role wasn't to find people work but to process the surrounding administration. Also unlike the recruiters, he did not work on commission, so any bonuses made for fake cases never went to him. 'The only bonus I ever received during my four years there,' he said, 'was when one of my children was born – I got a twenty-pound voucher.' As his salary was fixed, it therefore made no sense for him to do something illegal for commission. His only fault was to sign off the false scripts, which at the time he did not realise were false, and to create one script for an employee on the instructions of his boss, a script he didn't know would be used.[1] The court decided he should have known, and that made him liable. While six of his colleagues went to prison for fraud, the judge understandably took a more lenient view of Zabar, instead giving him a suspended community sentence.[2] 'Even so, I am still affected by it all today,' said Zabar, 'and I am not sure if the impact will ever go away.'

———————

The company Zabar had been working for was called A4e, and was one of the many companies to which the government had outsourced the task of getting unemployed people into work. To understand a little more about A4e and the role it played in our unemployment market, we must first travel back to the mid 1980s; to a time when the welfare system in the UK was undergoing major reform, unemployment in Britain was at its highest point since the 1930s Great Depression, and Margaret Thatcher's government decided, with no small anxiety, to begin tackling the unemployment crisis once and for all.

A key target of her unemployment strategy was to completely reform the benefits system, which she believed had made being unemployed more comfortable than it should be. Her Social Security Act of 1986 made it harder for people to receive and stay on the dole. Benefit payments would now be means-tested and time-restricted, with penalties and employment training awaiting anyone overstaying their welcome. As the historian Florence Sutcliffe-Braithwaite put it, the aim was not to abolish the welfare state entirely, but to slice away at it bit by bit, until only a sliver of breadline provision remained for the poorest minority.[3]

Making it harder to claim welfare support, however, was not Thatcher's only reform. It was accompanied by the promotion of a new narrative about what drove joblessness. Over the next decade, the causes of unemployment were decoupled in the public's imagination from unjust or bad social policy, and linked to a lack of personal qualities like willpower, effort and ambition (an idea celebrated in the early 1990s film *The Full Monty*, where the solution to unemployment was not economic regeneration but individual grit and initiative). As the idea took root that the unemployed were somehow liable for their jobless predicament, along came New Labour in the mid 1990s to rebrand Unemployment Benefit as Jobseeker's Allowance. This new phrase conveyed the idea that receiving benefits now depended upon you actively seeking work, implying that joblessness was a result of not doing so hard enough. In an era when 'things can only get better', the idea was that you could only blame yourself if they did not.

While all these changes over successive governments increased the stigma and anguish of the unemployed, the reforms would pale in comparison to what came next. Following the financial crisis of 2008, and the rise of austerity under the Conservatives, David Cameron's coalition government would tighten the welfare noose almost to strangle point. Following their 2012 Welfare Reform Act, receiving benefits would no longer just be conditional upon proving you were seeking work; it now became conditional on actually doing unpaid work. What had always been called welfare would now be replaced by workfare: working full-time for the benefits you received. While some workfare schemes had existed in small pockets since the days of Margaret Thatcher, the scheme would now be rolled out right across the country, in particular targeting long-term-unemployed people who had either physical or, more commonly, mental health and learning disabilities.

By the end of 2012, literally hundreds of companies were enthusiastically signing up to the government's workfare programme, profiting from the influx of free labour it provided. Stores such as Argos, Asda and Superdrug began recruiting people from the workfare scheme to meet their seasonal demands, instead of hiring extra staff or offering overtime to existing employees.[4] Private companies were scrambling to replace paid employees with non-salaried workfare participants sent from the job centre, who were effectively doing the work for free. A telling example concerns the food company 2 Sisters, which fired 350 workers from its plant in Leicester before moving its pizza production to Nottingham. While the company claimed this move was a result of 'several recent strikes', once settled in Nottingham it took on a hundred free workfare participants instead of recruiting paid employees. In defence, 2 Sisters said it was simply giving unemployed people invaluable experience of working in the food sector.

But it was not just the hundreds of private sector companies that were benefiting from workfare programmes; public sector institutions were also using free workfare labour to plug the redundancies and job cuts caused by austerity, with many hospitals, local services and councils making use of workfare participants to fill poorly staffed services. For example, in 2010, Halton Council shed 10 per cent of its jobs, using workfare placements to fill the gaps, while Lewisham Council closed some of its libraries, with free workfare labour helping to staff the replacement outsourced community libraries. By 2015, over 850,000 people in the UK had been sent on workfare placements. The government justified this expansion by stating that the programme offered crucial skills training and work experience. In reality, however, the placements involved doing unpaid work that nobody else wanted to do – the lowest and most stigmatised jobs of all: cleaning toilets, stacking shelves, working in warehouses or doing outdoor manual labour, jobs that positioned people, socially speaking, at the very bottom of the employment ladder.

The majority of these placements were aimed at people with mental and/or physical disabilities. While the government tried again to justify this on the grounds that this group required job training opportunities more than most, in truth, it occurred against the backdrop of the attempt to bring down the soaring disability benefits bill. As disability payments had doubled since 2004, getting disabled people into work became an overriding priority; which meant that those on disability benefits would bear the brunt of the workfare reforms.

An illustration of what someone could expect from a typical workfare placement was provided by the experience of Matthew, whose story I encountered during my research.[5] Matthew had a significant learning disability, but was quite happy to be given a workfare placement. In fact, he was excited to work, and in particular to work with people. But the charity shop where he was sent appeared not to want a working-class man with some learning difficulties on the shop floor. Charity shops were rebranding at the time to appeal to a more middle-class clientele that was used to customer service à la John Lewis. So they put Matthew in the warehouse, where he spent every day in the freezing cold, sorting clothes on his own. While the employment service told him this was good for him, he experienced it as lonely and demoralising, further depleting his already fragile self-esteem.

But perhaps the most insidious aspect of the workfare programme was that people, including disabled people, could not opt out. If you did not attend your placement, you would have your benefits stopped – or, as it was put, 'sanctioned'. As a result, thousands of people (and their families) were thrown into abject poverty, sometimes because the claimant had simply resisted a placement, often for health reasons, or because they had made minor mistakes such as filling in a form improperly or being late for an appointment. In fact, so strict were the sanctioning rules that by 2013, over a million unemployed people had been penalised – with the majority of the sanctions falling on either disabled people[6] or on those living in districts where it was harder to get a job.[7] These draconian policies, which did indeed help cut the benefits bill, had serious social consequences, significantly contributing to the rise in homelessness and food banks over the same period, and increasing severe anxiety and depression among the unemployed by 50 per cent[8] and, with that, the number of attempted suicides by 25 per cent.[9] Programmes like workfare were not only exploitative and stigmatising, they were also making people ill.

By 2016, the suffering that the workfare programme was causing had reached tipping point, finally provoking political action. As more and more unemployed people began to organise and fight back, grassroots protest groups like Boycott Workfare and Disabled People Against Cuts started listing and lobbying companies exploiting free workfare labour, organising public demonstrations outside their offices, warehouses and shops. Local and national media interest soon grew, and as the public learnt more about the underground exploitation taking place, any association with the workfare programme became almost toxic. One by one companies started opting out of the scheme; an exodus that was hastened when the High Court ruled in 2015 that the government had acted unlawfully by not providing enough information about the sanctions faced by those refusing to take part in workfare.

If the protests and lawsuits were not decisive enough, the final blow for the workfare programme struck hard in 2018, when the University of York published the first independent report on its effectiveness. Based on data gathered and analysed since 2013, the report concluded that workfare programmes were a resounding failure. Not only were they 'largely ineffective in facilitating people's entry into or progression into work', but benefit sanctions did 'little to enhance people's motivation to prepare for, seek, or enter paid work'. Additionally, it was found that sanctions and other workfare strategies had 'routinely trigger[ed] profoundly negative personal, financial, health and behavioural outcomes'.[10]

Although the workfare programme folded across the country, it would be wrong to say that every facet of it disappeared. On the contrary, one of its most essential yet insidious elements strode confidently onwards. Still widely operating across the country today, it is set to expand in the post-COVID era, though mostly below the public and media radar. To hear more about this clandestine aspect of workfare, it is time to meet one of the most important figures in exposing the harms it has inflicted: the academic and human rights campaigner Dr Lynne Friedli.

In 2012, Durham University hosted a research project funded by the prestigious medical research body the Wellcome Trust. The aim of the project was to understand the social and individual impact of the workfare programme as it was implemented across the country. After spending two years working alongside some of the UK's leading policy scientists, Dr Lynne Friedli and her colleague Dr Robert Stearn published what would become the defining academic study of the workfare system, a study that ignited a national media debate, rocked Number 10 and the DWP and ultimately helped to bring the entire workfare edifice toppling to the ground. The decisive move made by Friedli and Stearn was to expose a corrosive activity sitting right at the heart of the programme. They called this activity 'psycho-compulsion'.

To find out more about psycho-compulsion, I met Dr Friedli at her Victorian terraced house just off the chaotic Holloway Road in north London. After warmly welcoming me in her small front garden (purposely covered with fresh green spruce to shelter the nesting sparrows), she apologised for the pile of flyers on the doorstep, explaining that she'd just begun battling the council to reduce car emissions in the area. 'Over a thousand cars pass down our narrow road each day,' she said as she led me back inside. 'All the kids are getting asthma. But Arsenal FC down the road want every junction kept open.' It was something she was understandably upset about; an upset, I guessed, that Arsenal would one day regret, given her impressive campaigning track record.

Once inside with my recorder turned on, I asked Friedli to explain what she and Robert Stearn had meant by the phrase psycho-compulsion. 'It refers to a process that we never intended to study originally,' she told me, 'but that only emerged after we kept encountering benefit claimants who were being sent by their job advisers on what first appeared to be some kind of motivational training.' When they began digging deeper they soon found that these classes were rapidly spreading across the country, and that the unemployed were being threatened with having their benefits removed if they didn't attend.

To understand how these classes and interventions worked, Friedli and Stearn used a simple methodology: alongside gathering many personal testimonies (both positive and negative)[11] from those who had experienced psycho-compulsion, they meticulously assessed and analysed, over two years, all the training materials used by the private contractors being paid by the DWP to run the courses. They also assessed the contracts and training materials the DWP issued for these courses. As they sieved through these materials and testimonies, undertaking many interviews along the way, it became clear that the central intention of the courses was not to provide basic job-training skills, but to impose psychological explanations for why claimants were unemployed, while using interventions to make them more employable.

The DWP seemed to have a clear purpose in mind: to recast unemployment as a psychological deficit that compulsory training would somehow correct. 'And this is why we opted for the term psycho-compulsion,' said Friedli, 'because it reflected what we were finding across the country: the proliferation of compulsory and coercive practices designed to alter the internal attitudes, dispositions and psychology of unemployed people.'

To understand a little better how a typical psycho-compulsion class worked, allow me to introduce you to Izzy Koksal, one of the first claimants to speak publicly about her experience of the practice in an article she wrote for *Open Democracy*.[12]

As Izzy Koksal sat with a group of unemployed people who, like her, had been sent for job training under threat of losing their benefits, she sensed that something was not quite right. When the group leader suddenly exclaimed: 'Nothing is impossible!' – reading this statement from one of the many motivational quotations stuck all over the walls in the meeting room – Izzy stared back at him blankly, realising this session was not going to focus on improving CVs and interview skills. In fact, the course 'had much grander ideas' in mind, she wrote, such as teaching you how to tackle the true causes of your unemployment – the things buried deep down within you that allegedly impeded your ability to get a job.

We have already encountered the company running Izzy's course: A4e. It was where Zabar Kahlil had worked for four years before two police officers knocked on his front door that fateful morning. While Zabar was responsible for processing the administration around finding people work, he was also responsible for signing off on the courses that people like Izzy were forced to attend. A4e was one of many private providers required to offer psycho-compulsion courses if they were to win the lucrative contracts offered by the DWP.

'And so, for two days I sat with ten other unemployed people being told that we needed to "talk, breathe, eat and shit belief in ourselves",' wrote Izzy. 'The experience was like being in some sort of strange comedy sketch that just went on and on … Even the toilet signs were plain weird – the sign for the disabled loo had a man with a broken leg that appeared to be bandaged up with toilet roll.' Other oddities included being told how to be assertive in a way that would excite your prospective employers. There was 'no need to be nice and fluffy about it; tell them straight up: "I am the one you're looking for." Like *The Matrix* – "I am the one" – it was only when he believed he *was* the one that he became the one.'

She reported that the entire course felt like one long motivational psycho-boost, with very little real content. 'The main point, which was hammered home time and again, was that if we believed we could get a job, then it would happen. It was simply our mindset that was the barrier.' In fact, the trainer seemed so intent on this message getting through that he appeared to want all attendees to have 'mini epiphanies there and then', as if jobs would flow seamlessly in the wake of personal illumination. Izzy soon realised that the one thing all these messages implied was that the responsibility for getting a job fell on your shoulders alone – this was what you had to own and embrace. Forget about the state of the economy or any structural impediments or disabilities, if you were out of work then there were psychological reasons to be unearthed.

To illustrate the extent to which any political or sociological realism was banished from the course, Izzy used the example of a man in her group called James. He had lost his job at the age of sixty, finding himself unemployed for the first time in his life. But now no one seemed to want to employ him, despite his substantial professional experience. He felt the rejections were due to his age. His job centre agent agreed that this was probably the reason, suggesting that he start lying about how old he was. 'But our trainer did not accept that it was age discrimination and a saturated job market that were the issues here; rather it was the barrier that James had created in his mind about his age.' The trainer then proceeded to say: 'We are a product ... If we're not talking and bigging up that product, then we can't expect anyone to buy that product.' He insisted that the only barriers we erect to success are the false ones that reside within our heads.

Izzy reported how she felt exasperated as she watched this spectacle. She told the trainer that it was not James who was the problem, but age discrimination, which was a societal issue for which he could not be held responsible. She then pointed out that 50 per cent of urban young black men were unemployed largely for structural reasons, linked to a legacy of poverty, lack of opportunity, and discrimination. No matter how positively young black men envisaged their world, this would not change the brutal reality. 'We need to look at the bigger picture,' she insisted, 'and not focus on the individual.' At this point the trainer turned on her. 'You've got all these hooks on you ... you need to shift the way you look at it,' he said. 'You've got all this anger and frustration and that's stopping you from getting a job. It comes across on your CV.' Izzy was baffled at how he knew this, since he had never seen her CV.

While Izzy's story offers us just one anecdotal account of a psycho-compulsion course, Friedli and Stearn's research revealed that the dynamics she reported were broadly reflected across the board. As we will see, the emphasis these courses placed on personal motivation, change and responsibility was etched deep into the collective script.

––––––––––

To understand why the Department of Work and Pensions had become so excited by psycho-compulsion courses, and the positive psychology and behaviourist teachings that underpinned them, we must go back to the summer of 2010, when David Cameron asked his entire Cabinet to read the same book over the August recess. The book was called *Nudge*, and was written by the famous behavioural economists Richard Thaler and Cass Sunstein. Its central message was that through 'nudging' people (i.e. subjecting them to small and low-cost behavioural interventions), you could reshape their behaviour in desired ways. Classic examples of this included putting green arrows on shop floors that pointed towards the fruit and veg counters (increasing the amount of veg purchases); making recycling bins larger than regular bins (prompting people to recycle more due to limited space for general waste); or, more quirkily, putting an image of a fly at the centre of public urinals (leading men to aim their pee at the fly, reducing splashing).

Behind the nudge movement, then, was a simple idea: people's behaviour could be nudged by everyday prompts of which they were only dimly aware, and this could be done at the population level. Better still, as such influence could be exerted largely through subliminal means, the government need not always change social policy or legislation. Politicians could rather subtly compel people to behave in desired ways, without taking their freedom away. Nudging was therefore the paternal libertarian's dream – you could now change behaviour through gentle and unconscious coercion and correction rather than through always adjusting laws and regulations. Cameron became so enthused by the idea of 'coercion by nudge' that he insisted every government department embrace and deploy the philosophy. He even set up his own permanent nudge unit at Number 10.

As this philosophy began infiltrating all government departments, including the DWP, it was blended with features of positive psychology. For instance, the nudge idea that people are motivated by the fear of things being taken away was consistent with the policy embraced by the DWP of threatening to remove benefits if people did not comply with job centre demands. Again, the nudge idea that people tend to believe what they are told about themselves by those in authority was consistent with claimants being shown their go-getting job qualities (after sitting a test), which they were then invited to act upon. Furthermore, the nudge idea that positive and motivational messaging would lead people to act in more productive and driven ways cohered with the obsession on psycho-compulsion courses with getting the unemployed to embrace positive thinking. One of the workfare contractors, Ingeus, was so gung-ho with its positive messaging that it resembled what you'd expect to hear on a CEO away day at Goldman Sachs:

Nobody ever drowned in sweat

Failure is the path of least persistence

Success is getting up one more time than you fall down

It's always too soon to quit

The sin isn't falling down but staying down

No one can make you feel inferior without your consent[13]

In addition to the barrage of course affirmations, contractors sent positive emails to claimants. Each day a different nudge would pop into their inbox, declaring things like 'success is the only option', 'smile at life', 'we're getting there' or, more remarkably, 'This can be the greatest, most fulfilling day you've ever known. For that to happen, you have to allow it.'[14] At every turn, the manic blend of nudge and positive philosophy permeated psycho-compulsion, which rested on an almost quixotic belief in the unrelenting power of psycho-boosting people subliminally.

While the DWP was busy trying to nudge unemployment away, Friedli and Stearn's research was revealing how this constant positive nudging, rather than creating emotional uplift, was often experienced as depressing and confusing by recipients, evoking feelings of anger and humiliation. In a manner very similar to that found in the IAPT therapy programme, the call to positivity implied that the real cause of your joblessness was simply having the wrong mindset. 'You have to understand,' said Stearn, 'it might appear that there's a harmless absurdity to all of this, but it is directed at people who are extremely vulnerable to these messages. These give a psychologically reputable gloss to the wider societal idea that unemployment represents some kind of personal deficit or perverseness.'

As well as implying that the deficit is within the jobseeker, the upbeat perspectives of psycho-compulsion fly in the face of most people's experience of daily reality. These perspectives offer what the academic, David Frayne, has called a form of 'phony empowerment'. The idea that we have infinite power over our lives and fates, while initially seductive and uplifting for some, often leads to acute disappointment when things go wrong. Persuading people they have more power than they do and ignoring the very real social barriers to attainment primes them for self-blame when reality fails to deliver. The worst extremes of phoney empowerment, argues Frayne, can be found in the trite aphorisms of the self-help industry, where popular psychologists ascribe to us almost magical abilities to alter circumstances despite the harsh realities constraining us. In a world where problems like disadvantage, unemployment and work-related distress are so socially embedded, downplaying the very real obstacles to opportunity is regularly experienced as yet another form of punishment, yet another form of blaming and shaming the individual.

Consider, for example, the experience of single mother Sam, who was compelled on a psycho-compulsion course to become more positive and upbeat, despite being exhausted and at the end of her tether raising two young boys alone, living from food banks and having little social support. Or what about fifty-two-year-old Ed, who had just been made redundant in a town where all the industrial parks were closing due to outsourcing overseas? Or eighteen-year-old Sarah, who lived in an area where the only jobs she could find were zero-hour and insecure positions? What if your life experience makes embracing excessive positivity or 'phony empowerment' tantamount to denying the harsh realities around you? In such instances, your options are limited: you can accept the positivity on offer (becoming liable to self-blame if things don't work out); you can cynically feign positivity (to keep your advisers happy); or you can simply reject the positive tropes, as Izzy choose to do. As she wrote, 'Does the government honestly think that bombarding [people] with pseudo psychology about positive thinking will actually make any difference at all to unemployment? I would argue that it is actively harmful to unemployed people who spend their time being blamed for the situation that we find ourselves in and being offered "solutions" that will make no difference whatsoever.'

Defiance like Izzy's may seem reasonable enough. But when expressed in the world of psycho-compulsion, it has consequences. As Robert Stearn discovered during his and Friedli's research: 'When claimants criticise psycho-compulsion they often add the caveat: "but I really *do* want a job". They do this to try and fend off how they feel their criticism will be perceived: as yet another expression of their resistance to work, which will be penalised.' Indeed, Izzy ultimately paid the price for her defiance on the course. She was asked to undergo yet another psychometric test. Still, she escaped rather lightly, as dissent more often leads to benefit sanctions, or the threat of them. The contractor Ingeus even had a concept known as 'compliance doubt', where advisers would initiate the first stage of withdrawing benefits if they doubted a claimant's compliance with workfare demands.[15] Given that legitimate defiance is a sanctionable offence, it is little wonder that psycho-compulsion has directly contributed to an increase in family poverty as benefits are taken away.

Psycho-compulsion is therefore not just about instilling people with a so-called correct employability mindset. It is a mechanism for penalising deviation from what it defines as the right set of attitudes and behaviours. 'What psycho-compulsion therefore attempts to do is silence alternative discourses to the neo-liberal myth that you are to blame for your unemployment,' said Friedli. 'At the same time, it undermines and erodes alternative frameworks around which people can come together in solidarity to act against the social causes of worklessness.' In short, psycho-compulsion not only pathologises and punishes a claimant's dissent, it depoliticises the causes of joblessness (which discourages collective action), and it does so by resuscitating Margaret Thatcher's earlier myth that unemployment can be reduced to character deficiencies.

The depoliticisation of unemployment is not just achieved by rooting its causes in individuals. According to the DWP, individuals can be persuaded against employment by what it calls collective 'cultures of worklessness'.[16] These are family or larger cultural groups who supposedly possess shared values and behaviours that encourage unemployment and welfare dependency among their members. These cultures – epitomised in the UK Channel 5 documentary *Benefits Street* (which, incidentally, was highly praised by the DWP and its leader Iain Duncan Smith) – allegedly reinforce a shared 'poverty of aspiration' that normalises benefits dependency. This concept extends the fault of unemployment from rogue individuals to rogue families and communities, thereby exonerating wider social structures, factors and policies from bearing any causal responsibility.

The ungrounded nature of this narrative, however, has been exposed by organisations like the Joseph Rowntree Foundation, which when searching for evidence of these rogue groups was unable to locate any despite strenuous efforts. What it rather found was that in families where one or both parents were unemployed, working-age children were strongly committed to conventional working values and were keen to avoid what had befallen their parents.[17] This finding is consistent with most other research, which rather shows that the most significant obstacles to work for the unemployed are not psychological or cultural, but structural: lack of suitable jobs with sufficient pay to live on, or a lack of necessary skills and qualifications.[18] Given the paucity of evidence for these so-called cultures of worklessness, the DWP seems to have embraced the idea out of convenience; using the idea to justify its cost-saving benefit sanctions (which allegedly break these so-called cultures up).

———————

At the end of my meeting with Zabar Kahlil, he confessed that, five years after his court case, he still periodically returns to the courtroom where his ordeal had taken place. 'I take my lunch sometimes and listen from the gallery to other cases. But I always visit the same judge – the one who led my case. It brings back mixed memories.'

Zabar also frequently reads and rereads the many hundreds of emails that passed between him and his barrister all those years ago. 'Some part of me still feels caught back there, James, although everyone thinks my life has moved on.' I explored with him whether there were still some related things he needed to work through – perhaps the trauma had impacted him in ways he had yet to fully understand. 'Yes, I sometimes think I need to talk to someone about all this, get my head sorted. What do you think?'

'Well, Zabar, that might be a good idea. But it's a bit of a minefield out there, if you don't mind me saying. If you find the right person or group, then exploring what happened to you may benefit you in unexpected ways. In fact, this is actually what my book is all about – confronting and working through those experiences in your past or present that may be holding you back, including the harsh social realities you may face. Perhaps when it's finished I can send you a copy.'

When I left Zabar, I had a difficult drive back home to south-west London. The rain was still pouring and the traffic was slow. I was feeling unsettled about his situation, and wondered what would eventually happen to him. While of course his distress was not severe, certainly when compared with that of many people I had worked with therapeutically, his options were just as limited: if he was lucky, he might find a low-cost counselling service, but increasingly these were in short supply. Of course, he could always hunt out an antidepressant prescription and, at a push, a couple of IAPT therapy sessions. But these were clearly not what he needed; he was after some longer-term, more exploratory work, something our services don't provide. So what about paying for private therapy? Well, even if he could afford to make that investment, there is still the thorny issue of whether the therapy would work. On the other hand, while having money does not assure success, it significantly increases its chances. Those able to find and pay for the intervention that works best for them are clearly at an advantage. This is something we rarely consider when hearing about stories of personal recovery: how recovery is not a level playing field but is influenced by a whole host of social variables (such as a person's socio-economic status and their ability to access and afford useful resources) that dramatically impact outcomes. My fear was that Zabar, like so many others around him, suffered economic circumstances that disadvantaged him in an area of life where there should be parity.

But I couldn't let these matters distract me too much right now, as waiting for me at home was a pile of papers I needed to sift through carefully that evening. Two important interviews were scheduled for the following day, relating to how some of the depoliticising, medicalising and pathologising themes I've discussed aren't just reserved for clinics, workplaces and employment centres. In what follows we will see how they are now increasingly infiltrating our schools, thereby educating – or mis-educating – the next generation into a largely neo-liberal friendly vision of how to best understand and manage their emotional distress, with some concerning consequences.

6

EDUCATION AND THE RISE
OF NEW MANAGERIALISM

In the early 2000s, the number of children being labelled with special educational needs would speedily rise across the country. In fact, the rise was so rapid that the number of pupils diagnosed with special needs doubled in a mere ten years, capturing nearly 20 per cent of the entire school-age population (1.7 million children) by 2011. The special needs category was used to describe children who were considered to have either a learning disability or a mental/emotional or behavioural problem. While the number of those with learning disabilities did rise, by far the largest increases were found in the category of mental and behavioural problems, with half of all special needs children by 2011 being classed as having a diagnosable mental disorder, such as depression, anxiety, conduct disorder, Asperger's or ADHD.[1]

As the number of children labelled with special psychiatric needs grew during the 2000s, so did the number of psychiatric drugs being prescribed (with a 56 per cent increase in antidepressant prescribing to children and adolescents between 2005 and 2012).[2] By 2010, as special needs costs spiralled, the Department of Education finally took action by commissioning the schools regulator, Ofsted, to undertake the first top-to-bottom assessment of special needs provision in British schools. What was causing the special needs epidemic, Ofsted asked, and what could be done to put things right?

When Ofsted's report finally appeared in 2010, it was widely covered in the national media. But the factors many would identify as driving the epidemic – poverty, inequality, insufficient school funding, etc. – seemed to play almost no role according to the regulator. After all, during the period of rising special needs (the Blair years), many of these social problems were said to be improving. Schools were being better funded and staffed, leading to higher literacy, numeracy and overall pupil performance (as measured by examinations at least). Additionally, as levels of social deprivation in the areas surveyed had remained fairly stable or decreased, how could rising special needs be explained?

Ofsted's answer was unequivocal: the schools themselves were to blame. Too many of them were misdiagnosing underachieving children with special needs problems, when their needs were 'no different from those of most other pupils'. Many children were rather underachieving, Ofsted asserted, because there was still too much 'poor day-to-day' teaching and planning in schools. Some schools were therefore using these labels to explain away underachievement, to garner more expensive extra provision and, more importantly, to boost their position in league tables (as special needs labels gave schools higher grade weightings). As a result of misusing or 'gaming' these labels, stated Ofsted, as many as 457,000 children across the country had been ascribed them unnecessarily.

In response, the government called for a raft of school reforms, which included improving teacher training and introducing new measures to make it harder for pupils to attain special needs status.[3] The government's aim was easy to spot: if you raise the bar for receiving a special needs label, you'll inevitably bring the number of special needs pupils down, and, with that, any associated support costs. Over the next five years the strategy was highly effective, with the number of special needs pupils falling by around 480,000 (a number that, incidentally, almost matched the number that Ofsted had previously identified as misdiagnosed).[4] This see-saw-like symmetry was of course no coincidence.

And yet, as the number of special needs pupils began to fall, other cracks began appearing in the system. Soon, many schools would once again be accused of gaming the system, but this time by using other strategies such as 'off-rolling' difficult or underachieving pupils. This involved head teachers encouraging parents to remove their children from the school roll under the pretext that the school would alternatively have to officially exclude them.[5] When Ofsted surveyed over a thousand teachers as to why off-rolling was occurring, over half reported that it was to achieve or maintain a high position in league tables, such as those based on SATs scores or GCSE results.[6]

As well as off-rolling, other gaming strategies were alleged. These included moving low-attaining students onto vocational courses; shunting supply teachers into non-exam-taking years; reducing playtimes to create more class time; cutting academic options (especially in the arts) to force students to concentrate on English, maths and science; creating 'soft options' to circumvent difficult subjects;[7] and in some extreme cases engaging in exam malpractice (which has reportedly increased among teachers by 150 per cent since 2014, with the most high-profile case concerning Prince Harry's art teacher at Eton – hardly a state school, but you get the point).

The dominant story being told since 2011, in other words, was that many schools and teachers were suffering from basic miscarriages of professional morality – notions of cheating, of gaming the system, of malpractice and of mislabelling chimed throughout political and public discourse. Crackdowns and reforms were the watchwords used by sanctimonious public officials and Ofsted inspectors, who now appealed to their own audits, targets and inspections to hold schools, and their ailing morality, to account.

But as is so often the case with dominant public and political narratives, there is always another side of the story to be told; and in this instance, it's a side that raises crucial questions that neither Ofsted nor the government appeared willing to ask: if teachers and schools were in various ways trying to game the system, in what sense were the targets themselves to blame? Was such gaming really caused by flawed morality, or by the acute stresses of working under the new target culture? And given the pressing nature of such questions, why weren't they being asked in the places that counted?

––––––––

I met Professor Marilyn Strathern at her home on the outskirts of the Cambridge, where she had worked as a professor of social anthropology at the university for over thirty years. As Strathern is one of the foremost scholars internationally of target culture, I was keen to explore with her the effects this culture was exerting on both teachers and educational institutions.

As we settled down in her quaint and bookish living room, we began by discussing the historical roots of target culture, something about which she had written extensively.[8] For Strathern, the most recent wave of target culture, as I partly explored in Chapter Four, stemmed from the New Labour policies of the late 1990s, which introduced a new method of managing public sector institutions (schools, hospitals, universities) in the hope of making them more proficient and productive. This method was called 'new managerialism', and it stemmed from the belief, first propounded by Thatcher's government, that public institutions always tended to inefficiency, unlike the competitively driven institutions of the market. To reduce this alleged inefficiency, then, you must make public institutions behave more like competitive businesses. And you could do this by designing and imposing target-driven incentives and punishments to force behaviour in more industrious directions.

To this end, government league tables were used to rank schools, hospitals and universities from high- to low-achieving. Staff were increasingly audited in terms of their output and productivity, while the language of public service was entirely overthrown. Service users were now called customers. Managers were called CEOs. And a plethora of other business terms reframed all institutional operations. Instead of competing for custom and profit, public servants and institutions now competed for higher placing in government rankings, with penalties and rewards being issued accordingly. In the case of schools, those ranked low would be called out for their failure, bringing reputational damage and further special interventions and inspections. Conversely, schools ranked high would be held up as exemplars to emulate, creating better prospects for ambitious staff, more autonomy of governance and greater financial stability.

After Strathern had recounted the rise of target culture from the 1980s (a culture that would also come to dominate the NHS therapy programme, IAPT, as we have seen), we then explored how its implementation across our education sector has generated negative effects that the architects of new managerialism never foresaw. 'What target culture has ended up doing,' she said, 'is socialising a generation into judging themselves in terms of abstract measures that are continually making greater demands on their productivity.' And as people struggle to reach these targets, 'The temptation increases to gain an advantage in the system, especially if the resources you need to hit your targets are scarce.' This last point is particularly important given that government spending on schools has dropped significantly since 2010, by about 8 per cent in real terms.[9] In a period of deepening austerity, when we are trying to squeeze ever higher returns from ever fewer resources, cutting corners therefore becomes inevitable. 'And this is when benign corruption starts to occur,' said Strathern, 'because when people are under this kind of impossible pressure, it simply becomes intelligent to play the system.'

She then gave me an example of how she also once fell into the trap of playing the system, recalling a period in her professional life when she was under great pressure to bring research money into her university department – a target that most academics must hit if they want job security, promotion or research leave. 'So I applied for funding to study a new knowledge park here in Cambridge. As I made absolutely sure that my proposal hit all the right buttons to make it attractive, my bid was successful.' Unlike the work upon which she had built her distinguished career, this project was rather conceived under certain duress, 'to primarily hit a target' as she put it, rather than honour her genuine intellectual interests. For her, the irony was that once she'd begun her research project, it became clear that the knowledge park itself was built on exactly the same principle: 'It wasn't answering a real-life question about genetics and social science; its main purpose was to get funding from the Department of Health [funding that was ultimately cancelled due to poor outcomes]. The institution I was studying was therefore of the same bad faith as my research proposal.'

Strathern shared her own experience not only to illustrate how deleterious playing the game can turn out to be, but to make the broader sociological point that targets have the power to subtly corrupt, almost imperceptibly. From the standpoint of where she worked, she was doing exactly what was asked of her, and that deceived her momentarily into thinking she was doing the right thing. She was pressured to bring in funding, and so that was what she did, much to the appreciation of her department. She was simply being a good professional from the standards of new managerialism, which, after all, locates what is good and valuable in doing what targets dictate.

Strathern's work on target culture is replete with examples of how institutional gaming and corruption become inevitable outcomes of trying to satisfy unrealistic targets despite ever depleting resources and often being under 'surveillance duress'. And, of course, this is where her insights shed crucial light on the accusations made by Ofsted and the government that too many teachers and schools were gaming the system, mostly owing to some kind of lax professional morality. What Strathern's work rather teaches is that target culture played a central role in generating the very behaviour that Ofsted and the government highlighted. The failings in the schooling system weren't rooted in lax professional morality, but were the inevitable outcome of new managerialist policies trying to squeeze ever higher returns from an increasingly cash-strapped public sector. Because of these structural pressures, special needs labels were being overused to leverage more resources into overstrained schools, and certain pupils were being off-rolled to help relieve league table pressures. But more than this, as teachers struggled to play the game, professional burnout started to become endemic.

In 2018, a group of education and psychology researchers set out to discover what led teachers to develop mental health problems at work, at rates higher than found in the general population.[10] To enable this, they conducted multiple in-depth interviews with a wide range of teachers struggling with mental health issues. The first common problem they identified was unmanageable workloads, which were mostly driven by mounting paperwork, especially in service of satisfying Ofsted inspections. Teachers felt that these bureaucratic demands were eroding their job satisfaction as well as their creativity.[11] Many also felt that having to hit highly prescriptive targets was detracting from their expertise accumulated through practice, subtly telling them not to trust their professional experience and judgement. Others reported feeling under constant surveillance by distrustful management. Crucially, many teachers felt that these bureaucratic pressures negatively impacted their relationships with their pupils, making it harder for them to be responsive to the students' psychological and emotional needs. This research was supported by more recent findings that revealed the core reasons why teachers were leaving the profession. Two stood out: falling wages and the dislike of time-consuming, target-hitting bureaucracy[12] – factors fuelling the national recruitment and retention crisis in teaching, with four in every ten UK teachers wanting to quit within their first five years.

Given that target culture has generated a whole host of unintended results, to what extent might it also be responsible for rising mental health problems in schoolchildren and adolescents? And to what extent are those charged with childhood mental health care considering such questions in their efforts to bring down levels of mental health distress? Fortunately, I would soon be in a better position to answer these questions, as I had arranged to explore them with some of the relevant experts in the field.

———

Gothenburg is Sweden's second biggest city – a historic port straddling the banks of the Göta river. My hotel sat stoutly on the water's edge, with grand views spanning down the estuary towards the Kattegat Sea. I was there attending a large international conference on psychiatric drug interventions. The delegates – psychiatrists, psychologists, researchers and service users – had arrived from more than fifteen countries; some with tired eyes, many with high expectations, and all united in their commitment to improve mental health services.

After a busy day of seminars and discussions, I managed to sneak away with a fellow attendee, Professor Sami Timimi, a global expert in child and adolescent psychiatry, and a director of a large mental health trust in the NHS. For the last thirty years, Timimi has worked as a child psychiatrist, developing innovative mental health interventions for vulnerable young people, while at the same time researching and writing nearly a hundred articles, books and papers on child and adolescent mental health.[13]

I wanted to discuss with him a topic he had been considering for some decades as a professor, a psychiatrist and a parent. Given that he had worked closely with our school system for many years, I was keen to understand what he made of the new mental health interventions that have widely infiltrated our schools since 2010, and which are set to expand further following the COVID pandemic and its impact on mental health. Even before the pandemic, childhood distress was rising rapidly (by

48 per cent since 2004), with 1 in 8 children alleged to have a mental disorder. Despite this, only two-thirds of children referred for help actually receive any support, with half of those having to wait many weeks, months or even years for it to be delivered. Right now in the UK, the only way a child is likely to be seen by specialist services is if they have attempted serious self-harm.

To address this crisis in mental health special needs provision, there has been an explosion of initiatives and programmes specifically designed to identify and help vulnerable children early on, to safeguard against more serious interventions being needed at a later stage. These initiatives include in-class mental health literacy education, online self-help toolkits for teachers, pupils and parents (HeadStart, Mentally Healthy Schools, Young Minds, SANE) and, most significantly, new teacher training programmes where educators are instructed how to spot the signs of mental disorder and refer children to medical services if necessary. If this latter programme sounds familiar, that's because we encountered it in Chapter Three. Indeed, Mental Health First Aid has now also infiltrated our school system, training more than three thousand UK teachers to date.[14]

Given that Timimi is very familiar with this new raft of mental health initiatives, I was interested to learn what he felt were their pros and cons. 'Well, the main problem is that many childhood interventions are still far too medicalised, with scant provision for social and psychological treatment,' he replied. 'But the idea that an emotionally distressed child is medically ill or dysfunctional, needing expert biomedical care, is at best misleading.' At worst, it is stigmatising, disempowering and often frightening, upping the anxiety for all involved. 'I increasingly see this kind of fear in my clinic,' Timimi continued, 'where parents arrive with a medicalised perspective believing their child has a disorder that needs to be treated, when it is clear to me their distress is perfectly understandable given the circumstances they are struggling with. They have often been told they may have a condition by teachers, who themselves are under pressure to do all sorts of things that go well beyond educating children – like spotting these so-called disorders early on.'

The necessity of spotting disorders early on is a central theme around which all mental health initiatives in schools now coalesce. This approach is known as 'early intervention', and its core message is that if children are struggling emotionally and/or behaviourally, this may signal a more serious psychiatric problem looming on the horizon that needs to be tackled right away. Although the early intervention approach seems reasonable enough, in practice the picture is very mixed. While it is vitally important to offer good early social and educational support to children with learning difficulties and social problems, when we are talking about mental health issues, problems arise. After all, what counts as early intervention in this area often means prescribing psychiatric drugs, even though the trial evidence does not support using these as early preventive interventions.[15] Furthermore, it is highly risky to base such potentially harmful interventions on speculative predictions about a child's future. Early intervention programmes, then, if favouring biomedical over psychosocial support, may simply end up siphoning drug treatments of dubious efficacy and safety to children at ever younger ages.

These complications are often not considered by parents and teachers, who obviously just want the best for children. This is partly because these complications are concealed behind the facade of care and concern that early intervention programmes project. For example, the rhetoric of early intervention is very careful to avoid overly medical or biological language when describing children's problems, preferring more neutral and holistic terms such as 'distress' and 'intervention' over medical terms like 'illness' and 'treatment'. But despite this de-medicalised veneer, at its heart sits a decidedly medicalised logic: just as slurred speech, acute muscle pain and breathlessness may signal an early blood infection, difficult emotions may signal a gradually manifesting mental illness. Although this logic appears rational from the medical standpoint, when applied to our emotional lives, where bouts of suffering are often situational, self-correcting and certainly non-terminal, problems will ensue, as Timimi illustrated by referring to his own mental heath trust:

'In Lincolnshire we now have a new service called Healthy Minds, which employs fifty counsellors to cover the whole county (population half a million). The counsellors are attached to a number of schools and offer up to six sessions of CBT. The idea was to provide early intervention to reduce the number of referrals later on to secondary services. But when they opened their doors in October 2017, they were inundated, and very soon had over a thousand referrals. So what was happening?'

While Timimi accepted that the number of referrals may have partly risen due to a backlog of unmet need coming forward, he also knew this was only a partial explanation: 'This mass of referrals coincided with greater teacher training in "recognising" mental health problems, where early intervention is inculcated as a core pedagogical duty.' The hyper-vigilance created by the early intervention narrative is generating anxiety in children, parents and teachers regarding what should be flagged as requiring expert help. Could a child who becomes pensive and introverted following a painful loss be displaying early symptoms of clinical depression? Could night sweats and imaginary companions (very common in stressed-out children) herald an impending and more serious psychiatric disability? At what point does not pursuing professional help make you an irresponsible teacher, guardian or parent? Given the early interventionist belief that most forms of moderate to severe distress may herald a more serious psychiatric complication, it is little wonder that referrals for expert support are rising rapidly in almost every mental health trust.

While this critique does not imply that we should overlook our most vulnerable children, it is legitimate to ask whether this medicalised view of childhood distress is getting the outcomes we want: 'The threat of a looming psychiatric illness,' continued Timimi, 'is not just scaring the heebie-jeebies out of parents, teachers and children, it is dramatically narrowing the scope of what kinds of reactions children are allowed to have without everyone freaking out.' It is putting even greater strain on limited services and at the same time creating all sorts of odd dynamics within the schools themselves.

To understand this further, Timimi undertook research with his daughter, an educational anthropologist, to assess what effects school mental health programmes were having on teachers' perceptions of childhood distress.[16] They discovered that teachers today are more likely than they were only ten years ago to interpret children's behaviours and feelings as indicating mental health problems, creating a heightened anxiety about what childhood distress could mean. Fear about failing to identify problems early enough, coupled with living in an overly medicalised society, meant that 'much behaviour previously deemed ordinary and understandable was now more often thought of as mental health problems needing expert help'. Everyday experiences like peer break-ups, being young in the year group, failing to concentrate, or just going through important growing pains were increasingly falling under the rubric of disorder. As one teacher explained, 'We must never ignore anything that makes us worried about the well-being of the student.' The fact that our mental health discourse has rebranded ever more aspects of childhood experience as worrisome is something upon which teachers are not asked to critically reflect, which may partly account for why childhood mental health referrals have increased by over a quarter in the last five years.[17]

Another important theme emerging from Timimi's research was that teachers were finding it increasingly difficult to differentiate between children who had mental health conditions and those who were naughty or even misused their diagnoses to deny responsibility for their behaviour. 'We learnt that teachers are increasingly confused about what behaviour should be dealt with in a disciplinary way,' he said, 'and what problems need more sympathy or should be referred on.' As difficult behaviour can be read through a medical lens, discipline applied today may be reframed tomorrow as neglecting a child's mental health needs. The result is that teachers feel disempowered and more inclined to defer to medical authority, out of fear of making a mistake.

As Timimi and I meandered along the banks of the river, we moved away from discussing the problematic side of early intervention programmes to investigate the rise of another idea central to mental health interventions within schools: the concept known as 'resilience'. Anyone working in education today will know this concept, which is now used widely in relation to a whole host of childhood issues deemed problematic by educational and mental health authorities. In essence, resilience is defined as the capacity to endure and act optimally in the face of life's difficulties. This means that teaching resilience is about instilling capacities that will safeguard children against future emotional distress. While all of us will have some sympathy for the importance of learning to stand up to life's hardships, in recent years the resilience idea has been co-opted and reshaped by school-based mental health organisations in ways that are provoking critical concern.[18]

When I interviewed the well-known educationalist Dr Catherine Heinemeyer, she summarised such reservations well: 'The key problem is that children are now being taught that resilience is a kind of personal asset they must develop, as if not having it is their fault. But we know from research that resilience, or the capacity to bear difficulty, is an outcome of how you've been treated more than anything else.' For Heinemeyer, resilience is not developed in the classroom, but in the wider world: 'A child becomes resilient if their environment is loving and supportive, if they are economically secure, have good friends, a youth centre and so on – not because they've had resilience classes that try to correct some deficit.'

When I later raised Heinemeyer's observations with Timimi, he was broadly in agreement: 'Resilience, certainly when used in mental health settings, is another of these ideas being taught uncritically. When you tell young people they need to be resilient, the subtle message is that they need to toughen up. But for lots of kids this simply reinforces the idea that they are reacting in the wrong way – that there is something in them, and not their circumstances, that needs correcting.'

Timimi and Heinemeyer agree that low resilience is not caused by personal deficits, as many mental health initiatives imply, but by deficits residing elsewhere: in families, schools, communities or indeed society. To believe otherwise is to shift away from scrutinising and correcting the child's circumstances towards directly trying to reconfigure their inner self, an emphasis that resilience interventions broadly adopt. The problematic shift towards privatising the roots and solutions to childhood distress may partly explain why resilience-based interventions have largely been shown to be ineffective, having no enduring positive effects on life satisfaction or problematic behaviour.[19] Questions therefore arise as to why this approach is still so widespread.

'What concerns me most about all of this,' said Heinemeyer, 'is that the role of schools has always been to prepare young people for the economy – giving them the skills and qualities needed to thrive in the world they are entering. Yet that world today is a world of precarity, where there are no jobs for life, flatlining wages, too many zero-hour or short-term contracts.' Resilience training therefore becomes about developing the thick skin necessary to survive in inauspicious circumstances. 'And this is the problem as I see it,' she continued. 'At the moment our education system works to maintain this state of affairs by normalising these social realities – toughening kids up to bear them. But the system shouldn't just serve the economy. It should model an alternative so young people can understand there is another way of doing things.'

From this perspective, school mental health programmes, like workplace and IAPT programmes, subtly socialise teachers and children to think of childhood distress in individualistic and medicalised ways: escalating exam stress ceases to be a commentary on the harms of, say, target-driven culture (and, by extension, neo-liberal policy reforms), and instead becomes a problem of low resilience to be solved by more mental health training in our schools, à la MHFA. Rising childhood mental distress does not point to failing and unjust social policies or ongoing austerity, but generates calls for yet more early intervention, with the depoliticisation of childhood distress these interventions imply.

The radical position, then, is not to cry for more access to mental health services, or more mental health care in our schools, or more teachers trained in emotional literacy, or more mental health first aid. What we need is a profound rethinking of the nature of suffering itself, and what it is trying to highlight and ask us to change. We need to repoliticise emotional discontent in the minds of teachers, parents and policy-makers, rather than continue reducing it to dysfunctions that allegedly reside within the self. We need to acknowledge that suffering also reflects family/socio/political dynamics we would do well to better acknowledge and address. As the renowned clinical psychologist Dr Anne Cooke put it to me in conversation: 'The mental illness narrative encourages us to see mental health problems as nothing to do with life and circumstances, so no wonder we don't look at structural or social causes; and of course this perspective is a great fit with the current neo-liberal approach – where individuals have to reform themselves to fit with existing social structures.' The trouble with programmes that are blind to the perils of such adaptations is that they essentially neuter political reflection on why distress proliferates in our schools, certainly when compared to schools in most other developed nations.[20] Instead, we resort to medicalisation, which shores up existing conditions with depoliticised interventions and meanings.

'We need to move away from thinking we can just understand and fix kids in clinics,' said Dr Liz Gregory, a leading educational and clinical psychologist, and now head of the Welsh government's strategy for school well-being. 'Everyone who comes into contact with children should understand the role that communities, relationships and families play and the impact that poverty, trauma and austerity can have.' We must also understand 'how pressurised our schools have become', and how the target culture bearing down upon teachers and managers is adversely affecting pupils too.

Dr Gregory first became aware of this impact on children when she took her family to Canada for an extended sabbatical in 2017. She was surprised at what she found in their public schools. Her son was the first to notice the difference: 'Mum, in the UK it is all about being the best, but here it is all about doing your best.' Gregory reflected that this was from a boy who hadn't wanted to move to Canada, and who was used to winning prizes. Despite this, what he liked most about Canadian school life was that everything just felt far more relaxed. 'It suited his sister much better too, and her self-esteem blossomed. She even started taking part in sports because it was all about fun.'[21]

Life in Canada introduced Gregory to a style of education she had not encountered in the UK, either as a mother or as the consultant lead of a large child and family psychological service in the NHS. In Canada, the culture of target-hitting seemed far less entrenched. There was greater emphasis on cooperation, developing relationships and community building, being creative and learning from the arts – all things underscored in the national curriculum. The school-related stresses and strains she daily encountered in her clinic in the UK seemed far less prevalent in Canada; a perception that, as I later learnt, is also supported by the OECD, where, in a comparison of child well-being outcomes in thirty countries, Canada is ranked an impressive third for educational well-being, while the UK comes in at twenty-second, suggesting something is going seriously awry.[22]

After three years in Canada, Gregory and her family finally returned to Britain, to much reverse culture shock.

When her daughter went back to her local school – now slotting into Year 8 – she was immediately streamed in her PE class, and put right down into the bottom set. Her new-found confidence in sports disappeared overnight. 'When I ask her now how PE is going,' Gregory said, 'she just groans. At the regular cross-country race she tells me she walks at the back with her friends.'

This example is but one of many Gregory uses in her published work to illustrate how she woke up to the highly competitive nature of British schooling only after her Canadian experience – a competitiveness impacting teachers, pupils and parents too. 'When I came back to the UK, it was results season,' she told me, 'and exams seemed to be all that any parent wanted to talk about.' In these conversations, she picked up on a great deal of parental conflict and contradiction. 'On the one hand, parents complained their kids were under far too much pressure, but on the other they were fighting tooth and nail to get them into the schools with the best exam results.' Additionally, parents were also upping this pressure on their children by sending them to private tuition, something nearly every child in her middle-class state school was undergoing. For Gregory, this was yet another expression of the anxiety parents felt about their kids scoring well: 'But challenging any of this was profoundly taboo,' she said. 'If I tried to raise these issues directly with parents or on WhatsApp, there would be this tumbleweed moment. The only people who seemed to acknowledge the problem were the teachers themselves.'

Gregory's work on the effects of target culture gained added relevance in 2018 when the NHS published results from a major national survey that identified what children themselves regarded as the most stressful and upsetting pressures in their lives.[23] Contrary to expectations, they didn't report bullying or family tensions or even social media as the factors most adversely impacting their mental health. Rather, the most significant issue for them was the pressure of school examinations and tests. 'We must therefore develop a more holistic approach that is very mindful of context and circumstance,' said Gregory, 'and we need to stop tackling exam stress as if it were just a psychological failing within the child.'[24] What exams mean for children is shaped by the culture in which we live. So we must look carefully at the cultural messages being sent, their origins, their aims and who (or what) they are really designed to serve.

On the late flight back from Gothenburg, I sat gazing at the tapestry of lights twinkling thousands of feet below, pondering on the many conversations I had enjoyed. In the light of what I'd heard, I began reflecting on the experiences of my own two children, and in particular on an event that had occurred some months earlier. As I tucked my daughter into bed, she had asked me: 'Daddy, why doesn't Mr Joel play his guitar in class any more?' The kids all adored Mr Joel – he was kind, funny and childlike himself. But what they loved mostly about him was the songs they all made up together most days in class. I couldn't tell my daughter that Mr Joel no longer played his guitar because the SATs exams were just around the corner and he was running out of time to get the class prepared.

During that musically fallow period, many parents noticed a shift in their children. As the exam prep gained pace, more children seemed tired and stressed at the end of the day; many were tearful or reluctant to enter class in the morning. My wife and I noticed a change in our daughter too, and also a change in us, as tensions escalated around making sure all her homework was done, with extras. At the time, it was easy to forget that these new tensions were not entirely of our own or the school's making, but were the fallout from abstract political ideas contrived long ago, which gradually percolated down to schools, managers, teachers, children and their families. Their effects were now subtly accompanying us at the dinner table and during family walks, infiltrating our bedtime cuddles and conversations.

Most families have little time or resources to grapple with, let alone alter, the social causes of their distress. We are too busy trying to satisfy a thousand daily demands. And we are also told not to take on this added burden, as there are experts out there to help us when things go wrong. As the great mid-century sociologist Peter Berger once put it: the sheer business and complexity of modern life (the motors of which we rarely comprehend) makes it attractive to just spin incomprehension of social life into incomprehension of self, especially if simple and ostensibly credible solutions can then be offered that promise some kind of self-comprehension, self-mastery and relief. So we often opt for mental health toolkits, resilience training and early intervention schemes, rather than raising awareness of the complex social dynamics in which we are caught up and their capacity to have baffling, deep and disconcerting effects.

In the end, it is the ability of mental health interventions to obscure the social roots of distress that perhaps casts their longest shadow. An essential part of any remedy is learning to understand and critically assess the wider forces holding us back. We must accept that for many children, the truest and most effective therapy won't be found in a pill, a consultancy room or a classroom intervention, but in loving and meaningful human relationships that endeavour to mitigate the harsher social forces and impacts that they neither perceive nor understand.

———————

So far in this book I have taken us on a journey through mental health interventions as applied in various settings – workplaces, therapy clinics, employment centres and schools. I have tried to show that wherever we focus our attention, these interventions invariably privilege a common style of mental health ideology and simplistic pragmatism: one that medicalises, depoliticises and often commodifies our emotional distress in ways that neatly fit with the preferences of new capitalism. In what follows, I will move beyond these interventions to ask some more penetrating questions regarding how we as a society have arrived at this place, paying special attention to some of the mainstays of new capitalism: individualism, materialism and deregulation.

PART TWO

HOW WE GOT HERE

7

DEREGULATING THE SO-CALLED CHEMICAL CURE

In 1960, a little-known senator from Tennessee found himself at the heart of a congressional storm. His name was Carey Estes Kefauver, and he was responsible for initiating one of the most significant industrial battles of mid-twentieth-century America. The conflict began midway through Kefauver's time as chair of a government committee overseeing corporate fraud, consumer rights and fair competition in US industry, when he was handed some information alleging fraudulent practices occurring on a wide scale in the pharmaceutical industry. Such was the compelling nature of the supporting evidence that his committee committed to undertake the first ever congressional inquiry into the behaviour of US pharmaceutical companies.

As the inquiry unfolded over a period of three years, a worrying picture slowly emerged. Kefauver's hearings revealed that companies were marketing new drugs as dramatic breakthroughs, even though such drugs showed no improvement over medicines already on the market. It revealed that they were engaged in frenzied advertising campaigns designed to sell trade-name versions of drugs that could otherwise be prescribed under generic names at a fraction of the cost.[1] But worse still, they were being allowed to make excessive profits by bringing drugs to market without having to provide any evidence for their efficacy. As it stood, the government in effect had little authority to enforce either good manufacturing practices or the effective testing of drugs. The absence of any regulation in this area meant that billions could be made from prescribed drugs that possessed no medicinal value at all, or at worst, were harmful to patients.

While Kefauver's congressional revelations were certainly damning, the plain truth was that they did not go down well on Capitol Hill, especially when he tabled new legislation to rein in the drug companies. He was accused of threatening the viability of the industry, of seeking to insert Washington bureaucrats between patients and their doctors and of trying to expand the power of government unnecessarily.[2] The pharmaceutical lobbyists also took up arms, arguing that if greater government regulation was adopted, drug prices would rise inordinately, innovation would slow markedly and hundreds of thousands of people would lose their jobs in the pharmaceutical sector.[3] As powerful opposition rose to fever pitch, Kefauver's legislation seemed all but doomed. In fact, it almost certainly would have been doomed, had not some awful events turned in his favour.

At the time Kefauver's congressional inquiry was being conducted, a disturbing epidemic had begun spreading across Europe. Increasing numbers of babies were being born with severe limb-reduction defects – their hands and feet emerging directly from their torsos – disabilities that often caused extreme pain and were regularly accompanied by early death. Oddly, this epidemic appeared to be mainly affecting babies in Western Europe, while those in Eastern Europe were escaping relatively unscathed. Germany was by far the worst-affected area, leading to theories that the epidemic could be the product of chemical warfare programmes unleashed by the Soviet Union. But as cases began emerging in countries far from the Soviet Bloc (Japan, Australia, Brazil, west Africa), alternative theories soon gained momentum: perhaps the defects were due to unknown toxins, impure water, undetected parasites, even surreptitious nuclear testing. The theories mounted, but nothing seemed to fit, and all the while the number of children being maimed – now in their many thousands – continued to rise.

At the height of the crisis, an unknown German paediatrician called Widukind Lenz grew increasingly distressed as more and more babies in his own surgery presented with the disabilities. As a result, he embarked upon a study of his own, carefully inspecting the lives of 46 women whose children had been born with the painful deformities. He took extensive histories of the women to try to identify any factors linking them. After a long and painstaking analysis, one factor finally emerged: around 80 per cent of the women with affected children had been taking a particular antidepressant and insomnia drug during their pregnancy. Furthermore, when Lenz compared this 80 per cent with a large cohort of women who had not taken the drug during pregnancy, finding that none of their babies had been affected, he believed that he'd found the common link.

When he presented his findings to the manufacturer, demanding it remove the drug from the market, the company flatly refused, calling his research shambolic and unsatisfactory. It took another physician, located over ten thousand miles away in Australia, who published research supportive of Lenz's work in *The Lancet*, to convince the medical community that an allegedly safe and effective antidepressant and insomnia pill was at the root of the tragedy. The pill – innocuously small, white and round – is now infamously known as thalidomide.

Lenz's discovery eventually led to the enactment of a global ban on thalidomide, and consequently to a complete halt in the number of babies being born severely disfigured. But his findings had another crucial effect. They now made it almost impossible for Congress to ignore Kefauver's exposé of pharmaceutical misconduct, as well as his call for far tighter regulations on pharmaceutical companies – the most important of which being that companies must prove their drugs were both safe and effective *before* being prescribed or sold.

Given the highly emotive and shocking nature of the thalidomide scandal, the media and public leapt behind Kefauver's demand for the tighter regulation of the pharmaceutical industry. Even though thalidomide had never been approved in the US, owing to concerns about its thyroid toxicity, thousands of samples had still been distributed to US doctors to aid unregulated clinical trial investigations. The damage that could have thus ensued effectively silenced all congressional opposition. Kefauver's recommendations soon gained unstoppable momentum on Capitol Hill. And once President John F. Kennedy finally gave Kefauver his open support in 1962, they were at last signed into law.

From now on, the US government would ensure far tighter regulation of both the safety and efficacy of medicines, assessing what drugs should be approved for public use, communicating their risks and hazards to doctors and removing any harmful drugs from the market. Within a few years, many other countries had also followed suit, including the United Kingdom, where the new US-style drug controls were rolled out by the Department of Health through the 1968 Medicines Act. And while the period of stricter medicines regulation that followed this act certainly had its flaws and its critics (the most vociferous being the pharmaceutical companies themselves), during the next decade, the number of drug-related fatalities dramatically decreased, the proportion of sales of pharmaceuticals remained steady as a proportion of GDP, drug innovation progressed well and no jobs were lost as a consequence of tighter regulation.

The devastating effects that the companies had argued would follow Kefauver's reforms had simply not come to pass. In fact, the industry entered one of its most productive periods, during which vital new vaccines for polio, measles, mumps, rubella, chickenpox, pneumonia and meningitis were developed, alongside many new life-saving medicines like semisynthetic antibiotics, autonomous nervous system agents and cardiovascular drugs (diuretics, antihypertensives).

But the stricter period of regulation of the 1970s was soon destined to change once again. By the end of the decade, a new series of events would radically alter the fate of medicines. This time, it wasn't congressional inquiries or appalling epidemics that would shape the history of the medicines we are allowed to take, but an ambitious and charismatic professor from the University of Chicago – a man with a Nobel Prize not in medicine, or indeed any related discipline, but more tellingly, in economics. His name was Milton Friedman, and his ideas would help shape a generation.

———

Milton Friedman first met Margaret Thatcher at Number 10 Downing Street in 1980.[4] She had invited him and his wife for a small and intimate dinner with herself and her then Chancellor of the Exchequer, Geoffrey Howe. As they sat eating soup and lamb stew, they discussed the far-reaching new capitalism economic reforms her government was then implementing with gusto. Thatcher had invited Friedman to Number 10 not just because she held him in very high esteem (they broadly shared the same political and economic ideology), but because Friedman had rapidly become an economist of significant global influence. He was now a Nobel Laureate and one of Ronald Reagan's key economic advisers. He had also recently achieved almost celebrity status in the US owing to the success of his recently aired TV documentary series *Free to Choose* (which Ronald Reagan had partly introduced), in which he championed the virtues of free markets, privatisation, deregulation and the other mainstays of neo-liberalism. That TV series, reaching millions of viewers in the US, was now about to be broadcast on the BBC – in a prime Saturday-evening slot for five consecutive weeks. Friedman was about to receive mainstream media attention in the UK, and Thatcher, just before his public ascendancy, wanted to secure his full support.

As the pair sat consolidating a friendship and collaboration that would last throughout Thatcher's time in government, Friedman was busy championing the matter of deregulation, a subject close to his heart and on which a full episode of his TV series was focused. In sum, he argued that any government truly committed to the free-market enterprise must work tirelessly to deregulate all key industries; that is, to remove all government rules, regulations or red tape that inhibited their productivity and profitability. Industries such as banking, energy, communications, transport and pharmaceuticals should be allowed to bring their services and products directly to market without any government oversight or interference. He argued that in a truly free society, it should be the market and not the state that determines the fate of any product, innovation, service or company.

In *Free to Choose,* Friedman selected the example of medicines regulation to drive his point home. Sitting before a panel of experts in the University of Chicago's law library, from where the series was largely filmed, he began by critiquing the new stricter controls on drug safety and efficacy that Kefauver's congressional reforms had ushered in following the thalidomide crisis. He argued that these controls had given rise to a regulatory culture that had become far too risk-averse and even stopped potentially life-saving drugs from reaching market: 'Therapeutic decisions that used to be the preserve of the doctor and the patient are increasingly being made at a national level by committees of experts,' he wrote. 'And these committees and the agencies for whom they are acting ... are highly skewed to avoid risks. So there is a tendency for us to have drugs that are safer but not to have those that are effective.'[5]

Friedman's proposed solution was not merely to undo this regulatory culture, but to banish all regulation entirely. Medicines should be permitted direct access to markets, where consumers would ultimately decide any drug's commercial success. If a drug was harmful or did not work, people would stop consuming it and the drug would fail; and if a company acted fraudulently, the victims would prosecute it through the courts. As the threat of market failure or litigation was sufficient to keep companies in check, so the argument went, there was no need for any government regulation. Market forces and not government interference was the most efficient means of ensuring safe and effective drugs. People like Kefauver, Friedman argued, had got it wrong.

While Friedman's call to abolish all regulation may have resonated with Thatcher's free-market instincts, it was clearly a policy that would not win support from large sections of the electorate, who wanted to see regulatory controls on medicines maintained. The thalidomide scandal was still very much in recent memory, so to move from the stricter regulations of the 1970s to essentially having no regulation at all would have been a step too far for many UK citizens (and politicians). To solve this quandary, Thatcher settled on an ingenious compromise: rather than abolishing all regulation of medicines, as Friedman advocated, she would fundamentally reform the regulatory process, making it far more industry-friendly.

She would do this by taking regulation out of the hands of the state and giving it over, bit by bit, to a newly created semi-private regulatory agency, which was largely funded by the pharmaceutical industry itself, despite still operating under the auspices of the Department of Health. Furthermore, the regulatory agency would also start recruiting its leadership from the pharmaceutical industry, which would be progressively encouraged to help shape its regulations. All these changes effectively allowed industry to influence the very processes by which it was supposedly independently governed, and to do so in a highly industry-friendly direction, as we will see.

What Thatcher and subsequent governments appeared to have understood was that removing all regulation was unnecessary. A far less politically volatile solution existed: simply give industry unprecedented influence over the regulatory process. The resulting closeness between regulator and industry would mean that industry would no longer need to lobby government directly for lenient regulation, as it had open access to the regulatory process – almost co-creating the regulations by which it was overseen.[6]

Following these regulatory reforms, the economic fortunes of the pharmaceutical industry, unsurprisingly, rose rapidly. For example, from the 1970s to the early 1990s, the total value of the UK's pharmaceutical industry output increased seventeen-fold,[7] with prescription sales more than tripling from 1980 to 2002 and then growing steadily at a rate of around 6 per cent each year until the present day.[8] While a host of factors contributed to this inordinate rise in production and sales, deregulation was the key component. Rising drug consumption also meant substantially increased profits for pharmaceutical companies, dividends for shareholders and, in some instances, increased industry-led employment and innovation.

From the standpoint of those supporting deregulation, then, these results were a powerful vindication of all that Margaret Thatcher had started – deregulation had driven up sales, investment, consumption and profits, just as economists like Milton Friedman had argued it would. But as with other industries that had also begun flourishing under extensive deregulation, there was another story starting to emerge, a far deeper and more troubling story that would soon be encountered by a powerful group of British MPs, who, after realising the damage deregulation could do, became determined to act.

———————

On 17 July 1997, the backbench Labour MP David Hinchliffe was out and about in his local Yorkshire constituency when he received an important call from the media centre in Westminster telling him to return to London immediately, as the BBC wanted to interview him that evening. It turned out that Hinchliffe had just been appointed chair of the House of Commons Health Select Committee – one of the most prestigious select committees in Parliament. He was as delighted as he was surprised – he hadn't even known he had been in the running.

For those unfamiliar with what the Health Select Committee does, its remit is fairly simple. It undertakes reviews on current health policy, makes recommendations to government and generally holds our health departments and systems to account. At its best, it fights for the public good against vested interests, government inertia and outworn policies that may harm the public interest. Its more recent activities have included forcing the government to invest in tackling child obesity, pushing for a ban on smoking in public places, arguing the case for increased maternity provision and putting its considerable weight behind a new sugar tax. In short, it acts as Parliament's conscience on all health-related matters.

David Hinchliffe is now in his late sixties, with a reassuringly friendly Yorkshire accent. He spoke to me with great enthusiasm about his first two years chairing the committee: 'At this time it was a wonderful job ... As chair I had a key role in deciding what work should be done, and we were making some excellent headway implementing valuable reforms.' His relationship with the then Health Secretary was close and productive, and many of the committee's recommendations were taken up.

However, by late 1999, the atmosphere had changed considerably. This followed Tony Blair's decision to appoint a new Health Secretary – Alan Milburn – who immediately set about reforming Labour's relationship with the NHS along the lines of the previous Thatcher and Major governments, resurrecting the Conservative policy of marketising key NHS services along the lines discussed in Chapter Four. The role of private companies in running NHS services was expanded; patients were rebranded as 'customers', for whose business health providers would now have to compete; a new raft of managers was ushered in, trained in the new managerialism and charged with setting targets, streamlining services and refining employment contracts. Finally, many NHS functions were outsourced to private companies, which would come to provide, over the next ten years, key support services (in catering, portering, parking, laundry, cleaning and planning) and clinical services (in dentistry, GP provision, diagnostics and surgery). By 2015, private companies had become so pervasive that they were siphoning over £15 billion each year from the NHS budget.[9]

As the government embraced private contractors and corporate managerial techniques, critics like Hinchliffe argued that this would not lead to a better and cheaper NHS. Rather, it would harm services, insofar as private companies, under pressure from shareholders, would seek to extract profits by reducing the quality of patient care. Furthermore, now that private providers had to compete with each other for contracts, cooperation and communication between them would be undermined, threatening service cohesion, long-term planning and, again, patient care.

As the government pressed ahead nonetheless,

bringing to fruition the market reforms that Thatcher had earlier initiated, critics like Hinchliffe felt increasingly marginalised; a feeling that reached tipping point on 18 March 2003, when he joined a further 84 Labour MPs in voting against his government's decision to go to war in Iraq. To be at variance with his party on yet another vital issue was for Hinchliffe a decisive moment in his parliamentary career. 'If you are in a party and you profoundly disagree with the direction your leader is taking you in, and you don't see any end to that leader,' he said, 'something has to be done.' Hinchliffe decided to stand down from Parliament at the next general election, scheduled for 2005. 'I could have stayed frustrated in Parliament till my old age, or I could get out and do something valuable elsewhere.' But before his departure, he knew there was still time for some important work on the Health Select Committee. 'For years I'd wanted to do certain inquiries on the committee that I felt were absolutely critical,' he told me. 'One on my list, and a very important one, was an inquiry into the pharmaceutical industry's influence on medicine.'

During Hinchliffe's tenure on the Health Select Committee, many parliamentarians, on both sides of the House, were becoming increasingly concerned that healthcare in the UK was being unduly manipulated by pharmaceutical industry interests. 'I was hearing that we'd been hijacked by the industry in ways that were not in the interests of patients and the public,' he said, 'in ways contrary to the values of medicine.' As others on the committee began to learn more about highly self-interested harmful pharmaceutical industry influence, they unanimously agreed to launch an inquiry into the industry's influence on medicine – the first undertaken anywhere in the world since Kefauver's over forty years earlier.

Over a series of months, the committee cast its net wide, collating evidence and consulting expert witnesses from the health professions, Parliament, academia, the pharmaceutical industry, the media, patient organisations, medical charities and relevant government departments and agencies.[10] The ensuing report was as thorough and far-reaching as its results were damning. In short, it revealed that the pharmaceutical industry was aggressively advertising drugs to prescribers on a large scale, while often offering misleading information that downplayed harms and overplayed benefits. It was making significant payments (speaker's fees, consultancy fees and other honoraria) to so-called independent medical doctors, largely for marketing purposes. Likewise, it was offering promotional hospitality masquerading as education, while financially backing so-called independent patient groups and medical education programmes supportive of its products.

The industry was also engaging in dubious research practices: 'We heard allegations that clinical trials were not adequately designed – that they could be designed to show the new drug in the best light – and sometimes failed to indicate the true effects of a medicine on health outcomes relevant to the patient,' said the report. 'We were informed of several high-profile cases of suppression of trial results. We also heard of selective publication strategies and ghost-writing.'[11] In all, the inquiry revealed a litany of practices that appeared to serve industry interests at the expense of public health. Companies were engaging in unethical research, marketing and data reporting in order to cast their drugs in the best light and expand their market. But what surprised and concerned the committee most of all was that Big Pharma was just getting away with it. The regulation of medicines was failing on a huge scale, just as Kefauver had discovered to be the case before his reforms were implemented in the US.

What the Health Select Committee had therefore uncovered was that the agency responsible for regulating pharmaceuticals – today called the Medicines and Healthcare products Regulatory Agency (MHRA) – had simply become 'too close to the industry', a closeness underpinned by 'common policy objectives, agreed processes, frequent contact, consultation and interchange of staff'. The report concluded by calling for an overhaul of the system: for 'an effective regulatory regime to ensure that the industry works in the public interest ... Unfortunately, the present regulatory system is failing to provide this [as it is] insufficiently effective.'

To offer some insight into why regulation was seen as failing, just consider the following barrage of regulatory practices that the agency embraced, all of which still operate today, and many of which were criticised in the Health Select Committee report.

First, for the MHRA to approve a drug for public use, companies are only required to provide one or two positive clinical trials (i.e. trials showing that the drug works better than a placebo), even though two, three or many more negative trials may exist (trials showing that the drug works no better than a placebo). This is because the MHRA can discard negative trial data when considering a drug for approval. Critics point out that clinical research is all about probabilities – the probability that one thing works better than another – so if negative data are omitted, the evidence base is skewed in a positive direction, favouring the product (and the company) seeking licence. This issue is particularly relevant for the approval of antidepressants, as negative trials have been common (almost half of all trials into antidepressants have turned out to be negative). If we include this negative trial data in overall assessments of antidepressant efficacy, they show that antidepressants are only slightly more effective than sugar pills – and that is only for around 15 per cent of people taking them (the most severely distressed). For the rest of patients they are no more effective than placebos.[12] These facts were unearthed not by the regulator, but by independent researchers, who included in their large meta-analyses the negative data buried by the industry and ignored by the regulator.[13]

Second, the MHRA does not require a company to prove that its new drug is more effective than the most effective drug of that class already on the market. All a company need do is show their new drug to be more useful than taking an inert substance – that is, a placebo. This arrangement is justified on the grounds that if a patient has a rare reaction to a common treatment, then having an inferior alternative is better than having nothing at all. The rejoinder to this argument is that patients also have rare reactions to the inferior alternatives, and that most patients taking inferior alternatives are not doing so because of a rare reaction to a superior drug, but because they were prescribed the inferior drug in the first place (usually because the drug has been marketed successfully). Another justification for allowing inferior drugs on the market is that certain individuals may respond well to a drug shown to be less effective, so a trial-and-error approach is warranted. The problem with this argument, however, is that the approach does not apply universally. For instance, in the area of psychiatric drugs, there is no high-level evidence that switching an antidepressant is more effective than continuing the antidepressant you were initially given, even if that initial drug is known to be the weakest in its class.[14]

As the justification for approving less effective drugs is therefore weak, critics argue that the reason this practice is allowed is because it enables companies to market, distribute and profit from medicines that are inferior to ones already in use.[15] Not only does this undermine the incentive to make better drugs, but it regularly leads to marketing misdemeanours. A good example concerns the antipsychotic drug Seroquel. This was marketed by AstraZeneca as far superior to an existing competitor drug, Haloperidol, even though AstraZeneca knew that after a year on Seroquel, patients suffered more relapses and worse ratings on various symptom scales than patients on Haloperidol, while also gaining on average 5 kg in weight, thus increasing their risk of diabetes. By 2010, so many Seroquel patients were suffering from such awful side effects that about 17,500 of them were officially claiming that the company had lied about the risks of the drug. These claims were finally vindicated when AstraZeneca paid a large out-of-court settlement for defrauding the public.[16] Again, it was not the regulator that uncovered this fraud, but an independent group of victims.

Third, when a company submits a clinical trial to the MHRA to seek approval for its drug, the MHRA does not routinely examine the trial's raw data (i.e. the data as it stood before it was processed by the company). Rather, it can simply just examine a research summary of the data, written by the company. While this practice is justified on the grounds that it speeds up the approval process (something companies demand as it saves costs), critics argue that summaries of research are liable to be biased interpretations of the raw data, and may also omit data that is harmful to the drug's prospects of approval. Therefore, full inspection of all raw data is in the public interest. Such lax regulation may help explain why companies were able to bury trial data clearly showing that most SSRI antidepressants, when prescribed to children, increase suicidal feelings; data that, once it emerged, led to recommendations that most of these drugs should not be prescribed to children and adolescents. Again, it was not the regulator that spotted this problem, but BBC investigative reporters.[17]

Fourth, the MHRA has no 'anti-revolving-door policy', but actively encourages interchange of staff between itself and industry. For example, many members of the MHRA's executive committee were previously ex-pharmaceutical industry professionals, including former chief executive (Ian Hudson) and director of standards (Gerald Heddell), both of whom were directors at GlaxoSmithKline for many years prior to leading the regulatory agency. While such practices are justified by the MHRA on the grounds that insider knowledge may lead to more effective regulation, critics argue that the MHRA recruits those who are instinctively sympathetic to their previous (or future) employers, and that furthermore, there is no good reason why having worked in industry is essential to fashioning good regulation in the public interest. In fact, the evidence as it stands appears to support the opposite.[18]

Fifth, the MHRA approves psychiatric drugs on the basis of short-term clinical trials (2–3 months), while longer-term trials are not customarily requested. This is justified on the grounds that long-term trials are not only very costly for companies to undertake, but that their time intensity may impede effective drugs from reaching market. Critics point out that since many drugs are taken for periods far longer than those covered by short-term trials, long-term trials should be requested, not least because many drugs, while showing benefits in short-term studies, are harmful and/or ineffective when consumed long term. For example, while most psychiatric medications were approved on the basis of short-term trials, emerging evidence now shows the adverse effects of long-term consumption (something, as you may remember, we explored closely in Chapter Two).[19]

Sixth, the MHRA relies heavily on the idea of 'post-marketing surveillance' to justify approving drugs for public use even though significant concerns may still exist regarding their safety and effectiveness. This assumes that the drugs will be carefully monitored post-approval. But the reality of the surveillance means that the regulator has effectively allowed large numbers of patients to unknowingly become subjects in a public experiment into whether the drugs are indeed hazardous. The existence of post-marketing surveillance was recently used to justify approving a variant of the highly addictive party drug ketamine for the treatment of depression. The pharmaceutical company that manufactures esketamine, Janssen, only produced three clinical trials for the regulator, two of which revealed that the drug is no more effective than a placebo, with the third showing very minor (clinically insignificant) benefits over a placebo for a short period. The NHS prescribing guidelines committee looked at this data and concluded that the NHS should not pay for this drug. The supporting evidence was just too weak. But the pharma-fee-funded MHRA, on the basis of the very same data, reached a different conclusion, approving the drug's public use.

Finally, medicines regulation at the MHRA is exclusively funded by fees from the pharmaceutical industry. What is more, the MHRA has to compete for these fees with other European medicines regulatory agencies. This is due to an EU rule that if one national regulatory agency within the EU approves a drug, then the path to EU-wide approval is far easier. This arrangement has effectively created a market within which different national agencies compete with each other for lucrative licensing contracts. The competitive environment in which regulatory agencies now operate has been shown to incentivise light-touch regulation – if your regulatory process is too strict, you are likely to lose out on licensing fees to a more lenient competitor. Research has shown that this regulatory 'race to the bottom' favours industry interests over those of patients.[20] What happens now that the UK has left the EU remains unclear, but with Boris Johnson's government allegedly pushing for further deregulation[21] it is unlikely that standards will improve.

Five months after the Health Select Committee's report was published, exposing many of the problems with the MHRA outlined above, a headline appeared in the *British Medical Journal*: 'UK government fails to tackle weaknesses in drug industry'.[22] This referred to the government's response to the Health Select Committee's report, which was simply, as Hinchliffe put it, 'miserable on all our key recommendations'.

Regarding the points the report highlighted as undermining effective medicines regulation (revolving-doors policies; excessive conflicts of interest; low bars for drug approval; lax trials assessment), the government simply had no substantive reforms to offer. Mostly it advised, remarkably enough, that the MHRA look into these matters itself, as if a biased regulator could make an independent assessment of its own faulty procedures. This woeful government response also entirely and wilfully ignored the Health Select Committee's most important recommendation: that a full and independent review of the regulatory agency be immediately undertaken, in order to begin overdue reform in the public interest.

Over fifteen years has passed since the Health Select Committee's inquiry, yet there has still not been any independent review into the MHRA,[23] with the agency still operating in much the same way as identified in the Health Select Committee's report. Given the absence of any change, the question arises as to why the Select Committee's inquiry had no effect, or, as one committee member put it, 'has largely come to nothing'. There are at least four reasons.

The first is obvious: David Hinchliffe resigned from Parliament in 2005 over the Iraq war and so was no longer able to hold the government to account as chair of the Health Select Committee. As I was told by the Conservative politician Sir David Amess, who remained on the committee long after Hinchliffe's departure: 'After the election, the committee was overtaken by many new members, who had no involvement in the inquiry and no real interest in the issue ... Had Hinchliffe remained, he would have made things happen – but that just wasn't to be.'

A further possible reason the report wasn't acted upon may have been because the person who replaced Hinchliffe as committee chair – Labour MP Kevin Barron – was himself close to the pharmaceutical industry. It transpired that Barron's partner (later his wife) had been a lobbyist for the pharmaceutical industry during his tenure as chair of the committee, a domestic conflict of interest that may have amounted to very little. However, Barron, as chair of the Standards Committee, later broke the House of Commons code of conduct by agreeing to arrange events in Parliament for a group of pharmaceutical companies in exchange for many thousands of pounds. All this of course did not bode well for the implementation of Hinchliffe's report, which was, after all, highly critical of corrosive pharmaceutical financial ties and conflicts of interest.[24]

While such problems certainly damaged the impact of Hinchliffe's inquiry, these reasons were perhaps inconsequential compared to the next on our list, one to which the health minister at the time, Jayne Kennedy MP, alluded when issuing the government's response to the inquiry. While acknowledging that it exposed some problems, she concluded that the inquiry must nevertheless be 'mindful' not to impose 'regulatory burdens' on the pharmaceutical sector.[25] In other words, by asking for more balanced drug regulation, the report went against the dominant deregulatory ideology of the day.

I asked Hinchliffe's colleague on the Health Select Committee, David Amess, whether this could explain the aversion to reforming the MHRA, he was unequivocal: 'That's absolutely the reason; this was the height of New Labour – people said they weren't privatising things when they were. You'll remember how they exempted Formula One from certain advertising regulations; and how they deregulated the banks under Gordon Brown – we could go on ... It was all about advocating light-touch regulation.'[26]

Hinchliffe echoed Amess's view: 'To have done anything about the regulatory agency would have impacted on the commercial interests of the pharmaceutical industry, which deregulation served. This was the overall thinking in government. It has been no different from the conservatives, to New Labour, to the coalition, to Cameron, to May, and now to Johnson – the central philosophy has been broadly the same: we give what industry wants, the markets must not be unduly restricted, we should not interfere. And that philosophy is basically at the heart of the agency's closeness to the industry – so the industry can continue to pull the strings.'

The views articulated above were further corroborated in June 2014, when, as part of David Cameron's Red Tape Challenge, the MHRA pledged to further 'reduce bureaucratic burdens on firms' – ushering in an era even more industry-friendly than that criticised in Hinchliffe's Health Select Committee report, a lax regulatory environment likely to be further compounded now that Britain has left the EU. It does not bode well that Boris Johnson's government has already been accused of potentially making NHS patient data available to US companies while further deregulating pharmaceutical markets.[27] 'What do you make of all this?' I asked Hinchliffe, some time after our initial interview. 'Well, I just find it all astonishing,' he responded, aggrieved, 'especially in the light of the evidence uncovered by our inquiry: that deregulation and commercial power continue to dominate successive governments' thinking, to the clear and obvious detriment of the public interest.'

On 9 August 1963, Carey Estes Kefauver doubled over in sudden pain while delivering a speech in Congress. After being admitted to hospital as a cautionary measure, he was told he had suffered a heart attack.

Two days later, still in hospital, he died in his sleep. The day before he had allegedly been pensive, reflecting that his proudest achievement in Congress had been witnessing, only a year earlier, his medicine regulatory reforms being passed; reforms he sincerely believed would improve people's lives for many decades and generations to come.

Indeed, if Kefauver had lived into the 1970s, he could have taken succour from what unfolded: his work was seminal in creating one of the most productive and comparatively honest periods in pharmaceutical history. But that period was certainly not to last. As the seismic political shifts of the 1980s took place, the rise of neo-liberal economics, privatisation, marketisation and deregulation swept his reforms rapidly away, reshaping every area of business and industry on both sides of the Atlantic. Today, in the early 2020s, it is easy to forget how solid the deregulatory faith was among the post-Thatcher/Reagan political elite.

It took the events of 2008 to bring that delusion to its knees, when deregulation was exposed as the single most important factor in igniting the most serious economic crisis (at that point at least) since the Great Depression. It had allowed a culture of frenzied and fraudulent behaviour to become endemic in the global financial sector – banks, credit rating agencies, government agencies, regulatory agencies and accountancy firms had all become so financially intertwined and interdependent that recklessness and corrupt behaviour had become almost normalised. Revolving-door policies and financial conflicts of interest were endemic, resulting in lax oversight or just woeful regulatory enforcement; failings from which we all (or at least most of us) are still suffering today. And problems have been uncovered in other deregulated industries too: in the car industry, companies like Volkswagen, Mercedes and Opel-Vauxhall were found to be manipulating emissions data or simply gaming lax regulations.[28] In the energy sector, big providers were accused of price fixing, to the financial detriment of consumers.[29] In the food industry, there were cover-ups regarding additives causing child hyperactivity, and the toxic effects of aspartame and acrylamide.[30] In these and so many other instances, regulators were found to be too close to their respective industries (both financially and interpersonally) to be always trustworthy – they were either denying corporate misconduct, acting too slowly when it was exposed or just showing themselves to be impotent before powerful industrial interests and a competitive regulatory sector.

In the light of these reflections, the principal reason as to why Hinchliffe's parliamentary inquiry was ignored was that it violated the prevailing deregulatory faith to which the political class had largely succumbed since the 1980s, arriving a full five years before the 2008 financial crisis would powerfully shake our trust in regulatory bodies. While the palpable failings of our regulatory system will lead some to assert that Milton Friedman was right to demand the end of medicines regulation ('You see what happens when you regulate or deregulate rather than banish *all* regulation?'), others, including Kefauver and Hinchliffe, would respond that having bad regulation is better than having none, while having vigorous and independent regulation is best of all.

In sum, the progressive deregulation of the pharmaceutical industry since the 1980s has not only been one of the major causes of so many failings in our psychiatric drug sector,[31] but has been a primary driver of wide-scale over-prescribing. It helped enable the 400 per cent increase in UK psychiatric drug consumption since the 1980s, with nearly a quarter of our adult population now being prescribed a psychiatric drug each year. This corporate success story was not due to any wondrous new drugs (a myth I contested in Chapter Two), or to any leaps in psychopharmacological science, but to the rise of an ideology that has enabled industry to shape regulatory rules and medical opinion in line with its own interests. In the next chapter I will pivot towards inspecting how these regulatory changes have dovetailed with, and benefited from, the pervasive materialism of our times, which has endeavoured to sell consumption as the most viable way of assuaging the multifarious pains of modern living.

8

MATERIALISM NO MORE

In early autumn 2011, on a crisp Manhattan afternoon, I caught the subway from 116th Street at Columbia University to travel to the heart of New York's financial district. As I ascended the pockmarked subway stairs, I could already hear the chants and drums thumping in the distance. Following the crowd through police-cordoned streets, I soon arrived at the central hub of the protests: a spacious haven of trees and benches two blocks north of New York's Stock Exchange. 'Is this the place?' I asked a fellow protester with whom I'd been chatting on the walk down. 'Yep, you're here,' he said with a slight glimmer of pride. 'Welcome to Zuccotti Park, home of Occupy Wall Street.'

In those early days of the Occupy movement, very few people beyond the city had heard much about the protests in Zuccotti Park. What reporting there was had largely focused on discussing the legality of the protests and how the noise was disturbing those working in the offices above. The core messages of the movement were either not being clearly articulated by the protesters or were insufficiently emphasised by the media. But when I arrived in Zuccotti Park that day, it was immediately obvious that the situation was changing, and fast. Amid the dancing, the chanting, the spontaneous megaphone speeches and the fiery group debates, military-like rows of young people, seemingly oblivious to the din around them, were huddled over laptops with almost Zen-like studiousness, vigorously sending out messages to the world – tapping out press releases, memos, Facebook and Twitter posts. Occupy was rapidly organising its global messaging system.

What the protesters in Zuccotti Park wanted the rest of us to know was the damage being caused by the 2007/8 financial crisis. Only a few weeks before the protests had begun, governments across the Western world had confirmed that they had literally poured trillions of dollars into the global banking system, in an attempt to halt its total collapse; money that would soon be recouped through stealth taxes and massive cuts to public spending. In effect, the 99 per cent would have to pay retrospectively for the corruption and excesses of a small financial global elite – their holidays, apartments and champagne lifestyles. The political and corporate actions that had made the 1 per cent richer (unjust taxation policies and loopholes) would increasingly make the rest of us poorer – and that was why people were raging in Zuccotti Park.

One of the first people I spoke to in the park was a middle-aged college tutor from Philadelphia who'd been camping out there for the past two days. 'You got to understand,' she said insistently, 'most people here feel a whole lot of disgust. Families on my block have foreclosed on their homes. I know them. My kids know their kids. There is a real sense of desperation. The banks don't care – people have no place to go. We're here for those families, demanding social justice and political change.'

Amid the countless placards jutting from the sea of protesters, many decried other, similar forms of corporate callousness. In a section of the park dubbed 'The Library' (a matrix of tables filled with books to be taken or exchanged for free), I made a beeline for a placard that enigmatically read: 'Corporate Hurt is Good for Profit'. Richard, its holder, a doctoral student from New York University, was keen to explain what the statement meant: 'This financial crisis has broken many people down; some people have taken their own lives ... people are suffering and that distress is now being capitalised on – literally, it's being turned into *capital*. Our pain is being exploited for further economic gain.'

By claiming that our distress was being capitalised upon, Richard was referring to a process known in academic circles as 'commodification' – the process of assigning economic value to things (objects, services, human qualities and emotions) not considered in economic terms before. An example of commodification would be turning public spaces, such as free museums or national parks, into private spaces that now charge an entry fee; or turning things once seen as natural and so off-limits to private enterprise (water, air, space, organs, sperm and eggs) into items or goods that can be sold for profit. In short, like Midas and his golden touch, commodification turns all it comes into contact with into an economic opportunity – including our innermost emotional states.

'And this is how we've been taught to view our emotions,' continued Richard, 'as something we can almost manufacture through targeted acts of consumption. When we suffer, we are not encouraged to delve down and face reality; we don't learn about what is broken in our lives or in our society. We are not taught to read, to study, to think, to struggle, to act.' Instead we do what our economy wants, he insisted: we reach for the endless consumer products that falsely promise a better life for a price – the entertainment, the pills, the clothes, the *stuff*. 'We don't manage our distress through action but through consumption.'

As suffering is transformed into a market opportunity, it is stripped of its deeper meaning and purposefulness. It is no longer seen as a crucial call to active change, or as the organism's protest against harmful or traumatic conditions, or as anything potentially transformative or instructive. Rather, it becomes an occasion for yet more consumption and market activity, with an array of industries thriving on the basis of this logic, offering self-interested explanations and solutions for the many pains of living.

These were the kinds of topics I enjoyed discussing over the two days I spent in Zuccotti Park. People were ardently deliberating not only corporate misdemeanours and economic injustice, but also the dynamics of human pain, consumption and meaning, what defines the purposeful and good life. These themes were clearly interlinked and would soon come to play an even greater role in the Occupy movement as it spread far beyond the parameters of New York City. Indeed, within a couple of weeks, the movement had advanced to most major cities in the US, before spreading its tentacles internationally, with Occupy protests rapidly reaching urban centres across the globe. Soon similar conversations could be heard on the streets of Berlin, Paris, Sydney, Toronto, Rome, Hong Kong and, of course, London, where a sprawling tapestry of tents would rapidly spring up on the forecourt of one of the

country's most venerable ecclesiastical landmarks –
St Paul's Cathedral.

In a small coffee house on The Cut, near Waterloo
station, I sat with Dr Giles Fraser, a quixotic and
intelligent Anglican priest with a penchant for Marlboro
cigarettes and lively conversation. We were meeting that
early March morning in 2019 to discuss an event that
had occurred eight years earlier, when Dr Fraser had
still been the chancellor canon of St Paul's. He held
this appointment precisely at the time when the Occupy
protests rapidly took over the forecourt.

For weeks on end, the occupation of St Paul's would
dominate the evening news, dividing politicians,
the public and, in the end, the Church itself. Some
members sided with the government and the City of
London authorities, arguing that while the protests
were merited, there were trespassing laws that had to be
respected. The other side showed greater solidarity with
the protesters. What, they implored, would Christ have
done? Did he not expel the immoral money-changers
from the temple? Did he not give sanctuary to those
fighting corruption and greed? As the debate raged on
and Church division deepened, Giles Fraser decided to
put his full public support behind the protesters' right to
remain at St Paul's.

'The night before the cathedral committee voted on a motion as to whether to forcibly evict the protesters,' he told me, 'I gathered my kids around the kitchen table to show them some recent footage of how the protesters had been violently removed from an Occupy site in Montreal. I told them that if I voted for the eviction, then this was likely to happen in London as well. My kids were very shocked and upset, and implored me not to allow this to take place.'

The next day, when the cathedral committee decided, by a single vote, to forcibly evict the protesters, Giles Fraser immediately resigned. His resignation signalled not only his aversion to a potentially violent eviction, but also his deep intellectual and moral sympathy for the spirit of the Occupy movement itself. For Fraser, the protests were not just about the profound economic and social injustices of our 'rigged economy', as Bernie Sanders would later phrase it, but about 'the kind of society we actually want; the kind of values we want to live by'.

As these sorts of questions dominated the discussions among protesters, perhaps it was inevitable that Fraser would soon find himself on similar ground to that I encountered in Zuccotti Park: what effects was late capitalism having on our emotional, moral and mental lives – was it transforming how we understood and related to our suffering, and if so in what ways? 'These matters were particularly alive for the protesters,' recalled Fraser as we continued talking in the café in Waterloo. 'Some had been through difficult personal crises themselves or were suffering under the acute strain of living at St Paul's.'

Indeed, the makeshift clutter of tightly packed tents that sprawled across the forecourt offered no creature comforts at all. Life in the camp was hard, sometimes brutal. People lived with the constant threat of eviction and violence; passers-by would often hurl abuse, and sometimes hard objects. And sleeping in the city at night was cold, uncomfortable, noisy and frightening. In fact, the strain of camp life had such an effect that within two weeks, the cathedral put out a call to any volunteers, counsellors or therapists who'd be willing to come down and offer help and support to those protesters buckling under the stress.

Paul Atkinson, a seasoned psychotherapist of over thirty years' experience, and leader of the non-profit organisation Therapists for Social Responsibility, responded to the call straight away. 'A few of us went down and set up a small tent in the middle of the camp, advertising by word of mouth that there were some therapists around if people needed any support.' As the tent's thin canvas provided no real sanctuary from the mayhem outside, Atkinson had to be creative: 'We'd find quiet corners in local cafés to have conversations with protesters, or we'd do what we called "walking sessions" – where we'd just head out into the city, doing supportive and therapeutic work as we walked and talked.'

While the chaotic conditions of the camp weren't ideal for offering therapeutic support, these weren't the only impediments to helping people. 'There was a lot of suspicion about the whole idea of therapy among many people at Occupy. There was a belief that therapy is a kind of neo-liberal, capitalist project – taking people out of their social context and wrongly indoctrinating them with the idea that it is them, not the world, that is at fault.'

But Atkinson continued with his work nonetheless, trying to build relationships and dispel fear. 'It helped that I genuinely sympathised with a lot of the arguments the protesters were making against therapy, many of which I'd written about myself.' He agreed that therapy had often been misused to coerce people back to work (as we saw in Chapter Four), or to make them subservient to a so-called expert definition of what was wrong with them. He agreed that the pharmaceutical industry had created a vast and lucrative market by way of dubious practices, and that socially caused distress was often wrongly medicalised and psychologised. All these things might be good for business and the economic status quo, but not necessarily for the people therapists were trying to help.

Despite Atkinson's sympathy for these counter-arguments, his thirty years of clinical practice still convinced him that psychotherapy didn't inevitably have to depoliticise and medicalise people's suffering. In fact, in the right hands it could be used to deepen socio-political awareness and critique, and to inform and galvanise political action. To explore these ideas further, he decided to organise a series of large public lectures and debates in Occupy's newly erected university tent. 'We invited prominent speakers from around the country to offer a political critique of what we do, and to discuss with the protesters what we could do better as therapists.' By the end of the seminar series, the tent was crammed with people: 'You simply couldn't find a place to stand or sit ... we knew something really important was happening here.' People didn't want to be told they were ill or that their suffering was meaningless – they wanted the structural roots of their suffering understood and addressed. And this was precisely what the various seminar speakers agreed needed to happen.

Dr China Mills is an editor of the prominent mental health publication *Asylum Magazine,* and a young and dynamic professor of public health at the University of London. She is wrapped in a thick, bright rainbow-patterned scarf as we meander down London's equally colourful Tooting Bec High Street.

As China was one of the scholars invited by Atkinson to address Occupy at St Paul's, I was interested to hear about her experience of the event. 'It was really humbling to be there,' she told me sincerely. 'We all squeezed onto the floor and benches in a large circle in the university tent. There were no power points, no microphones; we just spoke directly to the people gathered there.' She recalled discussing with the protesters her research on mental health interventions in India, and how it resonated with many of their concerns regarding how powerful multinationals were shaping social policy and mental health provision here in the UK.

'I remember talking to the protesters about the terrible wave of farmer suicides that have blighted central India over the last fifteen years,' she continued. 'I explained how these suicides were related to the promotion of new farming practices by huge agricultural multinational companies.' These companies were replacing traditional crops with genetically modified plants that don't produce any seeds. At the same time they were patenting the seeds that were available, so that local famers could no longer continue to save their seeds for next year's crop. This made the farmers dependent on the multinationals as they now had to buy expensive new plants each year, which put many of them into crushing debt and poverty. 'Hundreds of thousands of farmers were killing themselves under the resulting stress,' China said, 'mostly by drinking toxic pesticide.'

The reason why China was discussing these events at Occupy was because, as she said to me, 'the research shows that the farmer suicides were directly related to these new agricultural policies. But rather than reform these new pro-industry arrangements, the Indian state just sent in teams of psychiatrists and psychologists.' In fact, the Indian government, along with the World Health Organization, actually launched a campaign to make antidepressants more freely available to the farmers – 'as if the primary solution to the suicide epidemic was psychiatric rather than political'.

The situation was made worse by the fact that the multinationals were promoting these psychiatric responses surreptitiously. 'As the World Health Organization, under its "Suicide Prevention Scheme", was busy widely distributing antidepressants to farmers,' explained China, 'one of the multinationals was helping fund this scheme from behind the scenes. Nowhere was suicide seen as a desperate response to a situation made unbearable by the multinationals.'

She recalled how when she spoke about these events at Occupy, the attendees were gripped. The issues she discussed resonated with some of their broader concerns about mental health interventions: how they are often a way of glossing over the real structural harms and solutions, creating the illusion of care while bad circumstances are left intact.

As news about the mental health talks at St Paul's Occupy spread, more people from the surrounding area started to attend. Some had mental health problems and were intent on reporting dire experiences of the treatment they'd received: of being forced to take drugs they did not want, of having their hope trampled by suggestions their illness was lifelong. Others complained that crippling adverse side effects were managed with yet more prescribing, while many reported that their harrowing life circumstances were entirely ignored. One woman, for example, reported being given antipsychotics at the age of eleven after being sexually abused – a domestic horror her doctors just seemed to overlook. As far as they were concerned, she was suffering from paranoid schizophrenia that needed to be treated, rather than a terrible trauma that needed to be understood and explored.

When I interviewed Professor Andrew Samuels, a leading UK psychologist and a speaker at the Occupy events, he recalled how the tensions in the crowd often boiled over. 'It could be a bit of a nightmare actually,' he said. 'I remember someone standing up and raging against his psychiatrist, and how he'd been given drugs that were far too weak. This person wouldn't stop – hijacking the whole event. But we all sat there in a kind of liberal paralysis, not really knowing what the hell we should say in response.'

The speakers saw these public flashes of pain as legitimate protests. People were angry that drugs were being used to paper over deeper fissures in their lives. This was what China Mills had been trying to convey by discussing how antidepressants were being used in India to sedate the suffering caused by profit-seeking multinationals. But China was also at pains to point out that these dynamics permeated our own mental health system too. 'In the UK, we widely use mental health explanations and interventions as a way of avoiding structural and institutional problems, no matter how benevolent or well meaning these interventions may seem.' For China, as for other Occupy speakers, the use of medicalised interventions to obscure complex human and social problems was yet another expression of our cultural inclination to manage distress in politically and economically convenient ways. Whether we are looking at the over-prescribing of psychiatric drugs or the advocacy of excessive consumerist living, people were being asked to manage their pain in ways that first and foremost privileged economic health.

Indeed, as Giles Fraser put it to me: 'Capitalism doesn't want your inner life to be completely fixed – it is happy for you to be a functional depressive or a functional alcoholic, because in both instances you are still a functional consumer and that's what really matters.' In this sense, the preferred emotional state for late capitalism is a state of perpetual 'functional dissatisfaction': functional to the extent that you will continue to work, and dissatisfied to the extent that you will continue to spend.[1] Late capitalism does not generate just the conditions of distress, but the materialist, apolitical and profitable interventions deemed to remedy it – interventions that, as we will now see, chime with the materialist zeitgeist of our times.

In 1986, an unknown psychology graduate student working at the University of Rochester, New York, sat alone late one evening in the computer lab at his university's science centre. His name was Tim Kasser, and unknown to him at the time, he was about to establish a whole new sub-field of psychology.

Kasser had been working for the past two years on a series of vexing problems: how might he determine scientifically the extent to which a person's goals and aspirations would shape their feelings and actions in the present? Are your behaviours and feelings today altered by what you aspire to achieve tomorrow, and if so, in what precise ways? Such questions were certainly not new to the field of psychology. For decades, leading academic and clinical psychologists[2] had together produced a vast body of theoretical and clinical literature exploring how our personal values and goals unconsciously influence how we think, feel and act. One of the most eminent of these psychologists was Erich Fromm, a mid-century social psychologist and psychoanalyst. Born in the German city of Frankfurt, Fromm emigrated to the United States in the late 1930s, taking up a post at Columbia University in New York. For the next forty years he would propound ideas that would disrupt and contest the overconfident capitalism of the day, becoming a confidant of the US presidential candidate Eugene McCarthy and soon establishing himself as one of the most important social, political and psychological thinkers of the time.

A central theme in all Fromm's work was the idea that our personalities are not solely shaped by our biology and our early family environment. As important as these may be, it is society itself that exerts the greatest impact on the kind of people we become. Social institutions like family and school are conduits down which wider social, political and economic values are transmitted to the self, shaping our development in their preferred directions. It is no mystery why a person is more likely to be a Christian than a Muslim if raised in a Christian society, or why someone reared in a Sudanese village will differ in values and outlook to someone raised in the affluent suburb of Hampstead.[3]

This theoretical perspective led Fromm to explore the ways in which the wider culture of capitalism had variously shaped us into the kinds of people modern capitalism needs in order to function optimally. In this sense, capitalist societies work like any other social system, educating people to behave in ways that secure that system's continuance. To explore this dynamic, he focused on the linchpin of capitalism, consumerism, and how modern consumption had distorted our values and behaviour in ways that served late capitalism but compromised us in the process. For Fromm, the materialistic way of life upon which late capitalism depended had undermined more authentic ways of living and being, and this was having adverse psychological effects.

To illustrate the psychological harms of materialism, Fromm spoke eloquently of what he called 'the having mode of living' – something that had always been part of human experience, but which had become unnaturally exaggerated under late capitalism. Under the pressures of modern life, we had all variously succumbed to the over-valuation of buying and consuming things. Those of us who had ended up predominantly in this mode of living had ceased to relate to consumption in any kind of rational way. Instead, we had come to derive our identity and self-esteem largely through what we owned and possessed – believing that we principally defined and created ourselves through the objects we consumed, and that by acquiring more high-status possessions we somehow increased our value and worth as persons. These possessions could be material objects (cars, gadgets, clothes), status symbols (titles, awards, prized group affiliations and memberships) or human possessions (lovers, employees, associates, followers and friends). The more we owned and the more we had, the more we believed we were. It was in this sense that Fromm declared that the primary goal for most people under late capitalism was to have much, rather than to be much.[4]

To illustrate this idea, he gave the example of the modern car. While a car may be necessary for navigating modern life, its practical importance is only a fragment of the picture. On the flip side, ownership has not only negative ecological effects, but as with any act of consumption, psychological ramifications: it can produce a false sense of strength and self-esteem ('the bigger the car, the bigger the man'); it invites a sense of identity based on the brand of the car and can stimulate increased competition (keeping up with the Joneses). 'One would need to write a book in order to give a full description of the irrational type of consumption that the private car represents,' said Fromm.[5] But just as with the car, we use the objects we buy to project ourselves, to speak for ourselves – to create an impression about ourselves (admire me for what I drive rather than how

I drive). We use them to compensate for our difficulties or failures, to distract from our losses, to renew our identities, to associate ourselves with desirable social groups, to measure our sense of progress (look at what I now have, compared with what I once had), and to conceal things we fear others will not like about us. Consumerism exploits our dreams, our hopes and our human vulnerabilities. And its pursuit (and promises) has orientated living to such an extent that consumption has become an endpoint for much of our activity, making it difficult to envisage a life lived outside the materialistic grind.

While the 'having mode of living', encouraged by late capitalism, exerts powerful influence over many of us, Fromm distinguished it from other more authentic ways of existing in the world, in particular from what he called the 'being mode of living' – a mode of life whose essential orientation is rooted in developing and using our unique human potentialities, our talents and powers, to their fullest extent. As he said: 'The mode of being [unlike the mode of having] has as its prerequisites independence, freedom, and the presence of critical reason. Its fundamental characteristic is that of being active, not in the sense of outward activity, of busyness, but of inner activity, the productive use of our human powers. To be active means to give expression to one's faculties, talents, to the wealth of human gifts with which – though in varying degrees – every human being is endowed.'[6]

'Being' means living in a state of creative becoming, deriving our sense of worth and integrity from our actions, values and endeavours – from our capacity to love, to relate, to create and to work in meaningful ways. It means living to realise our latent human capabilities – living to become the individuals we could potentially be. If we were to summarise the essential motto for the 'being mode of living', it would be 'I am what I do', or simply 'I am what I am', compared to 'I am what I have'. For Fromm, the essential question we must all ask ourselves, then, is: 'To have or to be?'

This was the question that deeply occupied Tim Kasser way back in graduate school as he worked tirelessly in the university science centre: how did our relationship to modern materialism shape the fundamental direction and orientation of our lives? Fromm had offered some powerful theoretical ideas, but would a 'having' or materialistic mode of living turn out to be as corrosive as he forcefully proposed? Would Kasser's scientific work confirm or disconfirm Fromm's theoretical speculations?

———

On a bright summer's day in 2012, on a busy street in downtown San Francisco, a group of scientists from the

University of Berkeley set up a fascinating experiment. They wanted to understand whether car drivers were entirely aware of why they chose to drive as they did, or whether their choices were rather governed by factors beyond their awareness. To assess this question, they carefully observed how different drivers would react to a pedestrian stepping out in front of them onto a road crossing.

After analysing hundreds of drivers' responses, as well as documenting each car's model, age and likely cost, the researchers noticed an interesting pattern: it appeared that the higher the status and value of the car, the less likely it would stop for pedestrians. What were classed as high-status cars – shiny new BMWs and Mercedes-Benz – were four times more likely to cut pedestrians up than were low-status cars such as cheap Chevrolets or Pontiacs. The same pattern could also be observed when the researchers measured how drivers treated each other on the road. When assessing the low-status cars, they found that only 7 per cent would cut in front of other drivers, compared to 30 per cent of drivers in high-status cars. The results appeared to show that people in high-status cars drove, on average, more dangerously and selfishly than those in lower-status alternatives.[7] Was there something about being higher status that led to more selfish and entitled behaviour?

In a series of follow-up laboratory studies, the same researchers showed that the link between high status and selfishness also obtained in relation to a whole host of other activities. Under experimental conditions, high-status individuals (defined in terms of their relative wealth and social standing) were far more likely than those with low status to display unethical behaviour in a range of different tests. For instance, high-status individuals were more likely to cheat to increase their chances of winning a prize, to take valued goods from others, to lie in negotiations, to exhibit unethical decision-making tendencies and to endorse unethical behaviour at work. In one laboratory experiment, researchers manipulated how study participants regarded their own status – making it higher or lower than before the test. Irrespective of where an individual's status started out, those who ended up believing they were of higher status began displaying more unethical behaviour on a variety of tests. At the outset of one such test, for example, participants were presented with a jar of sweets, being told they were for children in a nearby laboratory but that they could still take a few if they wanted. Those experiencing higher status ended up taking twice as many sweets as those of lower perceived status, again demonstrating increased selfish behaviour.

Overall, the researchers concluded, a key factor fuelling such unethical behaviour was the basic human propensity to greed. These experiments confirmed a notion that could be traced right back to the ancient

Greeks: that high-status and wealthy individuals, partly due to their more favourable beliefs about greed, were more likely to deceive and cheat others for personal gain. In short, the results showed that wanting more or having more was linked with possessing more selfish characteristics, and with a greater willingness to bend the rules for self-gain.

This series of studies was merely one in a long chain of research projects influenced by or related to the work of Professor Tim Kasser. Ever since those early lab days as a graduate student, Kasser had explored issues similar to those covered in the car and greed experiments, and those more theoretically discussed in the earlier work of Erich Fromm – an exploration that would see him soon help to establish an entirely new sub-discipline of psychology, now known as the psychology of materialism.

A key moment in the growth of this new sub-discipline was Kasser's development of what is now known in psychology as the aspiration index. This is a standard questionnaire designed to assess, among other things, the relative importance individuals place on materialistic values and goals. By getting participants to answer a series of questions, Kasser's team would use the index to assess the extent to which they prioritised money, possessions, high status and self-image as core aims for which to strive.[8] Once these evaluations had been made, they would then assess other areas of the subjects' lives too, such as mental health, self-confidence, self-realisation and the quality of their relationships. By this simple yet effective method, Kasser was able to explore whether being materialistic had any links with the quality of participants' emotional, relational and instrumental lives. Over the ensuing years he would work closely with many colleagues to produce a vast volume of scientific work – papers, articles and meta-analyses – that together revealed some astonishing associations between materialism and our general functioning.

Kasser's early research focused on some quite basic problems, such as how people relate to material objects, confirming that highly materialistic people are far more parsimonious and possessive than non-materialists. This early research also discovered some interesting nuances, such as that materialists prefer to own, keep or horde material items, rather than to borrow, rent or throw things out. Materialists also appear to display lower levels of generosity, being far less likely to share their possessions with others, and more likely to feel envy and displeasure if others own things that they themselves desire.[9] As Kasser's research gradually evolved, he began exploring why possessions are more important to materialists. In the first place, materialists seem more likely to use objects to compensate for feelings of personal inadequacy. The first suggestion of this dynamic came by way of research that analysed elite tennis players on college campuses. It showed that those who were less experienced at the game, and so relatively insecure and apprehensive, would be more inclined to buy high-status branded racquets and clothing, in an attempt to compensate for feelings of inadequacy on the court and elevate their status, almost by association.[10] Similar behaviour was also found in German law students, particularly when they were made aware of the discrepancy between what they would ideally like to achieve and their actual achievements. In the face of these insecurity-provoking discrepancies, fledgling lawyers would be more inclined to 'big themselves up' by emphasising their high-status purchases – for example, rating their summer vacation spots as more prestigious and fashionable – than those who felt more internally confident and secure.[11]

The above insights opened up new research vistas for Kasser and colleagues on why wealth and possessions were so important to materialists. Soon they found that materialists were far more likely than non-materialists to agree with statements such as 'I'd be happier if I could afford to buy more things' or 'the things I own say a lot about how I am doing in life'.[12] The belief that having more could increase happiness and well-being meant that materialists regularly used consumption to deal with difficult times, experiences and emotions. Despite these attempts at emotional regulation, however, Kasser's research showed that such 'retail therapy' would often backfire. For instance, a materialist might fixate on buying a particular item, say an expensive coat. But once the coat was bought and worn, the initial buzz would soon wear off, leading to further cycles of raised dissatisfaction followed by yet more consumption.[13]

Once Kasser's team had established that highly materialistic people use consumption to manage various kinds of emotional insecurity, they turned their attention to exploring the kinds of relationships materialists develop with others. Do materialists, generally speaking, enjoy better or worse interpersonal relationships than non-materialists? One important study addressed this question by interviewing around 140 young adults and their parents. It turned out that materialistic teenagers were more likely to have mothers who possessed fewer nurturing qualities. Materialistic teens were also more likely to perceive their parents as less inclined to listen to their perspectives, acknowledge their feelings or give them space to make their own choices, while parents of materialistic teens were more inclined to be possessive, use harsh punishments and be confusingly inconsistent in how they applied their rules for how their children should behave.[14] Summarising these findings, Kasser wrote that 'materialistic teenagers may be raised by parents who do not do as much as they might to help their children feel secure, valued and safe'.[15]

That troubled relationships and materialism appeared to go hand in hand was further supported by research that inspected the family backgrounds of 260 young adults. It found that those coming from divorced families were far more likely to display materialistic behaviours. They were more inclined to locate their self-esteem in acquiring status and goods, as divorce often meant that children would experience, at least temporarily, 'the diminution of interpersonal resources such as love and affection' – relational deficits that later materialist behaviour appeared to be trying to reverse, even if only unconsciously.

The above relational research was taken in a new direction when Kasser teamed up with the Indian psychologist Professor Shivani Khanna. Together they assessed, cross-culturally, the levels of emotional connectedness that US and Indian students experienced with people in their respective social groups. In both countries, materialists were consistently more likely to agree with statements such as 'I often feel detached from my social environment' or 'in order to relate to others, I have to put on a mask' or 'I often feel like I have to perform for others'. The higher the degree of materialism observed, the greater the degree of social alienation and isolation. It seemed that materialists were less likely to be themselves with others, perhaps because they feared rejection. One of the outcomes of this was that they were more inclined to use relationships mainly for instrumental purposes. For instance, when the researchers assessed how likely people were to use others to enhance their own popularity or status, materialists more regularly agreed with statements such as 'I like popular people' and 'if a friend can't help me get ahead in life, I usually end the friendship'.

In summary, Kasser found that materialistic values are linked with an array of relational problems, such as more conflicted and aggressive behaviours in dating relationships; shorter and less positive relationships; less open social connection with others; more inclination towards antisocial behaviour; and less investment in personal relationships and community. Materialists are also less likely to cooperate, less likely to show empathy or be generous, more likely to objectify people (using others for their own ends) and more inclined to experience feelings of interpersonal isolation. Indeed, as Kasser put it in summary: materialistic values clearly 'weaken the fibres that bind couples, friends, families and communities together, thereby working against the satisfaction of our needs for intimacy and connection'.[16]

Given that enjoying healthy interpersonal relationships is an essential part of maintaining our overall emotional health, what Kasser and his colleagues found next should hardly surprise us: that individuals who focus on money, image and achieving popularity report more depression, poorer mental health and less vitality than those less materialistic. Materialists also report more physical symptoms – headaches, backaches, sore muscles and sore throats – meaning that in both their mental and physical lives, poor health and materialistic values go together.[17] Other related studies showed that people with materialistic goals report fewer positive emotions and lower levels of life satisfaction compared with people who are less concerned with materialistic aims. Similar results are even found when you trace people over a period of time, noting what happens as they become more materialistic. Whether you are assessing Canadian students, US college graduates, Icelandic or Norwegian adults or Chinese business students, levels of overall well-being consistently decline as levels of materialism go up.[18]

Other researchers have confirmed the clear link between high levels of materialism and low mental health. When Professors Patricia and Jacob Cohen from New York University studied hundreds of 12–20-year-olds, they found that adolescents who admired materialistic values were also 1.5 times more likely to be diagnosed with a whole range of anxiety and personality disorders, concluding that 'the priority put on being rich was related positively to almost every ... diagnosis assessed in this study, for the most part significantly so'.[19] Their work thus established a close link between materialism and various forms of emotional distress – a conclusion consistent with findings from the largest meta-analysis yet conducted on materialism and mental health (reviewing 175 studies). This showed that materialism was linked to a diverse array of harmful effects, feelings and behaviours, such as more compulsive consumption and risky health-related habits (like smoking and drinking alcohol), a more negative self-image, fewer positive emotions, more depression, lower overall well-being, more anxiety, worse physical health and lower life satisfaction.[20]

After hearing all this, you might well be thinking, okay, I get the point, being materialistic is bad for your health. But this was not the message that Kasser intended. And this, I think, is the important bit. Tim Kasser's work never demonstrated that materialism was the *primary cause* of bad relationships, emotional insecurity, poor mental health and so on. His research rather revealed something subtler than that: that it went hand in hand with these undesirables.

Kasser pointed out that being materialistic or 'living in the having mode', as Erich Fromm had described it, did not cause poor mental health but was rather its outcome. To put it differently, materialism appeared to be a kind of disingenuous attempt to manage high levels of personal distress – a harmful coping mechanism that consumerist society encouraged and exploited. The distress itself, he argued, was rather rooted in other more fundamental human deprivations, such as many of our vital human needs sitting unfulfilled. If our basic needs were neglected (our need for safety, economic security, loving connection, autonomy, self-realisation and meaningful work; our need to feel equal and respected), then poor emotional well-being would be the inevitable result. Materialism was therefore an unhelpful response to various deprivations – a culturally endorsed coping mechanism that ultimately backfired. The more we used wealth, status and superficial attractiveness as a compensatory salve, the more we would de-prioritise those things that could make life rich and meaningful again. As a city financier once said to me at a social gathering: 'I can feel that my job is literally killing me. I hardly see my kids, but what can I do, it pays so well, and that has benefits.' Here, the spoils of materialism are framed as adequate compensation for the woes of living materialistically and as justification for enduring the evident harms incurred.

For both Tim Kasser and Erich Fromm, then, materialism isn't the primary cause of our distress. It is rather an attempt to compensate for other deprivations and neglected human needs. That it more exploits than fulfils these needs is precisely why they saw it as so psychologically pernicious. In the name of helping us, materialism actually harms, by conflicting with those values, activities and forms of support that make life satisfying and meaningful. The profitable continued spread of consumer capitalism, then, requires us all to act in ways contrary to our emotional and relational health, which may help explain why in countries where hyper-materialism is on the rise, so too are rates of anxiety and depression.[21]

When I interviewed Tim Kasser in 2020, I raised a point that we partly explored in Chapter Two. While we know that antidepressant prescribing is rising for a host of reasons, is there something about the high materialism of our times that is making antidepressants a more attractive choice for many people? This is something I had thought about for some time, and so I wondered if Kasser took a view.

'There are two things here,' he answered right away. 'The first relates to the solid evidence that materialism is linked with lower well-being and higher levels of depression and anxiety. From this, we know that materialistic people are therefore most probably over-represented among those who are seeking treatment for mental health issues.'

But does this increase in help-seeking among materialists have any bearing on what *kind* of mental health interventions they would prefer? I asked.

'The data certainly suggest that the more materialistic a person is, the more inclined they are to seek physical solutions for their problems,' Kasser replied. 'For instance, we know that materialistic people are higher in what is called alexithymia [i.e. they have lower emotional awareness, which negatively impacts their relationships]. As these people try to avoid emotional entanglements, it's understandable why they would prefer a pill to an emotionally demanding talking therapy.' Another fact consistent with this idea, he continued, is that 'materialists also have a tendency to believe that what is most real in the world are the physical things. So again, they would be more inclined to try and treat their depression with something tangible, like a pill, than something intangible, like psychotherapy.'

To support this argument, Kasser then referred to a large meta-analysis conducted in 2014 that showed that materialism is associated with a number of compulsive buying and risky health behaviours – most of the latter involving imbibing things (smoking or drinking alcohol) – as if materialists instinctively prefer solving their problems via acts of consumption. 'Once again, given that a pill is a much more material solution than psychotherapy, the evidence is consistent with pills being a preferred intervention.' Researchers at Stanford University, who conducted a large trial exploring patient treatment preferences, support Kasser's position. In their study, those who preferred medication alone tended to reduce their problems to brain-based, material causes, being more likely to endorse the chemical imbalance theory for why they were depressed.[22] This conclusion dovetails with other research, conducted at the University of Pennsylvania's Medical School, which showed that people who prefer psychotherapy are more likely to attribute the causes of their depression to non-material factors – such as incidents in childhood, relationship problems and complex social causes – than those who would prefer to take a pill, who again favoured material factors.[23]

Kasser's views, of course, have to be read carefully. He is not suggesting that people who take antidepressants are more materialistic or have lower emotional intelligence than others. We know that people take antidepressants for a variety of different reasons (not least because there is often very little else on offer). To conclude that antidepressant users are all materialists, therefore, violates what the evidence allows us to say, and would wrongly stigmatise users. What Kasser is rather getting at is more nuanced – namely that materialists may be more inclined to take antidepressants than non-materialists when given a choice of different mental health interventions.

The play on materialist tropes when promoting antidepressants has been a key feature of pharmaceutical marketing campaigns, which have, in a period of rising materialism, actively promoted material explanations for increasing levels of distress. The early mental health anti-stigma campaigns, for instance, which were largely funded and promoted by the pharmaceutical industry, marketed positive images of psychiatric drugs alongside biological understandings of emotional distress.[24] Behind the guise of tackling public stigma, these campaigns encouraged people to seek biological solutions (pills) for their depression.[25] By using biological ideas to make their pills a more attractive option, pharmaceutical companies had discovered not only a powerful way to increase sales, but a potent narrative with considerable appeal to an increasingly materialistic population. Acts of consumption were no longer restricted to improving your outer life and image; they were now being marketed as altering and improving the very dynamics of your deeper self.

———————

After our discussion about the role he'd played in the Occupy movement, Giles Fraser and I began walking slowly back to Waterloo station to catch our respective trains. It was during that walk that he opened up about how his life went into a tailspin after he resigned from St Paul's. 'The period that followed was very hard for me,' he said movingly. 'There were times when I think I was even suicidally low.' He battled to acclimatise to life outside the Anglican establishment. 'Being at St Paul's was good for the ego. It made you feel important just to be there, among important people, always at the centre of things.'[26] But once stripped of the uplifting proximity of power and influence, he felt isolated and exposed. The strain impacted his home life, and ultimately led to a painful divorce. What had begun as a courageous act of conscience very soon cost him his job, his reputation, his marriage and his emotional health.

As we continued walking, Fraser confessed that entering psychotherapy for many months played a pivotal role in helping him get back on his feet. 'I'm completely with Wittgenstein when he said that solutions come by going the bloody hard way through.' This meant seeing his private turmoil as an invitation for introspection and change, engaging with his suffering as though it had something vital to teach him. 'For me, suffering is never meaningless. When the issues are spiritual, existential, social or psychological, to have faith in finding the right drug "treatment" is simply to make a category mistake.'

On the train home to south-west London, I began reflecting on the topic I knew I would have to explore next: if the rampant materialism of late capitalism was surreptitiously siphoning people towards particular forms of mental health intervention, what kinds of subjectivity were these interventions promising to manufacture or restore in return? What internal states was our dominant mental health ideology marketing as healthy and functional? Was there something about the medicalised and materialist approach that dovetailed with new capitalism's definition of what it means to be a successful and productive person? And insofar as our state-run services had become unwitting emissaries of this neo-liberal health ideology, were they now serving neo-liberal interests rather than our own? These were the questions I wanted to explore as I prepared for my next set of interviews.

9

DEHUMANISING PRODUCTIVITY

On a blustery October afternoon, I ducked and dodged my way through the crowded streets of central London, dashing to meet one of England's foremost political journalists. As he'd been editor of the *Daily Telegraph*, the *Sunday Times* and also the *Spectator*, it was important I did not miss this meeting. Once I'd entered the bustling café on London's Piccadilly, breathless and just on time, I immediately spotted my interviewee sitting serene and upright at a table in a far corner. Charles Moore rose to greet me, immaculately dressed in an English three-piece suit; an attire fitting the assured Etonian accent with which he asked whether I'd prefer tea or coffee.

I had wanted to talk to Moore for some time now, as I knew his expertise perhaps eclipsed that of most others on the subject of our interview: the life and person of Margaret Thatcher. Having spent many years writing and publishing the first two volumes of Thatcher's official biography (a combined tome of over fifteen hundred pages), he was now busily working on the final part of his trilogy, a task he'd been engaged with that very afternoon. As we settled into our chairs, I pushed my recorder close to him, hoping to circumvent the steely sound of cutlery being stowed away nearby.

After I'd briefly outlined my project, I then put to him my central question. It concerned a fascinating essay I first read some years ago by perhaps the greatest economist of the twentieth century, John Maynard Keynes, the Englishman who had ushered in the social democratic style of capitalism that dominated many Western nations between 1950 and the mid 1970s – the man whose economic vision, you'll remember, was finally upended by the Thatcher and Reaganite neo-liberal revolution that still dominates our economy today.

The essay in question was entitled 'Economic Possibilities for our Grandchildren', and in it Keynes envisioned how the world would look by the 2020s, should his style of economics be allowed to unfurl unimpeded. His most salient prediction was that by today, none of us would be working for more than fifteen hours a week. He believed that the advances in technology, science and accumulated wealth would, in the long run, have solved the economic problem of scarcity and inequality, extending the leisure once enjoyed only by the elite to the wider working population. No longer having to dedicate most of our waking hours to wage earning,[1] we would be free to devote ourselves to more nourishing pursuits: to 'experimenting in the arts of life as well as the activities of purpose' and learning how 'to live wisely' and 'agreeably well'. We would learn to develop our relationships and creativity, finally casting off the 'pseudo-moral principles which have hag-ridden us for two hundred years'; we would learn that 'the love of money' or the 'money motive' was not only a 'disgusting morbidity' but acted against our best human qualities – just as the materialist way of living diminished our humanity.

By envisaging a state of relative freedom from excessive work, Keynes was describing an economic future he believed society must one day embrace. Like Adam Smith and Karl Marx before him, he saw economics as a servant of the good life, as a mechanism for solving inequality, for cutting levels of demeaning work and for facilitating the highest human values and characteristics. The future society he envisaged, to use Erich Fromm's words, would ultimately elevate living and loving over attaining and acquiring – would put 'being more' over 'having more'.[2] While Keynes's vision never advocated the end of market capitalism, as did Fromm's, both men shared the view that cutting the amount of meaningless work would progress our behavioural, intellectual and interpersonal potentialities, assuming we learnt to use our new-found freedom properly. The end of economics wasn't therefore a system serving the economic engorgement of a privileged few (riches that would apparently somehow 'trickle down'), but one that served the interests, betterment and well-being of the greatest number of citizens.[3]

Given that Keynesian economics imagined a world of work radically different from that which the new capitalist economic reforms would eventually usher in, I asked Charles Moore what Thatcher would have made of Keynes's vision of a fifteen-hour working week, and the relative freedom for self-development it would have accorded. 'If we held that vision up before her,' I put it to him, 'do you think she would have embraced it?'

'Now this is me talking, not her,' coughed Moore, 'but, I have to say, it is a misunderstanding to think that economic and scientific innovation will create more time to do nothing much. If anything, the tendency of a more successful society is to get *busier*. Now, you may criticise the idea that getting busier is a good thing, but I think Margaret Thatcher saw a successful society as one that is more active. She was always thinking about how people could move on, develop and achieve more.

So Keynes's vision [of an economy where we all work less] wouldn't have appealed to her.'

I was interested in Moore's suggestion that freedom from wage labour was the same as doing 'nothing much'. This seemed to misunderstand Keynes's central point, that freedom from wage labour should be used *productively*. Not in the economic sense of being productive in the market, but in the humanistic sense of productively developing and using one's intellectual, creative and relational capacities. Did not Thatcher have sympathy for that?

'Well, Margaret did not think of productivity only in economic terms,' responded Moore. 'She had a romantic idea about all attainments – musical greatness or artistic endeavour. The people she admired the most were great thinkers and scientists. So hers wasn't a narrow vision, but based on a valuation of achievement and effort rather than self-discovery.'

I wanted to point out that Keynes's idea of living productively had little to do with battling for achievement or greatness (whether artistic or economic), but was about living fully, ethically and humanely within the community – using one's intellectual, creative and interpersonal qualities for the good of self and others. As I was about to mention this point to Moore, he raised the issue of Thatcher's disinterest in self-discovery. This topic seemed somewhat important, so I didn't interrupt:

'Thatcher wasn't at all interested in herself,' he continued. 'Of course she was quite self-critical – that's because she was a perfectionist. But she didn't look inwards. In fact, she was rather frightened of looking inwards. And that's why she had to be busy all the time. She was a real workaholic. Her staff would always get very worried if, during a weekend at Chequers, there wasn't something else for her to do – they just knew it would be trouble. And even when there was leisure time, she'd still want to achieve something with it – she'd want to repaint the house or something, not watch the television or read a thriller.'

'And that constant activity, that level of industry,' I enquired, 'is reflected in her economics? In her vision of what people should be doing in society?'

'Yes, of course,' answered Moore matter-of-factly.

Given that a successful society was, for Thatcher, a busy one – people working, achieving and attaining more – I was interested in what she made of those who weren't particularly ambitious for achievement, but who valued humanistic values more – living 'wisely' and 'agreeably well' for their families and communities, serving others and being good citizens. 'She was never unfriendly about people who didn't seem to have much ambition,' answered Moore, 'but sort of more uncomprehending. She'd say things like – "well, they have their hobbies". She couldn't understand people who just wanted to go and make balsa-wood boxes in their shed, or knit, or do things like that.'

'And what of people who *did* have ambitions but nevertheless failed to realise them despite hard work?' I asked.

'She believed that if people confront a barrier they should still try to overcome it rather than be discouraged by it,' replied Moore. 'That was her experience being a woman rising in a man's world. Don't allow yourself to be put down – you get up and keep going. So she admired grit and determination. For her, calling someone a "bonnie fighter" was a very great compliment.'

As I sat listening to Charles Moore's views on Margaret Thatcher, nothing contradicted what I'd already learnt about her through reading and conversation. While Thatcher certainly had her cultural interests, she seemed to value artistic drive and ambition perhaps a little more than what was actually produced. She instinctually admired the battling sort, and believed that perpetual striving and busyness indicated a kind of higher species of living – something her economy would both encourage and reward. She had less imagination for the happy minutiae of everyday life, for more local ambitions, hobbies and affiliations – for the multitudes of little kindnesses upon which communities and societies are built. Hers was an entrepreneurial, striving and competitive world, to which familial things were often sadly sacrificed (for her, this was sometimes bypassing her children's emotional needs in their important years). She was in no sense psychological or introspective, but pragmatic, industrious and achievement-focused. The hearts and souls she most admired, and those her economy rewarded, most closely mirrored the contours of her own. For her, success was understood in highly individualistic terms – people succeed because they have exceptional fighting qualities (rather than exceptional privileges and advantages), just as failure is largely rooted in a deficit of talent and effort (rather than a deficit of opportunity, equality and social support). For her, to blame failure on our social predicament was to offer up an excuse.

After I said farewell to Charles Moore in Piccadilly, I headed towards the leafy sanctuary of Green Park. Once inside, I meandered along a narrow tree-lined path towards the triumphal Wellington Arch. As I walked, I reflected on how, in so many respects, Thatcher's lack of introspection, her incessant busyness and her admiration for outward achievement and success chimed with many features of the materialistic personality that Professor Tim Kasser had spent his career trying to understand. As I pondered on this link, I couldn't help but think about something else Moore had said during our conversation: 'Margaret probably did go too far in admiring people who had got rich – she perhaps did not have very good emotional understanding of people who weren't any good at it.' The constant striving, the five hours' sleep per night, the dedication to personal image and credibility, the relative sacrifice of family and friends was not simply because she was, well, a prime minister, but because she was a particular kind of prime minister – one whose specific character style instinctively gravitated towards the style of economy under which we now all labour and live. Margaret Thatcher therefore still demands our attention because her values almost spiritually align with the new materialistic capitalism dominant today – the neo-liberal vision first hatched by Fredrick Hayek in the 1930s, elaborated by Milton Friedman in the 1960/70s, and enacted by her and Reagan in the 1970/80s.

In 1964, in the heyday of John Maynard Keynes's influence on the economies of Western capitalism, a group of eminent psychologists met in a modest and dimly lit conference room on the outskirts of Saybrook, Connecticut. Their intention was to share and consolidate their ideas on the fundamentals of human psychology. What resulted was more than just a sharing of minds but the inauguration of what would become known to psychology undergraduates today as the 'third force'. Until that time, psychology had been dominated by two traditions: behaviourism (first force) and psychoanalysis (second force). The first force explained human behaviour as an outcome of how we are conditioned by our environment; while the second explained it in terms of dynamic forces between our unconscious and conscious minds. Now a third force would not just stake its claim, but gradually establish itself over the next ten years as a leading light in the psychological professions.

This third force was known as 'humanistic psychology', and it prided itself on being in alignment with a long and venerable tradition in Western thought.[4] It held that once our basic human needs had been satisfied, self-betterment for the good of oneself and others became the highest occupation of life. Whether self-betterment came in the form of developing our 'virtue' (as in Aristotle's ethics), or our unique artistic and intellectual powers (as Francesco Petrarch and Pico della Mirandola claimed),[5] or our critical and scientific reason (as Benedictus de Spinoza, Adam Smith and John Locke stated),[6] or our individuality and creative possibilities (as John Stuart Mill and Wilhelm von Humboldt insisted),[7] the humanistic psychologists valued the development of our highest human qualities as the epitome of health-seeking activity, as of course did John Maynard Keynes.[8]

But these psychologists also offered something new. For them, self-realisation was not just a goal for which to strive, but an innate human compulsion and necessity. Just as our physical development could only be fully realised under the right conditions (proper nutrition, exercise, health care), so our psychological development was dependent upon having supportive conditions around us. To illustrate this idea, the humanists used the analogy of a young seedling struggling to grow. If it was given sufficient light, nutrition, space and water, it would flourish into the plant it was meant to be. But if denied these vital resources, it would at best grow in a compromised direction, failing to reach its inherent potential. As with seedlings, so with us – if our needs for love, security, physical, emotional and intellectual nurturance were left unmet, our development would be impeded, despite our best efforts. Self-development was therefore not just a matter of trying and fighting harder (as Thatcher supposed), but of receiving the social support necessary to facilitate our growth (as Keynes supposed).

The humanists, then, became very interested in identifying and removing those obstacles that held back our natural development. And with this they once again aligned with a long tradition of social and political philosophy. A key humanist occupation of the eighteenth and nineteenth centuries was, after all, identifying and removing all social barriers to human betterment, whether these were irrational leaders and institutions (as the Enlightenment *philosophes* stated), absent or poor education (as Humboldt and John Dewey said), poverty and inequality (as emphasised by Max Weber and Karl Marx), slavery, racism and discrimination (as Frederick Douglass and William Wilberforce argued), or unequal rights (as Mary Wollstonecraft and Emily Pankhurst insisted).[9]

While the humanistic psychologists agreed that all such social barriers would hinder growth, they were equally interested in removing any blocks that existed within our own minds. After all, harmful social and environmental conditions could set up damaging psychological impediments (traumas, anxieties, distorted beliefs, entrenched thinking patterns, conflicts and compulsions) that could also adversely impact our physical, mental and emotional health. For the humanists, then, emotional distress, even at its most acute, was largely rooted in the social and psychological factors that impeded our growth, and against which our distress was a painful protest.

Throughout the 1950s, 1960s and 1970s, humanistic psychology gained huge momentum. It dominated many university psychology departments, academic journals and conferences, giving rise to a host of new interventions. These included the practice of 'counselling', new forms of psychotherapy (more humanistic versions of psychoanalysis and existentialism), as well as new schools of social work, advocacy and person-centred education. It also established the foundations of many self-help and peer-support groups (charities like the Samaritans and, to a lesser extent, Mind still broadly operate today along humanistic lines). In the political domain, humanistic psychology also played a critical role in the civil rights movement, women's liberation and anti-war movements, lending scientific and ethical legitimacy to ideas of self-expression, equality and human rights. In short, humanistic psychology won widespread cultural influence not through the financial support of a massive corporate sponsor (as the pharmaceutical industry sponsored biological psychiatry), but via the compelling power of its ideas.

———————

As humanistic psychology grew as a cultural force in the 1960s and 1970s, the new capitalist elite was busy pushing in the opposition direction, trying to shake off the humanistic aspirations of John Maynard Keynes. They did this by arguing in the mid 1970s that Keynesian or 'regulated capitalism' had failed owing to the serious economic problems over which it presided. One of these central problems was low and falling productivity (namely, the output of each worker per hour of their labour). In fact, solving the productivity problem became a key rationale for many of the policy initiatives introduced by Thatcher and Reagan, such as curbing wage growth through de-unionisation (making people work harder for less), boosting competition through more privatisation (making people work harder to keep their jobs) and establishing 'work incentives' through reduced welfare provision (making losing your job a far more dangerous prospect). This suite of measures was instituted to nudge our hearts and souls in the supposedly more productive direction new capitalism demanded.[10]

At the same time as this new economic ideology took over, the culture of the mental health professions transformed too, moving in a far less humanistic direction. The psychiatric profession in particular would come to emphasise the importance of our performing optimally at work. This change can be traced to the very year that Reagan became president: 1980. This was the year when psychiatry's centrepiece, DSM-III, began medicalising, for the first time in its history, workplace underperformance. This vastly influential diagnostic manual, which I discussed in the introduction, would no longer see distress as a protest against bad circumstances, as the humanists did, but as 'a behavioural, psychological or biological dysfunction in the person'[11] – one that also significantly threatened our productivity at work.

Going forward, DSM would define poor work performance as a key characteristic of mental disorder, obliging all patients to be assessed with its Global Assessment of Functioning scale. This linked poor work performance with mental dysfunction and thus with a greater need for treatment.[12] For example, if you had few friends at work, experienced conflicts with co-workers or simply found yourself uninspired and demotivated by the work you did (working at a level 'below expected'), you would score high on its mental illness assessment scale. By pathologising poor work performance, DSM-III had established at the very outset of neo-liberalism a conceptual link between mental illness and low labour productivity, something that would dovetail nicely with Thatcher and Reagan's medicalising reforms, which also included, in the US, drastically cutting social, disability and community support for mental health, while dramatically increasing funding for psychiatric research by 84%.[13]

These changes to DSM now gave many mental health organisations a potent economic rationale with which to lobby government and the corporate world for financial support. The big sell was that while governments would raise productivity through social policy, mental health interventions would work on our subjectivity, increasing productivity by altering our internal states. The pharmaceutical companies in particular embraced this new message, by commissioning and/or conducting studies that linked low worker productivity with poor mental health – a malady, they implied, that their drugs could correct. In influential reports funded by the drug company Eli Lilly in the 1990s, for example, depression was cast as posing substantial losses to employers, who must therefore 'invest in the treatment of this widespread problem'.[14] Interestingly, when the psychologist Robert Krause analysed these reports, he identified them as typical of the broad marketing agenda at the time, which ignored the possibility that the nature of contemporary work (increasingly stripped of previous labour protections) was the key driver of low worker productivity and satisfaction. Instead, 'corporations are presented as potential victims through losses in productivity'[15] – losses caused by ailing mental health.[16]

As the mental health and productivity agenda of new capitalism became ever more aligned, psychiatric drugs were given a boost in another way. Interventions like psychoanalysis and humanistic therapy were deemed comparatively less cost-effective, which of course mattered in the new economy. After all, in the space of one hour of psychotherapy, you could treat 3–4 people with psychiatric drugs, increasing output per hour of clinical labour. Furthermore, unlike with psychotherapy, prescribing psychiatric drugs did not involve paying for multiple costly therapy sessions. These arguments became all the more important during the 1990s and 2000s, as the DSM began medicalising huge swathes of everyday distress, placing greater strain on services, especially in primary care. See-saw-like, psychiatric prescriptions would consequently soar, while payments for psychotherapy would go down, by insurance companies in the USA and by NHS commissioning bodies in the UK. In fact, the only therapy that benefited the NHS was the back-to-work interventions offered by IAPT – therapies designed to help the economy. As IAPT's fortunes therefore rose, what little funding that existed for GP-based humanistic therapy was siphoned into IAPT services. That a therapy promising to raise workplace productivity was the one that thrived was of course no coincidence.

This marriage of mental health and new capitalist ideology meant that therapeutic interventions serving economic productivity (as defined by Friedman, Thatcher and Reagan) were preferred over those serving humanistic productivity (as defined by Keynes and Fromm). This radical shift would reshape our whole therapeutic ethos, generating manifold and unanticipated consequences.

———

Throughout Tim Kasser's twenty-five years working as a university professor, he kept his working week down to three or four days. He was fortunate enough to have that option, as academic salaries are still relatively generous in the US, certainly when compared with what the average citizen earns. So even with his reduced workload his family could still get by comfortably. He and his wife, Jenny, chose this option to avoid organising their lives solely around work (which meant that Jenny too, as a clinical psychologist, would only work part-time). Their primary motivation was dedicating time to their children and to other nourishing pursuits: playing the piano, spending more time in the garden and getting involved in local community work. 'What drove our choices were our values,' said Kasser. 'We traded money for having more time,' a trade-off that has paid dividends, and in ways that John Maynard Keynes long ago outlined.

When Kasser was in graduate school, he learnt how precious time can be. Back then, he was living with a woman and they were very much in love. But during their second year together, she was diagnosed with stage four stomach cancer, and was told she only had a month to live. Kasser dropped everything he was doing professionally to be with her. She lived for a further four months. When he recounted this experience, I could tell the pain still cut deep.

The second major trauma that awoke Kasser to the limits of time was when his son, at two years old, was diagnosed with leukaemia. His life went into a total tailspin, as any parent's would. But the little boy slowly recovered against the odds (and by the time you have this book in hand, he will have graduated from college). 'Yet there were other kids at St Jude's Hospital who didn't make it through,' said Kasser, 'many families who would never fully recover.' These experiences left a profound mark on him, bringing home the truth that we must live right and fully while we can.

Kasser's life choices also very much reflect what his many years of accumulated research findings have taught him: that life becomes fulfilling not by way of having more stuff, but by way of living more authentically, relationally and meaningfully. As Kasser falls squarely within the humanist camp, I therefore wanted to know whether he also sensed, as I did, that the political demise of humanism had deeply impacted our mental health interventions. Did he agree that the fall of Keynesianism precipitated a radical shift in our mental health ideology, to one now favouring economic over humanistic productivity?

'I think that is precisely what we have seen,' he responded. 'The heyday of humanistic psychology was in the 1960s and 1970s, when Keynes dominated. But since the rise of neo-liberalism from the 1980s, we've seen an influx of cognitive behavioural approaches and psychiatric drugs – technologies that put the cause of the problem right between your ears. The therapies our governments now want all focus on internal not external reform. They don't see suffering as a call to change external circumstances for the good of our development.'

To illustrate the implications of this ideological shift, Kasser recalled what he believed to be one of the most compelling allegories on suffering he had read. It was the alleyway scene from Victor Hugo's *Les Misérables*, where the young revolutionary, Enjolras, takes over some Parisian streets with his fellow fighters. When he implores people to join him in the fight for freedom, the doors and windows close one by one as those inside reject the opportunity to fight for a better world.

'This scene made a powerful impression on me,' said Kasser, 'as it offers an important parable on the nature of suffering.' People rejected Enjolras's call not primarily out of fear, but from a kind of resigned apathy. They had become so accustomed to their poverty and disadvantage, to using anaesthetics to compensate for their difficulties, that their suffering had become politically impotent. Sedation had neutered the vital energies that make change possible – an effect that many humanistic psychologists have long warned against, owing to the restorative power of facing your predicament head-on. As such painful confrontations are integral to raising awareness of what holds us back, suffering is often the precondition for positive change. 'If a way to the better there be,' as Thomas Hardy once phrased it, 'it first exacts a full look at the worse.'

While many humanistic psychologists never intended their views on suffering to also apply to social change, it is true that communities must endure similar painful confrontations with reality before social reform can follow. When a group wakes up and understands the causes of its predicament, social and political action then becomes possible. 'And this is what we witness time and again,' said Kasser. 'Suffering is what ultimately motivated the civil rights movement of the 1960s. It also drove the women's liberation movement of the 1990s. In these cases groups of people experienced their distress acutely, but they also experienced it as a community. And this helped them find their collective political purpose, enabling organisers to unite them behind a shared agenda for social change.' The trouble with the medicalised approach, on the other hand, is that it dissolves collective experience, dispersing our socially caused and shared distress into different, individual, self-residing dysfunctions. In this way, diagnostic tribes come to replace political tribes, as we identify with a given mentally ill social grouping. Now our suffering has been politically defused. Then follows an emphasis on self rather than social reform, which is facilitated by individualist treatments. This is to say, whether we are talking about consuming antidepressants to manage difficult symptoms, or undertaking IAPT therapy to get us back to work, the negative upshot is that we are diverted from joining Enjolras on the streets, so to speak.

———————

Both Kasser and I agreed that the fall of Keynesian social democracy enabled the assertion of a new vision of self, aligning with a novel kind of mental health paradigm that served high materialism, consumption, commodification and the fetishisation of economic productivity. As this new vision began reshaping mental health ideology, depoliticising interventions (chemical and cognitive) gained unprecedented governmental support, while pharmaceutical interests thrived through deregulation, and humanistic therapies were progressively devalued or decommissioned (they promoted the wrong kind of productivity, after all). In the next chapter, I will show that in addition to all these changes, cognitive and chemical interventions were further boosted by their conformity with another mainstay of new capitalism – namely, 'hyper-individualism', with its concomitant blaming of individual selves.

10

YOU ONLY HAVE
YOURSELF TO BLAME

Emma arrived for her first therapeutic session looking tired, demoralised and much older than her twenty-two years. Behind her struggle to project a posture of confidence and strength, her sadness and vulnerability easily came through. This was most evident when she spoke about her four-year-old daughter, Mimi, with whom she no longer lived. Since Mimi had gone to live with her grandmother, Emma's mood had degenerated significantly, leading her to sometimes feel suicidal. When she finally visited her GP, he diagnosed her with clinical depression and prescribed her antidepressants. He also gave her a leaflet about our therapy service – a small, no-fee family-centre charity located in the middle of the council estate where she lived.

The story Emma told of her life was harrowing.

Between the ages of nine and sixteen she had been moved between four different foster homes, living with people whose names she mostly could no longer remember. She dropped out of school at fifteen, taking on various low-paid retail jobs. She met Mimi's father, Pete, when she was only seventeen, hoping he would whisk her off to a better life. But this was no love story. Pete soon began abusing her emotionally, physically and sexually. After about six months of enduring this, she became pregnant, but the abuse didn't stop. If anything, it intensified, continuing right through her pregnancy. When Pete finally left her, eight days after Mimi was born, Emma's relief was sporadic, as he would periodically turn up at her flat demanding money, and become violent if she refused.

The world changed for Emma when one day she fought back. Mimi had woken during one of Pete's abusive visits and was crying uncontrollably in her basket. Pete grabbed the basket and started shaking it violently, shouting for the baby to 'shut the fuck up'. Emma fought frantically to get him off. But Pete was far too strong. Now screaming and desperate, she grabbed a mug and shattered it across the side of his head. As he stumbled, she grabbed her baby daughter and ran out into the street. The police were called and Pete was arrested. Since then, almost four years later, neither Emma nor Mimi had seen him.

When I began working with Emma in that family centre, Mimi was living with her grandmother (Pete's mother) under the pretext that Emma's mild epilepsy somehow posed a danger to her. Emma saw her daughter only three days a week, but this was not a legally binding arrangement. Rather, Pete's mother had originally offered it as an unofficial short-term measure to help Emma out during the difficult period after Pete's arrest. After sixteen months, this short-term arrangement had taken on an aura of permanence, even though Emma desperately wanted Mimi back with her at home.

A few months into my work with Emma, Pete's mother, for no apparent reason, decided to reduce her access to Mimi to just two days. While this left Emma distraught, she feared that if she protested too hard, she'd be cut off from seeing her daughter altogether. She felt trapped, but she reasoned that at least she still had two days alone with Mimi – days around which her life now entirely revolved.

The whole week she would prepare for Mimi's visit. The sheets would be washed and pressed, the entire house scrubbed, Mimi's favourite foods bought and stored. She would even write a little bedtime story for her daughter, and buy a new toy with what little spare cash she had. She and Mimi would stay up late reading, cuddling and laughing, while planning imaginary trips they would one day take together. When Mimi would ask, 'Mummy, when can I come home?' Emma would struggle to hide her tears. And when the next morning came and the little girl was picked up by her grandmother, Emma would feel devastated, often repeating the same ritual: retreating to her room and hiding away alone.

Six months into my work with Emma, something decisive occurred. She took the step of speaking to a community solicitor about her situation with Mimi. Soon the solicitor and I were working together, eventually through the courts, to increase Emma's contact time. After a protracted struggle, the court declared that Mimi was entitled to live with Emma for three days a week, with a view to eventually moving in full-time if all went well. As these changes were gradually implemented, the effect on Emma's mood was remarkable. Her entire demeanour transformed, her hopes for the future returned and her self-esteem and confidence visibly increased, not least because she experienced the court's verdict as validation of her as a mother.

After my work with Emma eventually came to an end, every once in a while I would hear from her, until the spaces between her messages gradually stretched out into silence. She told me that she and Mimi were doing well. Mimi was now living with her largely full-time and was enjoying school, and Emma herself had enrolled at college part-time to train as a nurse.

I recount Emma's story here because it illustrates something that I, as a fledging therapist, had not expected to encounter when I started working in my very first placement: that the vast majority of people making use of mental health services, those who had been diagnosed and prescribed psychiatric medication, were not mentally ill or dysfunctional in any substantiated or biological sense. They were rather people experiencing the inevitably painful human consequences of being engulfed by life's difficulties or severe misfortunes. This is not to diminish their suffering in any way, nor to deny that they deserve care and support, as Emma evidently did. It is just to say there is nothing scientifically valid or indeed clinically helpful in reclassifying understandable human suffering as mental pathology, especially when this often just leads to more stigma and individualistic interventions, like being prescribed psychiatric medication, often long term.

I have told Emma's story because in many basic characteristics it mirrors the stories of most people I encountered in that family centre. Like her, the majority of people were living with very difficult situations, and yet most also experienced having the human and social causes of their suffering largely ignored. Instead, like Emma, after a seven-minute consultation, they ended up being prescribed psychiatric medication (antidepressants, tranquillisers), which they took for extended periods, while nearly every one of them had been given a psychiatric label, usually that of a depressive or anxiety disorder. Yet for most, just like for Emma, there were fathomable reasons as to why they suffered as they did, and these had nothing to do with having a mental illness, a chemical imbalance or any other unsubstantiated pathology with which patients are regularly regaled when prescribed antidepressant drugs.[1] Rather, they were suffering from entirely understandable human responses to intolerable life events. Far from being pathological reactions, these were sane reactions to factors like social disadvantage, marginalisation, poverty, trauma, social discrimination and dislocation – to legacies of abuse, social neglect, denied opportunity and so forth. Despite such suffering being invariably caused by complex socio-political, interpersonal and psychological factors, then, it was still invariably medicalised and medicated and nothing else. In those early years I constantly asked: how did this wide mismanagement of our suffering come to be?

After twelve months working in that family centre, I took on a second clinical placement, this time in an outpatient psychotherapy unit within the NHS. The clinic was set in a far more affluent part of the city, serving mostly white, middle-class, well-educated and financially secure clientele. But here the suffering I encountered was no less real or immediate: there were relationship problems, sexual problems, unhappiness at work, low self-esteem, thwarted ambitions, bereavement, loneliness, meaninglessness and ennui. Most people, once again, had been prescribed medication, and most had been given labels that dressed their suffering in medical terms – anxiety, depression and sometimes more severe diagnoses: bipolar, personality or psychotic disorder. But here too I never met a person I felt comfortable calling mentally ill in any biologically verifiable sense, even though, after a brief consultation, most of their understandable yet painful experiences had been recast as symptoms of a specific psychiatric disorder, to which a specific psychiatric drug was then matched.[2]

Working on the front lines in mental health services is an instructive experience. But the most striking lesson I learnt in those early days was how little time there is available to understand the lives of people who seek our help – their work life, their home life, their early life; the circumstances and relationships in which they have become deeply embroiled. On the occasions when time and attention is allowed, professionals at least have a chance to work towards a meaningful and shared narrative of why a person suffers as they do, one that can give meaning and hope and inform what specific changes should at least be attempted, with ongoing psychological and, ideally, social support appropriate to that individual. During this process, if all goes well, a confiding, trusting and facilitative relationship may also be established, which is now recognised as the single most important factor in any service in aiding a person's recovery.[3] In short, the very things most likely to bring good mental health outcomes – enduring and facilitating relationships that increase understanding, hope and expectation for recovery – are often the very things lacking in the services charged with improving our mental health.[4]

From the mid 2000s, two short patient questionnaires were gradually introduced into the NHS. Their arrival from the US passed without much comment or notice. Together they covered two sides of A4, and each asked a series of standard questions. There was nothing to suggest that these seemingly inconsequential tick-box questionnaires would become, over the next fifteen years, two of the most powerful documents in our mental health system, helping to reshape how countless mental health and primary care professionals would come to understand and respond to emotional distress.

The first was called PHQ-9, and the second GAD-7, and they were designed to enable your average doctor to determine within five minutes if a person had depression (PHQ-9) or anxiety (GAD-7), and if so, how severely.

They were quick and efficient, short and to the point, and by the end of the decade were being administered in practically every GP surgery in the country.

But there was one major criticism of PHQ-9 and GAD-7: both set a very low bar for what constitutes having a form of depression or anxiety for which a drug should be prescribed. For instance, if you tick the boxes indicating that in the last two weeks you have experienced poor appetite, troubled sleep and low concentration and energy 'nearly every day', you will qualify for 'moderate depression', which, according to NHS guidelines, is sufficient grounds for being prescribed an antidepressant.

Given that this is a low bar for getting a drug, it should not surprise us that eight out of every ten people who complete PHQ-9 end up being prescribed antidepressants.[5] In fact, since PHQ-9 and other such diagnostic tools entered the NHS, the UK has seen one of the most dramatic leaps in antidepressant prescribing across the developed world – from around 25 million prescriptions per year in 2002[6] to nearly 75 million per year in 2020. The fact that many, if not most, of these prescriptions were issued by GPs using PHQ-9 and GAD-7 raises the question as to what role these documents have played in fuelling this inordinate rise.

But the story does not stop here, because what the tens of millions of Brits who have filled in PHQ-9 and GAD-7 almost certainly did not know is that both documents were developed by, their copyright owned by and their distribution throughout the NHS paid for by Pfizer Pharmaceuticals – which, incidentally, makes two of the most prescribed anti-anxiety and antidepressant drugs in the UK: Effexor (venlafaxine) and Zoloft (sertraline). So here we have a company setting the bar very low for receiving such drugs, while at the same time making and profiting from those drugs. And this has been going on unchecked in the NHS for many years.[7]

In 2017, I was asked to consult for a BBC documentary on the over-prescribing of antidepressants in the NHS.[8] I raised the topic of PHQ-9 with the producer, who, like most others who hear the story, found the whole affair rather shocking. The upshot was that the production team tracked down one of the Pfizer-funded developers of PHQ-9, a leading US psychiatrist called Kurt Kroenke, and interviewed him, later broadcasting his defence, which went something like this: we developed PHQ-9 not to promote drugs (in fact, neither PHQ-9 nor GAD-7 advocates any specific treatment) but to help GPs distribute more care to more people. At that time primary care physicians were under criticism, largely from the pharmaceutical industry and psychiatry, for under-diagnosing and under-treating depression and anxiety. These questionnaires would help put that right by bringing the psychiatric diagnostic system for depression and anxiety right into the heart of primary care in a convenient and user-friendly way. Pfizer's work was therefore necessary and benevolent, helping people get access to treatments they might otherwise miss.

That is one way of explaining the purpose of PHQ-9 and GAD-7. But here is an alternative account: as the questionnaires were introduced at a time when primary care offered almost no alternative to drugs, it was clear that drug prescriptions would rise as an upshot of more people being classed as depressed or anxious – which, of course, is precisely what ultimately happened. To believe that a pharmaceutical company would spend millions of pounds developing and distributing new diagnostic questionnaires out of sheer corporate benevolence implies that this initiative was never seen by the company as an investment from which a definite financial return was expected, and that, more importantly, the rise in prescriptions (and thus profits) that ensued was an entirely unanticipated and unsolicited result.

However you personally choose to interpret the story of PHQ-9 and GAD-7, the history of these documents informs far more than current debates around rising prescriptions, the over-medicalisation of everyday life and the ethics of allowing private interests to infiltrate and shape our health provision. It reveals a story more ideological in tone, about how these questionnaires would never have been allowed to medicalise (and medicate) millions of people had the surrounding cultural, political and economic climate not been uniquely supportive. They do not, after all, exist in a cultural vacuum; they speak to wider and more powerful narratives about what constitutes the right state of mind in contemporary life, ideas they clearly exploited and profited from.

In the late 1970s, no one could have predicted how dominant new capitalism would become. Back then, it had few political supporters in the great Western centres of capitalism: Westminster, Washington, Berlin and Paris. And this lack of support was for good reason: when compared to the more socially democratic style of capitalism that had dominated the West since World War II, new capitalism seemed to offer no enticing ethical or moral vision with which to ignite and inspire the electorate. The ethical power of post-war social democratic capitalism, on the other hand, had been tried and tested for decades, even if actual circumstances often fell short of its ideal: a strong state would keep taxes high, especially for the rich, to ensure a more balanced distribution of resources across society. The state would make strong public institutions and long-term public investments; it would support wage equality and low unemployment, and endeavour to restrain the rapacious behaviour of the markets via robust regulations. A strong state would balance the interests of all citizens, discouraging extremes of wealth and poverty to create a more equitable middle ground.

The problem for new capitalism, then, was that it directly challenged the existing economic ideal in which large sections of society fundamentally believed. It called for lower taxes on the wealthy, for weaker corporate regulation, for a smaller state and fewer social services, for the dominance of an entirely free market where people would battle for the spoils of success – a world where there would be more winners (and, of course, more losers); a world where competition and enterprise would reign supreme. The people who appeared most excited by this vision in the mid 1970s were mostly those who could make the best use of it: the powerful, the entrepreneurial, the well connected and the well resourced. But as this group comprised only a minority of the electorate, new capitalism seemed destined to fail at the ballot box. For this reason, its champions in the 1970s (right-wing economists, politicians and captains of industry) began eagerly exploring how to best convince voters that new capitalism was not just for the few, but for the many – that it would create and preserve a better world for all. What its champions therefore required was an inspiring ethical vision around which all sections of society could enthusiastically rally; a vision that could turn a minority philosophy into a majority one. The question was: what would this new vision be?

One of new capitalism's most eloquent spokespersons, Milton Friedman, the Nobel Prize-winning economist we met in Chapter Seven, was convinced he had the answer. As he argued vociferously through various writings over the 1970s, new capitalism would win popular approval by aligning itself with the central pillar of Western culture: by promoting itself as the only economic vision that truly protected freedom. Exploiting the fear and anxiety provoked by the rise of the communist Soviet Union, Friedman put the 'fight for freedom' at the epicentre of new capitalism's economic message. It was the last true guardian of Western liberty, he said, defending the West against the communism that threatened our borders; the only version of capitalism that could push back against communist authoritarianism – and this was what the populace needed to understand.

To make this narrative take hold, Friedman set about critiquing the idea of freedom that had been embraced by social democratic capitalism since World War II. Such an idea went like this: the state is the true guardian of the freedoms we all enjoy. It exists to emancipate us from the harms that impede the good life, by freeing us from the chains of poverty (by providing social security), the ravages of illness (by providing free health care), the inequities of inequality (by redistributing wealth) and the blight of ignorance (by providing universal education). By fighting the social ills that hold us back, the state will liberate us to realise our potential.

But for Friedman and others on the economic right, this state-centred vision of freedom was not only misleading, it actually imperilled our liberty in a fundamental way.[9] Invoking the earlier work of the economist Fredrick Hayek, Friedman argued that the problem with every state was that it had an inbuilt tendency to gather ever more power unto itself, becoming continually more expansive and dominant in the process. As this happened, it became more centralised and totalitarian until it finally took people's democratic freedoms away. What Friedman argued so passionately, then, was that social democratic capitalism, if left to its own devices, would ultimately morph into socialism and then communism (just as had happened in the USSR). The best way to halt this inevitable stride towards communist subjection was to replace social democratic capitalism with a free-market version, thus cutting the ambitions of the state down to size.[10]

Whatever the weaknesses of Friedman's argument, his linking the 'big state' with Soviet communism and the 'small state' with Western freedom chimed with the deeply pervasive anti-communist sentiments of the day. And this was the key to endowing small-state market fundamentalism with the moral vision it had previously lacked. All that now remained was to persuasively communicate this new-fangled vision far and wide. What new capitalism therefore required was a group of highly charismatic politicians who could take the message to the people.

Margaret Thatcher rose to political prominence in the mid 1970s, a period during which only a small handful of parliamentarians championed the central ideas of new capitalism. Thatcher had encountered these ideas many years earlier through reading the work of both Hayek and Friedman, and she would soon come to promote them aggressively during her bid to become Conservative party leader in 1975, and then prime minister in 1979. Throughout this time it would often sound as though she was quoting directly from Friedman's playbook, by energetically representing her small-state and pro-market economics as the only viable option for truly free Western societies:

> There is no freedom where the state totally controls the economy. Personal freedom and economic freedom are indivisible. You can't have one without the other.

> Unlike the socialists, who trust the state, we
> trust the people. That is why we are the party of
> freedom.
>
> The British are individualists, who do not respond
> to state direction and control. We like leadership
> – yes. But above all, we like freedom.[11]

As Thatcher's new freedom-loving, pro-market economics helped pave her way to Number 10, Ronald Reagan took up the mantra in his 1979 presidential campaign. His equivalent to the slick 'Yes We Can' or the ironic 'Let's Make America Great Again' was the more gassy yet no less powerful 'We'll take government off your backs to free you to do what you do so well'. Across each mighty American territory, Reagan would reiterate different versions of this liberty-loving refrain: because big government weighs you down, we will remove it to raise you up, and with that the whole of America will ascend again. In statement after statement, in speech after speech, whether hatched in Washington, Chicago or Westminster, the new economics of freedom would super-charge popular faith in new capitalism.

So how, you may ask, does this new economics of freedom apply to depression and anxiety tests? What is the relevance of this interlude? Well, as we will soon see, by understanding what freedom means under new capitalism, we are in a better position to also understand how it gave prominence to a new set of cultural ideas about what it means to be an effective, healthy and successful person in contemporary society. As we have seen, those ideas were used over subsequent decades to justify not only the central policies of new capitalism (privatisation, de-unionisation, marketisation, austerity and deregulation) but also the widespread medicalisation of distress, facilitated by documents like PHQ-9, GAD-7 and DSM.

––––––––––

To understand these important processes, I want to take you back briefly to 2013, when the former UK Foreign Secretary David Owen described the first occasion he properly met Margaret Thatcher. The meeting took place in the House of Commons some years before Thatcher was elected prime minister. On that day, Owen was in the Commons with his wife when they encountered Thatcher in a corridor. She had in tow someone whom Owen recognised: a psychiatrist he had once worked with at St Thomas's Hospital in London (David Owen, for those of you who don't know, had trained and worked as a psychiatrist). Thatcher therefore invited Owen and his wife to join her and her guest for coffee.

As the conversation unfolded, she began to talk about one of her constituents – a mother who had become so concerned about her son's mental health that she had arranged to meet the doctor treating him. Owen recalled what she made of the son's ailments: 'It soon became apparent that she neither accepted nor wanted to understand that any adolescent could be depressed. For her, it was all due to a lack of personal drive, effort and will.' As she continued speaking, her argument became more fervid: 'Her voice hardened and she became ever more assertive about the impossibility of the adolescent's condition having anything to do with depression.' Owen's wife, who was normally very talkative, had clammed up in bemusement at what Thatcher was saying. 'I have never forgotten that conversation,' said Owen. 'It showed Thatcher conscientious to a fault, yet insensitive to someone she perceived as a non-achiever.'[12]

The above sketch will illustrate different things to different people. For me, it captures how faithful Thatcher had already become, by the mid 1970s, to the tenets of new capitalism; how her views on this occasion perfectly cohered with something that the new capitalist faithful *had* to believe: that many difficulties previously seen as matters to be resolved by the state could in fact be better dealt with by individual endeavour and responsibility. People should therefore primarily look to themselves, and not to the state, to solve intractable problems. As Thatcher confirmed in what has now become one of her most infamous interviews: 'We have gone through a period when too many children and people have been given to understand "I have a problem, it is the government's job to cope with it!" or "I have a problem, I will go and get a grant to cope with it!" or "I am homeless, the government must house me!" and so they are casting their problems on society ... [But] there is no such thing as society!'¹³ Rather there are only individuals and individual actions, so stop looking for state-based social solutions.

While this view was used to justify cutting social services, such small-state individualism was also reflected in countless other particulars, even down to how Thatcher responded to David Owen: the boy's problems were due to something within him that need immediate reform, rather than anything more socio-culturally or economically caused (her antinomy for this latter perspective was, interestingly enough, symbolised by her deep aversion for the discipline of sociology).

The upshot of the rise of individualism from the 1980s, therefore, was that people were increasingly encouraged to look within themselves for the causes and solutions for their plight. The moral task became to reshape internal selves through personal effort, self-will, self-help, consumption or other emotional interventions. As the self became the ultimate site for reform (it is down to *me* alone, what I consume and do, to change my lot), it is unsurprising that a new kind of national selfishness flourished, something about which Margaret Thatcher experienced much unease and bemusement at the end of her life. In fact, when asked in the late 2000s about her biggest regret as prime minster, she answered that it was actually failing to tax the rich enough: 'I cut taxes and I thought we would get a giving society, and we haven't.'[14] While Thatcher located rising selfishness in unequal tax policy, a far more obvious driver, of course, was the rising individualism that her freedom-loving small-state economics invariably obliged; a driver she simply couldn't see.

While we are all familiar with the arguments as to how individualism undermined local community spirit and engagement, it is less appreciated how it also individualised our framing and responses to emotional and mental distress; how it denigrated the importance of exploring, understanding and reforming the social and situational drivers of our suffering. What Thatcher's exchange with David Owen captures for me, then, is how her views are a logical outcome of what small-state economics directly obliges: the answer to personal crises has less to do with social policy than with individual change, initiative and responsibility – a view that implies an almost Darwinian understanding of why people fail or succeed within any social system. By stripping back the state in the name of preserving our freedom, so the thinking goes, we are unleashing people to make the best of themselves – creating a level playing field where success or failure is decided by our personal choices, ambitions, actions and capacities alone. Just as in other areas of the natural world where success is to be explained in terms of the survival of the fittest, new capitalism frames our trials and tribulations in similar ways. Our social success is seen as a sign of high personal fitness (rather than of social privilege or advantage), and our social failure of low personal fitness (rather than of poverty, discrimination or inequality). Here the suffering resulting from social failure – misery (dysthymia), fear (anxiety) and demoralisation (depression) – is seen as owing either to personal deficit (the boy is not ambitious enough) or to a medical malady that will, if possible, one day be technologically swept away.

Some time ago I delivered a seminar to medical students at Imperial College London, and raised the above points with them. One thoughtful student confidently responded, 'This is all very interesting, Dr Davies, but how is any of it relevant to our clinical work?' I answered that the philosophy of suffering that now dominates our services is consistent with new capitalism's preference for rooting the causes of problems in self. I said that such hyper-individualism influences how we understand, manage and respond to the suffering we daily confront. The philosophy we embrace matters, as it ultimately shapes all the work we do.

To illustrate this, I asked the students to make sense of the following fact: why is it that in the UK, the highest rates of psychiatric drug prescribing are found in the areas of highest socio-economic disadvantage, poverty and unemployment?[15] Is this really just a coincidence? Or is there something causal behind the correlation? They naturally responded that it was no coincidence at all, because these are precisely the kind of social circumstances (high deprivation, poverty, etc.) that cause higher rates of mental illness.

I then asked them to pay attention to what they had just said – in particular, to their use of the phrase 'mental illness'. While it is true, I continued, that people in deprived situations are likely to suffer a great deal more than those who are more affluent, on what grounds are we correct to use medical language to describe that suffering? Do we use it because we have simply been taught to use it, or because we have objective evidence that it is somehow better to medicalise such suffering than it is to view it, as many social scientists might, as a non-medical, non-pathological, yet understandable human response to harmful social, relational, political and environmental conditions?[16] Perhaps the reason why inequality, poverty, social disadvantage (and indeed pandemics) are good news for the antidepressant market, I continued, is because our response to socially induced suffering is so medicalised and drug-friendly – a response consistent with new capitalism's hyper-individualism.

———————

Over the years I have met, both professionally and personally, many people who filled in questionnaires like PHQ-9 and GAD-7, just as Emma had done. But not one of these people had ever, to my knowledge, thought of themselves as bit-players in a larger economic saga. They did not see these diagnostic tools as political documents that reframed and privatised their suffering in ways predominantly advantageous to the neo-liberal status quo. Nor did they consider these documents to be intimately connected to marauding pharmaceutical ambition and over-medicalisation. By articulating misery as a personal failing, they were unaware that these tools were warping their distress into a commodity from which profits were accrued, while enabling governments to leave undisturbed the deeper structural determinants of emotional pain. In the next chapter, I will more carefully assess some of these structural and social determinants that medicalising tropes and resources help relegate, also broaching the vexatious question of where do we go from here, given that the current dominant medicalised approach is clearly not working.

11

THE SOCIAL DETERMINANTS OF DISTRESS

Jack Graham cut a larger-than-life and jovial figure when I met him at his private sports club just outside London. He greeted me with a warm smile and an easy handshake. He was wearing a three-piece suit and a bright yellow tie, which proudly ballooned out from the top of his herringbone waistcoat. Jack is married, in his mid fifties, and has three teenage children. He is a successful entrepreneur, owning a large printing firm on the fringes of Berkshire. He left school at sixteen and blundered about from job to job until at the age of twenty-five he had a revelation about where he wanted to go in life. This led to him found his first company. Starting out with two employees in a small, damp garage loaned to him by his uncle, he now employs over a hundred staff in a suite of buildings. All his kids attend private school, a privilege from which he himself felt excluded, growing up in a low/middle-income household in south London. He works twelve hours most days, but still makes time to enjoy his success. Before COVID-19 hit, he would take regular spa breaks as well as travel abroad at least twice a year, always flying first class.

There are so many things we could focus on in Jack's colourful life, but let's now hone in on that final point: his choice to only ever fly first class, paying special attention to its economics. One of Jack's favourite trips is flying from London to New York, for which a first-class ticket costs about £5,000 – a full £4,500 more than an economy seat on the same flight. This extra cost does indeed purchase a more luxurious experience: lounge access, priority boarding, tolerable food and wine, highly attentive service, and now, more commonly, a lie-back neon-illuminated privacy pod where you can blow your £4,500 in attempted somnolence – all extras he highly appreciates. But given that they amount to an extra £650 an hour (for a seven-hour flight), I asked him whether he really considered them value for money.

'When you put it like that, probably not,' he laughed, rocking back in his chair as we shared lunch, 'but you have to remember that people fly first class for different reasons. You've got the guys who've been upgraded because they've accumulated Air Miles, or those whose company picks up the tab, and those who can pay without even thinking about it. Then you have people like me, who are not in the super-league but are wealthy enough to be willing to take a small hit for something a little special.'

I asked him why he didn't use the £4,500 he'd save by rather flying economy to buy something else instead. If it was luxury he wanted, why not purchase something a little more durable? 'You're missing the point,' he responded, 'because you're only focusing on the perks you get. I think what I'm really paying for is a lifestyle – how sitting up there makes me *feel*.'

He then told me about how he hated flying economy, and how, as a younger man, he'd always felt a certain shame when walking through business to the cheaper seats behind. 'The whole experience always felt demeaning in some way, as if it said to me: *they* are better than *you*, which is a message I was very sensitive to when growing up.' For Jack, the existence of a first class symbolised deep inequality in social relations between the haves and the have-nots. It undermined his instinctive feeling that he mattered just as much as anyone else – that he was just as worthy and valuable. The very notion that you could simply *buy* higher status, irrespective of whether you deserved it, violated his deep sense of social justice: 'It's wrong to be told you are at the back, in every sense, because you don't have the money to sit up front.'

Jack recognises that by flying first class today he is exploiting the very dynamic that meant he suffered as a young man. But he will continue to buy his first-class ticket, because for him it shores up a particular kind of desirable identity, sparing him the humiliation of what being at the back represents. In the language of the French social thinker Jean Baudrillard, his ticket does more than satisfy a desire for comfort. It additionally buys the sense of higher status that comes from believing you are part of a privileged social group. In fact, without knowing it, Jack is embroiled in a social dynamic about which sociologists have long written. He is consuming a sense of *distinction* from those he perceives as lower down the social scale, using his money to purchase the status that as a child his family so sorely lacked.

———

From the 1980s onwards in many Western democracies, the gap between the richest and poorest sections of society became ever more acute. To give some sense of how quickly this gap grew, just consider what happened with respect to income inequality from the 1980s onwards. While in the late 1970s the top 5 per cent of British households had an income four times higher than the poorest 5 per cent, that gap would gradually widen over subsequent decades to reach the ten times difference we endure today. And the income extremes become ever more glaring when looking at the very top 1 per cent of all earners. Today, that tiny minority of the population takes a full 13 per cent of all the income paid in the UK. This is treble that paid to them during the 1970s and almost double the corresponding figure in present-day Belgium (7 per cent) Sweden (8 per cent) and Norway (8 per cent).[1]

If these facts still don't really hit home, then let's look at rising inequality in another way: right now, the richest fifth in our society enjoy almost 50 per cent of all income in the UK, compared to the lowest fifth, who receive a lowly 4 per cent.[2] But perhaps the most striking statistic, for me at least, is derived from considering Britain's relationship to the rest of Northern Europe. While it is true that the UK possesses by far the wealthiest region in Northern Europe (west London),[3] it also happens to possess six out of the ten poorest regions (Tees Valley, Cornwall, West Wales, South Yorkshire, Lincolnshire and Outer London).[4] Thus the most extreme divergences of wealth and poverty in Northern Europe reside within just one country – the United Kingdom.

When you ask what has caused these huge economic disparities, a number of causal factors clearly present themselves, most of which are a direct result of deliberate choices made by successive governments since the

1980s. The more nuanced factors include technological progress (with highly skilled workers demanding higher wages); trade liberalisation (with cheaper labour abroad undercutting already low wages at home); the dismantling of the unions (leading to weaker worker representation); and shifting employment patterns (with an increase in workless single-parent families, despite lower unemployment rates overall).[5]

But perhaps the most significant factor driving inequality has been the changes to taxation policy since the 1980s. For example, while the top rate of income tax was 83 per cent on earned income in the late 1970s, that would drop over consecutive decades to the 45 per cent we witness today. Additionally, since the 1980s a whole host of 'wealth-friendly' taxation policies have also been steadily introduced, bringing down the average tax paid by the richest 10 per cent even further. For instance, as the wealthiest derive a greater proportion of their income from financial investments and family inheritance, they are disproportionately advantaged over the less wealthy, since governments have progressively lowered the tax rates on these additional forms of income. This is to say, when all tax advantages are taken into consideration (as well as national insurance, VAT and council tax), the richest 10 per cent of UK households pay an average of 13 per cent less of their total income on tax than the poorest

10 per cent.[6] So the poorer you are in the era of new capitalism, the more tax you invariably pay.[7]

In 2011, a bestselling book emerged that explored in detail how growing economic inequality affected the heart and soul of a nation. It was called *The Spirit Level*, and was written by two leading British health epidemiologists, Professor Kate Pickett and Professor Richard G. Wilkinson. The book represented the culmination of their career-long research into the relationship between inequality and human and social well-being. Could the former affect the latter? And if so, in what precise ways?

Drawing upon hundreds of national and international data sets from organisations such as the World Health Organization, the World Bank and the United Nations, Pickett and Wilkinson analysed the relationship between inequality and well-being in 23 of the wealthiest developed nations. They were particularly interested in identifying whether higher rates of inequality had any impact on our quality of life and well-being. The many measures of well-being they focused on included levels of life expectancy, infant mortality, obesity, drug use, teenage pregnancy, bullying, imprisonment, social connectedness, educational attainment, social mobility and the status of women. After correlating all these variables with income rates across international data sets, a clear pattern emerged: the bigger the gaps between rich and poor in any society the more severe and prevalent each of these social problems would be.

Overall, greater economic inequality was associated with a whole array of social and health problems. And this association, it turned out, adversely impacted not just the poorest members of society. An affluent person in a highly unequal society, for example, could also expect to die sooner, experience less connection to the community, and see their children perform less well at school than an affluent person living in a more equal society. Pickett and Wilkinson summarised this association (Figure 3), with the more unequal societies on the right.

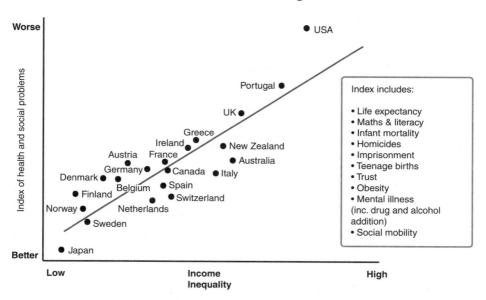

Figure 3 Health and social problems are worse in more unequal countries[8]

When Pickett and Wilkinson published their work, it garnered substantial scientific and political attention. Positive reviews appeared in *Nature*, the *British Medical Journal*, *The Lancet* and the *London Review of Books*, with the *New Statesman* ranking it among the top 10 books of the decade and the *Guardian* in the top 100 books of the twenty-first century. It inspired the Conservative party's flirtation with 'raising national well-being' and brought keen endorsements from politicians like Will Hutton, Ed Miliband and Roy Hattersley. US president Barack Obama and the head of the IMF, Christine Lagarde, both cited its arguments positively. But of course, there was also a powerful backlash, especially from the economic right, whose ideology was threatened by the book's main conclusions. Pickett and Wilkinson were accused of using data selectively, of confusing causation with correlation, of using obscure statistical methods and of overplaying the scientific consensus on the harms of inequality. The criticisms were many, but each time the authors pushed back convincingly with highly detailed counter-arguments.[9]

Ten years after *The Spirit Level* was published, Pickett and Wilkinson released their second book, *The Inner Level*. Unlike the first, this focused on just one variable: the relationship between inequality and mental distress. When I spoke to Richard Wilkinson in 2020, I asked him what he and Kate Pickett wanted to achieve by undertaking their new study. 'As we'd already focused on how inequality impacts so many facets of social life, we now wanted to know about the personal and psychological effects of inequality too.' After replicating the statistical analyses deployed in *The Spirit Level*, Pickett and Wilkinson found something unnerving: that unequal societies experience over twice the prevalence of mental distress as their more equal counterparts. This is illustrated in the Figure 4, with the most unequal societies again placed on the right.

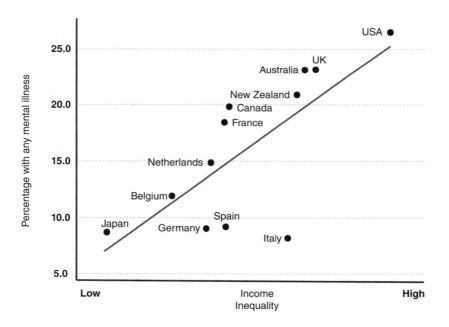

Figure 4 The prevalence of mental illness is higher in more unequal rich countries[10]

So why were inequality and mental distress so closely related? I put this question directly to Wilkinson, who drew on evolutionary theory to offer an answer: 'The vast majority of our evolutionary history was spent living in small hunter-gatherer societies, where we adapted over a very long period to an egalitarian way of life where status was evenly distributed,' he said. 'Back then, group cooperation was essential to the survival of all – so a cooperative person was very useful to have around.' Women would prefer partners whom they regarded as less selfish, and the community would value those who put the group first. 'In fact, we know that if you were selfish and out for yourself you could be ostracised or even killed. And so our early environment selected pro-social characteristics like relatedness and cooperativeness.'

Given that most of our biological history evolved in these more egalitarian and cooperative settings, I asked Wilkinson how that might affect people today, living in societies with large material and wealth disparities, and with significant gaps and splits in the social fabric? 'Well, we begin to experience a huge accentuation in competitiveness and division,' he replied, 'and this significantly increases our insecurity and anxiety about our place within the system – about our status relative to others and how we are judged.'

For Wilkinson and Pickett, the rapid rise in economic

inequality over the last forty years can therefore explain the dramatic rise in what they term 'status anxiety' – that is, the fear of being seen as lower or less valuable than others, something that we are evolutionarily primed to avoid. 'What supports this point,' continued Wilkinson, 'is that the highest levels of status anxiety are found today in the most unequal societies.' Indeed, according to research that maps results from large cross-sectional surveys, status anxiety and inequality consistently go hand in hand, as Figure 5 shows.

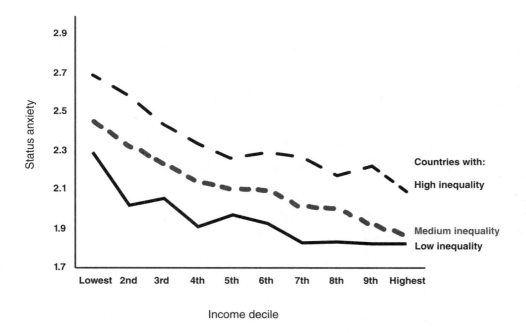

Figure 5 Status anxiety across income deciles for high, medium and low inequality countries[11]

As Wilkinson and I continued our conversation, he gave me an example of how status anxiety plays itself out in real life. It concerned a young woman called Martha Beck, who shot to notoriety after describing in a leading US magazine how she felt in social situations. In short, she characterised herself as 'one of the millions of party-impaired people – social-phobes who dread party talk, who are petrified of saying something stupid; something that will reveal us as the jackasses we are, rather than the social maestros we wish we were'. She described needing 'a whole armoury full of impressive weapons to survive a party, things like cleverness, thin thighs, social connection and wealth'. For Martha, 'every act, from choosing clothes to making small talk, is a fear-based defence against criticism'.[12]

While we can all relate to these anxieties to some degree, we may be less aware of how they undermine our capacity to enjoy the benefits of social interaction and intimacy – all things vital for supporting mental and emotional health. In today's society, Wilkinson insisted, these anxieties are increasingly common. For instance, between 40 and 70 per cent of people, depending upon the study you consult, now admit that they would largely prefer to stay at home watching TV than to go out at the weekend and mix with other people, even close friends. Many of us are also reducing our face-to-face interactions, replacing them with social media exchanges, where our image can be carefully manicured and we have more presentational control. 'A large part of this reticence about real interpersonal exchange has to do with the effort of self-presentation,' said Wilkinson. 'Anxiety about how you will be seen in the light of day. Will you be clever or entertaining enough – can you muster the occasional joke?'

For Wilkinson, our growing status anxiety contrasts with earlier periods, such as the 1960s, when there was far less inequality. 'Then, people talked about communes and living together, about sharing and supporting each other in social groups.' Collective action and organisation were also stronger, and community hubs (pubs, social clubs, kids clubs, fairs) were far more common and regularly attended. While this earlier period was certainly not exempt from social tensions, it was far less atomised when compared with the more unequal contexts of today. Indeed, Wilkinson and Pickett cite many studies revealing that leisure activities that support community and social connection occur less frequently in more unequal societies. 'This not only undermines the very clear health benefits of good relationship, connectedness and community,' said Wilkinson, 'but raises levels of distrust and fear between people and groups.'

One such study on rising distrust is of particular note. It was undertaken by the American economists Samuel

Bowles and Arjun Jayadev, who uncovered something intriguing when they studied what they called 'guard labour'. After assessing employment statistics in many different societies, they found that the proportion of people employed as police, prison officers, security guards, bouncers, etc. – basically the people we use to protect ourselves from each other – actually increases with inequality.[13] It is as if levels of fear and distrust grow proportionately with the social distances existing between us. In the era of extreme inequality, what matters is not whether you are safe but whether you feel safe. And as the feeling of being unsafe increases in unequal societies, so too does the use of guard protection.

For Wilkinson and Pickett, then, one of the worst effects of inequality is rising status anxiety, which separates, divides and breeds fear between us. It is also associated with spending less time with our families and more time at work. It is linked with higher levels of depression and with greater levels of consumption, as we buy more stuff in an attempt to win social approval and acceptance. This use of consumption to mitigate status anxiety is even reflected, interestingly enough, in the fact that highly unequal societies like the UK and the USA spend almost twice as much on advertising as their more equal counterparts like Norway and Sweden, presumably because advertising in the former societies is more likely to get a good return.

Pickett and Wilkinson's work, then, closely chimes with the extensive research on materialism we explored with Tim Kasser in Chapter Nine. For Kasser, you'll remember, high levels of consumption and materialism were an attempt to satisfy essential needs left unmet by our social and relational environment. For Pickett and Wilkinson, the equation is essentially the same: through consumption we try to satisfy the need to feel accepted and valued (and so safe and supported as part of the group), a need that highly unequal societies frustrate.

I have focused closely on Wilkinson and Pickett's work as it supports a view that has gained wide credence over the last fifteen years: that mental distress is mostly psychosocially determined. This does not mean we can reduce mental distress to inequality or any other single social factor. Nor does it mean that our biology has no impact on our social and psychological lives. What it does mean is that social determinants must sit at the heart of our understanding and management of mental distress, whether that management is dispensed through our clinics, workplaces, employment centres, communities or schools. As an almost endless stream of new research is confirming,[14] whether we look at the harms of poverty, trauma, abuse, meaninglessness or work dissatisfaction; consumption, inequality, materialism or inner-city living; over-medicalisation, pollution or low educational attainment; sexism, unemployment, debt or discrimination; ageism, economic insecurity, loneliness or marginalisation; community fragmentation, racism or bullying; overwork or any other social determinant, all adversely impact our mental health. We must, therefore, bring the world and its happenings into the centre of what we do, designing mentally healthy social policies and ensuring that all our interventions are sociologically informed. As one of the UK's most illustrious professors of public health, Michael Marmot, recently put it: 'We must build a society based on the principles of social justice; reduce inequalities of income and wealth; and build a well-being economy that puts achievement of health and well-being, rather than narrow economic goals, at the heart of government strategy.'[15]

To now explore how this might be done, let's take a trip to one of the great institutions of mid-century capitalism, from where some of the most compelling and promising calls for immediate mental health reform are now emerging.

———————

A week before Christmas 2019, I met Professor Dainius Pūras in the twinkling Swiss city of Geneva – the European headquarters of the United Nations, and the first city to sign the Universal Declaration on Human Rights. Just outside the festive hub of the central district, nestled away on the nondescript Rue de Montbrillant, sits a small and traditionally decorated Swiss hotel, popular with foreign dignitaries, politicians and UN officials. After meeting in the hotel's lobby, we found two plump armchairs draped in warm sheepskin rugs sequestered in a corner just off the main atrium. Pūras, now in his late fifties, had a surprisingly lively manner given that it was still only 7 a.m. (the only time in our schedules, after weeks of trying, that we could both manage).

In 2014, Pūras rapidly became one of the most important figures in global health after being appointed by the United Nations as its Special Rapporteur. His role, as defined by the UN's Human Rights Council, is to promote the rights of all people to the highest standards of health care, and to expose any health system not achieving those ends. Having trained as a medical doctor and a psychiatrist, and now holding professorial psychiatry positions at Georgetown (Washington DC) and Vilnius (Lithuania), a central focus of his UN appointment was to understand why mental health interventions have fallen so far behind the success rates of other health disciplines, something, as you will recall, that I discussed in my introduction. Today, Pūras is a leading global voice on the challenges facing mental health provision in the twenty-first century, having visited more than thirty nations on UN fact-finding missions to assess where our mental health systems are going wrong and how we can put them right.

I had travelled to Geneva to explore with Pūras two hard-hitting UN reports, led and authored by Pūras himself.[16] These aimed to identify the main barriers to creating successful mental health services in the twenty-first century. The first report, published in 2017, drove a wedge into the heart of the mental health establishment by arguing that a proper human-rights-based approach to solving mental health problems was being sidelined in most countries, including the UK. This rights-based approach essentially argued for two fundamental changes. It requested much wider implementation of psychological and social support for people with mental health difficulties (relational, community and group support) and called for greater attention to be paid to tackling the social causes of distress: inequality, poverty, discrimination, overwork and social exclusion. Both reports argued that this rights-based approach was being neglected due to three serious obstacles.

The first obstacle, and perhaps the most important, was the dominance of the biomedical model in mental health care – an approach that, as I covered in the introduction, frames most mental distress as medical illness and favours biomedical explanations and interventions like psychiatric drugs. This approach, Pūras explained, had increased the amount of needless prescribing, neglected effective psychological and social alternatives, and misrepresented the nature and causes of mental distress. It had also largely led professionals to overlook the complex social and psychological determinants of distress, to the detriment of individual health. On this final point, he offered me an illustration as our coffee arrived:

'During a recent trip with the UN, I met a woman who told me about her nine-year-old daughter, who had an autism diagnosis. They lived in a high-income country with a relatively good level of medical support, so the child was in inclusive education and receiving special school support for her difficulties. One afternoon when the mother came to pick her up from school, however, the teacher said her daughter had been very agitated all day, beyond what was usual. The teacher suggested they go back to the doctor to assess the problem. The mother asked the teacher what had happened. The teacher answered that she wasn't a doctor so she couldn't be expected to understand her daughter's brain. When the mother told me this, she said: "You see how ignorant professionals can be, even after a university education." It took the mother less than a minute to discover the cause of her daughter's agitation. There was a small stone in the girl's shoe.

'So you see the common mistake,' Pūras continued. 'Once the person has a diagnosis, everything that then happens is seen through that prism, and then only biomedical decisions and treatments will be applied.'

While this approach will be appropriate when dealing with many physical conditions, in the realm of mental health it is rarely appropriate. For Pūras, this simplistic biomedical vision strips suffering of its broader context, leading it to be managed in technological rather than relational ways. For these reasons, he stated at the UN's Human Rights Council in 2019 that 'too heavy reliance on this biomedical model has failed'.

What made matters worse for Pūras was that this biomedical approach was not scientifically substantiated. 'Despite billions spent on research, we have yet to discover biological causes for any mental disorders,' he said. 'What we have discovered, mind you, are power imbalances – between doctors and patients and between the biomedical and other approaches that will pay more attention to the social and psychological determinants of a person's distress' – to the stone in the shoe, so to speak.[17] 'Yet when you ask psychiatrists informally why the biomedical approach is failing, about 90 per cent will blame lack of resources. They say that there is a funding gap that we need to close if things are to improve.' For Pūras, though, ploughing more money into the same failing approach will simply not turn things around. Rather, we must redirect funding towards tackling the social causes of distress and implementing effective psychological and social interventions.

As Pūras and I continued talking, our attention

was occasionally drawn through the nearby window towards the trams periodically passing by. The sound of their heavy wheels grinding on the steel tracks symbolised for me how I have always felt about the other two obstacles to reform outlined in the report. These were obstacles I had also written about (and critiqued) for some time,[18] and have already alluded to in the introduction: the mutually beneficial financial links between psychiatry and the pharmaceutical industry and the biased use of evidence to shore up their biomedical approach.

On this latter point Pūras was unequivocal: the influence and interests of the pharmaceutical industry had corrupted research and the dissemination of information to the extent that 'our collective knowledge about mental health has become tainted'. A troubling example of this bias, he wrote, 'is the use of evidence to inform people with mild and moderate forms of depression that they should receive psychotropic medications (antidepressants), despite the clear evidence that they should not. This is even more shocking when we know that other non-biomedical interventions are more effective, such as the ones targeting relationships and the social and underlying determinants of mental health, rather than the brain.' For Pūras, then, the excessive use and misuse of psychiatric medications had ultimately created a serious human rights issue, by denying us the right of access to safer and more effective forms of mental health care.

———————

After this hard-hitting UN report was published in 2017, there was substantial controversy. But this did not stop Pūras from further developing, with the UN's full support, the preferred 'human-rights-based approach' in a second report, published in 2019. While this new report affirmed that mental health services must be provided for anyone in need, it called for them to rather focus on the social and interpersonal drivers of distress, placing healthy relationships at the heart of everything. As the report put it: services 'should not be based on an excessively biomedical model', but reflect the wider societal need to build 'connections between individuals, families and communities over the course of life and across generations'.

In 2019, the *Guardian* covered Pūras's UN report through an exclusive interview with him. The resulting article implied that the changes called for by the report directly challenged many core policies of late capitalism. For instance, it quoted Pūras's views on how, since the 2008 financial crisis, austerity policies had accentuated the very things we know worsen mental health: social division, inequality and social isolation – all problems also having greater prevalence in the most neo-liberal of the developed nations (the UK and US).

The article also emphasised that if governments weren't prepared to challenge these social determinants of distress, but instead continued to scale up biomedical and individualistic interventions, then mental health outcomes would not improve. We therefore required policies that tackled the social roots of distress, such as better (and de-medicalised) early-years and school programmes, fairer taxation, stronger workforce unionisation, better social welfare, more community support and the reduction of inequality and social exclusion. We also needed to develop social arrangements – in homes, schools, workplaces, health care settings and communities – that built up therapeutic support. In short, said Pūras, 'we need to target relationships rather than brains', bringing people together, de-medicalising their distress, and tackling difficult social and environmental causes.

As I discussed the *Guardian* interview with Pūras, I couldn't help but think how interesting it would be if Professor Richard Wilkinson were able to join us, as the two men appeared to have so much common. What I now wanted to know was whether Pūras, like Wilkinson (and, indeed, myself), agreed with something that the *Guardian* article strongly implied: that our current mental health crisis would remain unchanged until some core social policies of late capitalism were rejected.

'Well, the *Guardian* piece certainly did a great job

at highlighting the emotional harms of austerity, inequality, poverty and the damage caused by hyper-capitalism.' He smiled. 'So of course those on the left said, "Hey, look, he is with us!" and even Jeremy Corbyn began tweeting me. And yes, it is true I am with the left, but it is also true that there is another side of the argument that the article didn't fully reflect.'

This other side, he then elaborated, was his rejection of the idea that communism, or pseudo-socialism, as he called it, was the only real panacea for mental illness. He strongly warned against this view given his experience growing up in the Soviet Union during the Cold War, and training there as a doctor and psychiatrist. From these formative years, he knew how damaging such political systems could be: 'There was lots of propaganda in the 1980s claiming that we in the Soviet Union had solved all mental health problems because we had defeated capitalism. Mental illness was a Western disease, it said – suicide, alcoholism and depression all occurred because capitalism exploits people. But in reality, of course, we had exactly the same problems in the Soviet Union. We were just hiding them in vast institutions – locking children and adults away; oppressing people's civil rights and freedoms, and saying to the world: "Look, we don't have your Western sicknesses here." We then extended this model to all disabilities. In fact, when Moscow hosted the Olympics Games in 1980, the government actually refused to host the Paralympics too. They just said, we don't have any disabled people here! It's only you in the West who have this problem.'

Such Soviet propaganda during the 1970s and 1980s did not lead just to the mass incarceration and maltreatment of people with mental health and other disabilities, but also to the failure to develop any community mental health services, because if all mental health problems were defeated by communism, no such services were required. 'During that time there were no social workers, no psychologists, no therapists, only psychiatrists who were prescribing huge dosages of psychotropic medication and incarcerating people. So when we now reflect on capitalism and mental health, we have to remember recent history and recognise that from the Cold War onwards, both sides got it wrong. Capitalism largely ignored [and continues to ignore] the economic and social drivers of distress [putting the emphasis on individual failings rather than social policy] while the pseudo-socialism of the Soviet Union simply hid the entire reality of mental distress, leading to widespread denial and human rights violations.'

———

On the afternoon of my meeting with Dainius Pūras, I took a walk into the centre of the old town, first to meet some colleagues from the University of Geneva, and then to take a final hike through the city. I was feeling a little nostalgic, as I knew that my interview with Pūras would be one of the last I'd undertake for this book. And so, once I'd left my colleagues at the Uni Dufour, I headed straight for the stately Parc des Bastions, from where beckoned the enticing smell of warm chocolate fondue and sweet burning pine. Along the park's central boulevard stretched and glittered the most delightful Christmas market, replete with log cabins, fire pits, cosy sofa chairs and the dulcet hum of jazz. Above our heads, vast silver baubles hung from branches forty feet up, showering their wisps of dancing light across the ground below. Families were now pouring into the park from the Conservatoire de Musique directly opposite, where an early matinee of *The Snow Queen* had just been performed. The whole atmosphere was joyous, festive, enlivening even, and certainly oozing prosperity. Geneva, after all, is one of the great beneficiaries of new capitalist success: a global banking hub with extraordinarily low corporate and individual taxes, and so a magnet for a tiny financial global elite. Central Geneva is a conurbation for the 1 per cent – and of course this was *their* Christmas fair.

Once I had left the Parc des Bastions and begun my long walk towards a less affluent quarter, I could not shake from my mind Pūras's final comments about the politics of mental health – about how both capitalist and communist systems had exploited and promoted different mental health narratives for their own particular ends. For communism, mental illness was characterised as a Western disease from which its own superior social system was mercifully exempt, while for new capitalism, it was a problem to be reframed and used to economic advantage. While the communists would bury and deny suffering, the new capitalists would medicalise, depoliticise and profit from it; they would turn it into a productive threat, and exonerate neo-liberal policies for causing it.

With these thoughts in mind, I recalled the three obstacles to mental health reform that Pūras's UN reports had outlined (the biased use of evidence, pharmaceutical power and biomedical dominance). I now wondered whether Pūras would agree that there is in fact a fourth obstacle to reform, the most seminal obstacle of them all, and the one I have tried to illuminate throughout this book – namely, the general style of political economy that since the 1980s has favoured the medicalised and individualistic approach that his UN reports indict.

As I continued my walk through central Geneva, now meandering through the colourful student quarter, I found a café, ordered a coffee and started pondering some more. Why had Dainius Pūras seemed so non-committal when I asked him about this fourth obstacle to reform? Why did he appear unsure how to answer? Perhaps it was a matter he needed to give more thought to, or perhaps he feared where a radical critique of capitalism might lead, given his experience living in the Soviet Union. But there are many forms of capitalism. Some that came before the 1980s and many that will follow our current time; and some that might one day look back at our present version as an unjust and damaging outlier.

As I continued ruminating in that café, I soon remembered my earlier conversation with Professor Richard Wilkinson and the response he had given to the same question: did he feel our style of economy had hindered mental health reform? His answer had been more decisive: 'Whenever we hear in politics or the media that mental disorder, stress or self-harm is going up, the response is almost always a call for more services – more psychiatrists and psychologists. But we rarely ask why a society living with such unprecedented levels of physical comfort suffers such an appalling burden of mental and emotional difficulties. The fact is, there are structural explanations for this, and that's the central problem.'

In this book I have tried to explain that these structural explanations are largely ignored in mental health care because its ideology props up, rather than challenges, the socio-economic status quo. Whether we are looking at the medicalisation of worker dissatisfaction, at the rise of back-to-work therapies, at the alignment of materialistic values and treatments, at the pathologisation of the unemployed, at recovery being measured in terms of economic productivity, at pharmaceutical regulation that puts industry interests first, at the use of diagnostic labels to plug school funding cuts, or at the widespread commodification and depoliticisation of mental distress, we are referring to a system that has become handmaiden to the ideological needs and wants of new capitalism. Only once this subservience is fully acknowledged can we explain why our failing mental health system continues to expand nonetheless.

As I left the warmth and buzz of the café and made my way up Rue de Chantepoulet towards Geneva's central station, it became clear to me that I would need to end this book by reiterating a point raised at its very beginning: that the alignment of mental health with new capitalism was never purposely plotted behind the scenes. The actual truth, in my view, is far less enticing. Our mental health system has, like most other major social institutions, simply come to embrace those ideas and practices that have best secured its own perpetuation. It has become what it is, and has continued to thrive, by following the path of least resistance – by moving with, rather than defying, the dominant neo-liberal tide. Indeed, as the mid-century social philosopher

Michel Foucault once put it: power embraces the ideas and practices that best serve its own aims and interests – ideas and practices that come to shape reality on the ground. In the light of these comments, we cannot forget the Conservatives trying to 'nudge' people into work to bring the disability bill down; or New Labour trying to raise worker productivity through its new therapy programme; or successive governments attempting to increase profits through ongoing pharmaceutical deregulation, or government/corporate alliances trying to mitigate pervasive worker dissatisfaction via new mental health workplace consultancies.

As I stated at the outset of the book, these enthusiasms take hold of the powerful not because their overriding political goal is to improve our mental health (well, at least not primarily), but because our politicians enjoy solutions that are sold to them as killing two or more birds with one stone, or that appear, behind the banner of helping people, to also serve their more deeply held ideological commitments. The great movers and shakers of our mental health systems (the purveyors of IAPT, the mental health consultancies, the pharmaceutical companies and psychiatric opinion leaders) have all understood this at a deep intuitive level and have played the politicians well: the stuff that gets heard, funded and implemented is that which ignites the ideological passions of those holding the strings of the public purse.

The great fault in our services, then, lies just as much with those who have funded bad ideas as with those who initially contrived them, and then marketed them in politically enticing ways. Unfortunately, the outcome of this mutually beneficial alliance has been ongoing poor outcomes, and the almost endless string of costly systemic/service failures we witness everywhere today.

CONCLUSION

I sit alone on the top floor of my university library. The view stretches far off towards central London, where multiple steel and glass turrets jut up on the horizon. The sun is setting, and an orange glow drapes the city in the shape of a vast segmental dome. Close by sit a few tired doctoral researchers, wearing the obligatory face masks. They've been huddled over their laptops since early morning and now appear to want to call it a day. I have one hour remaining before I must dash home, undertake a superficial tidy-up, help bath the kids, read a couple of stories, prepare an evening meal, and then, probably in the early hours of the morning, submit this manuscript.

And so, at the final hour, I confront a question that has been close to me throughout this book, constantly petitioning my attention and intruding into my many conversations and interviews. The question is as deceptively simple as it is difficult to answer: where do we go from here?

One response is to say that it should not be up to any single author to write the charter for how the mental health crisis might be managed in this country. It should be up to government, policymakers and local authorities to advance ideas and solutions. But this answer, I know, is unsatisfactory, least of all because these aforementioned institutions are bound by the same economic rationale governing our mental health services during their period of failure and so are in no position to be innovative or radical beyond what this rationale will permit.

Perhaps there is an alternative answer, then. Perhaps we could wait for the mental health profession to reform itself, in spite of an unsupportive political/economic environment? Perhaps it could surreptitiously carve out spaces that take collective suffering and solutions seriously, that put the nurture of community and relationships at the heart of what they do, and that favour health outcomes that are not primarily economic. This answer certainly feels more palatable than the first, especially since such work is already long under way. In important areas of the mental health landscape, many people and organisations are spontaneously joining together to resist decades of neo-liberal subservience – calling for less medicalisation, medication and depoliticisation while implementing more trauma-focused, relational and community care, more humanistic, psychosocial and non-biomedical alternatives.

These calls for reform are gaining support in many mainstream mental health organisations, and are being variously implemented by a number of influential professional, campaigning and service-user groups.[1] While this diverse progressive movement espouses a multiplicity of views and practices, it broadly agrees that our distress has been wrongly commodified and privatised in recent times: robbed of its capacity to illuminate social ills, galvanise social action and facilitate lasting and meaningful personal and social change.

This movement's unwillingness to serve neo-liberal interests commends it. But it also hinders it, as I believe its aims will struggle to materialise fully until our political economy shifts in a more accommodating direction. Until this happens, vital pockets of transformative mental health thinking and practice will continue to wrestle for salience in an arena where neo-liberal dictates still come first. This means that any approach that decouples services from raising productivity, that demands independence from industry influence, that defies the over-medicalisation and privatisation of distress, and that aims to facilitate healthy relationships, communities and social justice will struggle to see the full light of day.

And so this brings me to my final answer regarding where we go from here. And it is the answer with which I most closely align: fundamental mental health reform is most likely to occur only once our political economy permits it – only once we have changed the economic approach and instituted more regulated, progressive and socially democratic arrangements throughout our economy. While this answer may feel less than satisfactory for some, as it implies such a major prerequisite for change, it is also true that socio-economic reform looks far less implausible than it did even in early 2020.

Since then, the world has changed irrevocably. As COVID-19 spread globally, it triggered the sharpest and deepest economic contraction in the history of capitalism,[2] graphically exposing the deep faults in our current economic paradigm. It seemed that the more neo-liberal the economy, the more perilous its predicament became, with the UK and US faring especially badly on a whole host of economic and health measures.[3] Years of austerity and deliberate dismantling of state capacities left the UK struggling to meet basic public health, hospital and welfare needs. The UK also failed to act swiftly with testing and tracing, and even strained to provide, week after week, basic PPE to doctors, nurses and carers. This translated into the worst care-home death crisis almost anywhere in the developed world,[4] and was only resolved once the UK government finally sourced foreign supplies that it could not manufacture at home.

As depleted public services left the UK particularly exposed, gaping economic inequalities, widened by decades of new capitalism, also became glaringly visible again. Lockdown did not treat us all the same. It discriminated heavily against low-income and BAME groups, who were more likely to be found working on the front lines or to be sequestered in cramped living spaces, their health and well-being suffering disproportionally.[5] It also discriminated against people living in poor areas, who were nearly two and a half times more likely to die of COVID than those living in affluent regions.[6] Then came the schools crisis to expose and deepen social inequity. While the private schools delivered daily online teaching to pupils (sparing their families the many stresses of forced home-schooling), nearly half of all state school pupils received almost no teacher contact at all during the first major lockdown.[7] And as the lowest home-schooling rates were found in the most disadvantaged homes, the attainment gap widened further. These imbalances were compounded by the A level algorithm debacle, which lowered the grades of university-bound disadvantaged students more than it did those who were privately educated.

As major social inequalities were foregrounded by COVID, protest movements like Black Lives Matter highlighted the linked themes of racism and social injustice, especially in the US. The killing of George Floyd symbolised the wide structural violence of racism and urban poverty. These iniquities were compounded by black, Asian and minority ethnic (BAME) people being dramatically over-represented in the COVID-19 death statistics.[8] Their distress was not caused by strictly biomedical factors, as some would have it. It was a product of living in a rigged economy where inequality, racism, ailing services and poor wealth redistribution saw BAME people filling the COVID front lines of essential work.

Neo-liberal ideas of individualism and non-state-intervention also took a hit. After all, it was no accident that it was leaders located on the economic right who mostly embraced the failed anti-interventionist policy of 'herd immunity'. Donald Trump (US), Boris Johnson (UK) and Jair Bolsonaro (Brazil) all adopted this policy to varying degrees, even though the most vulnerable in the herd (the elderly and chronically ill) would be the worst affected. This anti-interventionist, survival-of-the-fittest policy only collapsed after the UK public, out of incredulous self-protection, began spontaneously locking themselves down in early March 2020. This symbolic revolt forced the government's hand, making it change tack. But the delay was still costly, leading to the death rate soaring, lockdown extending and the recession, in the end, further deepening.

As neo-liberal economies struggled to defy their anti-interventionist instincts, another mainstay of new capitalism – belief in the superiority of the markets – also looked fatally strained. No matter how inadequate the government's response, the markets simply could not save themselves. Instead, government used hundreds of billions to shore them up. A decade of neo-liberal sermonising about the absolute economic necessity of fiscal austerity and there being 'no magic money tree' was exposed as ideological after all. Vast debts were incurred to fund private enterprise bailouts and furlough schemes, which, as it turns out, many employers fraudulently misused (six million furloughed employees continued to work during lockdown).[9] These necessary state interventions were conducted in the spirit of saving the neo-liberal economy, a potent injection of socialism to boost neo-liberalism's immunity. But as the UK still reels from the worst economic downturn in the league of developed nations, the question arises about the extent to which short-term interventionism is a busted flush, with the only viable long-term solution being a full pivot towards embracing a more progressive and equal economy.

As new capitalism, in the midst of lockdown after tired lockdown, was put on life support, we would soon face another epidemic: worsening rates of mental ill health. By April 2020, lockdown was taking its toll, leading the Royal College of Psychiatrists to warn of a coming 'tsunami of mental illness'.[10] By July, the Office of National Statistics had followed suit, reporting that 'rates of depression' had doubled in four months,[11] while a major report by the LSE concluded that by the end of the year, the nation as a whole had pretty much reached the threshold for psychiatric morbidity (that is, psychiatric illness).[12] Yet despite this excessive over-medicalisation of COVID distress, very little new provision arrived in response, apart from a few million pounds to boost some impoverished services and a new mental health hotline (which by many accounts was always engaged). The inevitable result was more psychiatric drug prescriptions, which vaulted to unprecedented levels,[13] and a feedback loop of yet more medicalisation.

What was being medicalised as a mental illness epidemic by the mental health establishment, however, did not look like illness at all to most people on the ground. Rightly, people understood intuitively that their suffering was not pathological, psychiatric or disordered in nature, but a natural response to the ills of lockdown: whether to increased interpersonal isolation, economic insecurity, domestic tension, abuse, unemployment, loss or an uncertain future. This was reflected in data emerging during the 2021 lockdown. The worst-affected people were women with small children, the ill, the bereaved, those losing their jobs, and young people aged between 18 and 24.[14] At the root of this distress were not misfiring chemicals or biogenetic liabilities, but the obvious social stressors to which these groups were exposed. Medicalising such distress now appeared as theoretically obtuse as it did pragmatically and morally bankrupt, especially since social stresses needed social responses: economic security, family support, jobs, community and rekindled hope for the future – all things the pandemic, for many, had snatched away.

Rising distress did not just strain the credibility of medicalisation as a plausible explanation for the suffering, but also demanded that we de-professionalise the management of our mental health, due to the restricted NHS provision during the first and second major lockdowns. Public Health England set out to empower us, knowing that yet more medicalisation would simply overwhelm an already overstretched health system. It asked us to take charge of our distress – to eat, sleep and exercise well, to engage with and nurture supportive relationships.[15] Another major report, commissioned by the Wellcome Trust, reiterated the importance of such measures, warning us that pathologising COVID distress would inadvertently make our suffering worse by 'catastrophising the conversation around mental health' and by 'undermining informal and communal coping mechanisms ... that sit outside the medical system'.[16]

The message rang out: there are things you can do to improve your predicament. And some of this messaging soon took on a more political tone. When Michelle Obama publicly declared that she was suffering from 'low-grade depression', for instance, she was quick to declare why: lockdown, police brutality and five years of Donald Trump. It wasn't long before she translated her pain into social action, igniting Joe Biden's presidential bid with her moving speeches and fiery campaigning, which helped turbo-boost his road to victory in November 2020. Her pain was her motivation; her political action her therapy. This approach could also work for others.

While suffering afflicted many during lockdown, others, less exposed to its various stresses, began to flourish in unexpected ways, which was the side of the story that new capitalism, judging by the coverage, was far less likely to report. In fact, when YouGov undertook the largest survey into the national outlook, only 9 per cent of people reported wanting life to return to 'normal' after the pandemic was over,[17] while research conducted at University College London showed that lockdown was enjoyed by a full third of the British population.[18] Our COVID confinement, it seems, had brought deep questioning of our pre-COVID neo-liberal lives. Many people were relieved to be temporarily away from jobs they disliked or found dissatisfying and unengaging. Others found unsought-for opportunities to spend more time with immediate family, to rekindle and deepen connections, to read, to reflect, to walk and to exercise. As the everyday maelstrom of neo-liberal living dissipated, so our vision also provisionally cleared. With fewer distractions, many were able to adopt a more philosophical cast of mind, bringing neglected feelings, thoughts and life questions to the fore. We were forced to shop and consume less, to live life more slowly and modestly. Ecological awareness also grew,[19] as more of us connected with nature again, and as the air around us felt cleaner. The crisis punctured our sense of hubris, too. If our technology could not avert a global lockdown, perhaps we weren't invincible after all. Maybe climate catastrophe could not be rapidly reversed should the point of no return be reached as climate scientists warned.[20]

So in the end, COVID has changed everything. It has changed the viability and sustainability of new systems of economic production. It has changed our sense of what matters most and least in life, and it has transfigured, to some extent, our understanding of what makes us tick, what brings us down and what is necessary to raise us up. All these changes provide hope that a new paradigm of mental health care may soon have a winning chance, given that systemic economic reform may be closer than only recently supposed. No economic paradigm, after all, has ever existed in perpetuity.[21] And this one won't buck that historical trend. When change arrives, and it will arrive, alternative ideas in the realm of mental health will only be poised for implementation if we keep putting in the effort right now; if we work to defy the neo-liberal pressures and enticements, and if we develop interventions adapted to serve the needs of people rather than the commandments of neoliberal doctrine.

ACKNOWLEDGEMENTS

I have so many people to thank. First off, let me offer my sincere gratitude to all those people who set aside time out of their busy schedules to grant me interviews. Without their generosity this book simply would not have been written. I must also thank my colleagues and collaborators at the Council for Evidence-based Psychiatry and the All-Party Parliamentary Group for Prescribed Drug Dependence: Luke Montagu, Dr Anne Guy, Professor Peter Kinderman, Professor John Read, Dr Jo Moncrieff, Lord John Montagu, Professor Sami Timimi. There are others too who deserve special mention, such as Dr Lucy Johnstone, James Moore, Jo Watson, Dr Mark Horowitz, Dr Ruth Cooper, Dr Michael Hengartner and the prescribed-harm community. Your confidence and intellectual collaboration are an invaluable source of support for which I am truly grateful. I also wish to thank my colleagues at the University of Roehampton for keeping the environment in which we all work supportive, collegiate and intellectually stimulating.

I must also especially thank Andrew Lownie, for taking me on those many years ago, and for his wise guidance and steady confidence ever since (it can't always be easy for him, given that he is also prone to writing books of his own). Also, my sincere gratitude to the excellent team at Atlantic Books, and in particular its factual editor, Mike Harpley, whose sharp eye and intellectual acumen were vital in helping shape this book.

I must also thank my clients and the many other people who have written to me with their stories over the years, often sharing the harms they have experienced at the hands of interventions that purport to help. I learn with each encounter. My gratitude also to my students (undergraduate and doctoral) for always keeping me on my toes and ensuring that things remain intellectually vibrant.

Lastly, I have to thank my wife, Alex. It cannot be easy living with someone who decides once in a while to write a book. Alex, you have helped in so many vital ways, often doing so at times when your hands have already been too full. Your confidence and support during the choppy times was more crucial than you know. Finally, this book is dedicated to my two young children, Oliver and Rose, who, like all children across our pandemic-ridden land, have had to bear challenges that will leave their mark. They have done so with humour, imagination and grace and have been, when all is said and done, the most important solace and loving distraction during difficult times, especially since they have absolutely no interest in the pages of this book, which is, of course, absolutely as it should be.

NOTES AND REFERENCES

Introduction

1 For this illustration I must thank Prof. Richard Bentall, who has used it in presentation.

2 I will explore this argument in greater depth in Chapter Eight.

3 In the US alone, around $20 billion has been spent on psychiatric and neurobiological research, but has failed to move the needle on reducing suicide, reducing hospitalisations, and improving recovery for the tens of millions of people who have mental illness. See: Henriques, G. (2017), 'Twenty Billion Fails to "Move the Needle" on Mental Illness', https://www. psychologytoday.com/gb/blog/ theory-knowledge/201705/twenty-billion-fails-move-the-needle-mental-illness (accessed Jan. 2020).

4 Around 17 per cent of our adult population was prescribed an antidepressant in 2019 alone. See: Public Health England (2019), *Prescribed Medicines Review Report*, https://www.gov.uk/government/ publications/prescribed-medicines-review-report (accessed Jan. 2020).

5 For the US figures alone, see: NIMH (2020), 'Mental Illness 2020', https://www.nimh.nih. gov/health/statistics/mental-illness.shtml#:~:text=Mental per cent20illnesses per cent20are per

cent20common per cent20in,mild per cent20to per cent20moderate per cent20to per cent20severe (accessed Aug. 2020).

6 In 2013 alone, more than 100 critical editorials, op-eds and articles were published in the broadsheet media, alongside an array of articles in prestigious academic journals such as *Nature*, the *British Journal of Psychiatry* and *The Lancet*. These charged DSM-5 with over-medicalising human suffering by lowering diagnostic thresholds and expanding the number of 'mental disorders'. Such criticisms gained professional support in late 2012, when more than 50 mental health organisations internationally (including the British Psychological Society, the American Psychoanalytic Association, the Danish Psychological Society and the American Counseling Association) signed an online petition calling for a halt to the manual's publication. See: Davies, J. (2019), 'Deceived: how Big Pharma persuades us to swallow its drugs', in Watson, Jo (ed.), *Drop the Disorder*, London: PCCS Books.

7 Frances, A. (2013), *Saving Normal*, New York: William Morrow.

8 For a more recent analysis, please see: Kendler, K. S., and Solomon, M. (2016), 'Expert consensus v. evidence-based approaches in the revision of the DSM', *Psychological Medicine* 46 (11):2255–2261

9 Quoted in Davies, J. (2013), *Cracked: why psychiatry is doing more harm than good*, London: Icon Books.

10 Davies, J. (2016), 'How voting and consensus created the *Diagnostic and Statistical Manual of Mental Disorders* (DSM-III)', *Anthropology and Medicine* 24 (1):32–46. Decker, Hannah, S., (2018), *The Making of DSM-III: A Diagnostic Manual's Conquest of American Psychiatry*, Oxford: Oxford University Press.

11 Quotes from Davies, J. (2013), *Cracked: why psychiatry is doing more harm than good*, London: Icon Books.

12 A full 21 out of the 29 members of the most recent edition, DSM-5, reported previous ties to the industry. See ibid.

13 Cosgrove, Lisa, and Shaughnessy, Allen F., 'Mental Health as a Basic Human Right and the Interference of Commercialized Science', *Health and Human Rights Journal* (2020), https://www.hhrjournal.org/2020/06/mental-health-as-a-basic-human-right-and-the-interference-of-commercialized-science/ (accessed Sept. 2020).

14 I refer to it as a claim, as what the professor suggests still remains to be definitively established. However, six months after this exchange, while undertaking research in the DSM archives at the American Psychiatric Association in Arlington, Virginia, I decided to try to verify her statement. Even though the archivist did confirm that most sales of the DSM were indeed bulk purchases, I was also told that the publisher, the APA, was unable to disclose or gather 'customer-end' information.

15 Carlat, D. (2010), *Unhinged: the trouble with psychiatry*, London: Free Press. Gøtzsche, P. (2013), *Deadly Medicines and Organised Crime: how Big Pharma has corrupted healthcare*, London: Radcliffe Publishing. Whitaker, R., and Cosgrove, L. (2015), *Psychiatry Under the Influence: institutional corruption, social injury, and prescriptions for reform*, New York: Palgrave Macmillan.

16 Campbell, E. G., et al. (2007), 'Institutional academic-industry relationships', *Journal of the American Medical Association* 298 (15):1779–80.

17 Whitaker, R. (2017), 'Psychiatry Under the Influence', in Davies, J. (ed), *The Sedated Society: the causes and harms of our psychiatric drug epidemic*, London: Palgrave Macmillan.

18 Angell, M. (2011), 'The illusions of psychiatry', *New York Review of Books* 58 (12):82–4.

19 Spielmans, G. I., and Parry, P. I. (2010), 'From evidence-based medicine to marketing-based medicine: evidence from internal industry documents', *Bioethical Inquiry* 7: 13–29. Turner, E. H., et al. (2008), 'Selective publication of antidepressant trials and its influence on apparent efficacy', *New England Journal of Medicine* 17:252–60. Kondro, W., and Sibbald, B. (2004), 'Drug company experts advised to withhold data about SSRI

use in children', *Canadian Medical Association Journal* 170:783.

20 Spielmans, G. I., and Parry, P. I. (2010), 'From evidence-based medicine to marketing-based medicine: evidence from internal industry documents', *Bioethical Inquiry* 7: 13–29. Turner, E. H., et al. (2008), 'Selective publication of antidepressant trials and its influence on apparent efficacy', *New England Journal of Medicine* 17:252–60.

21 For just a few of these studies, see: Lexchin, J., et al. (2003), 'Pharmaceutical industry sponsorship and research outcome and quality: systematic review', *BMJ* 326:1167–70. Orlowski, J. P., and Wateska, L. (1992), 'The effects of pharmaceutical firm enticements on physician prescribing patterns', *Chest* 102:270–3. Adair, R. F., and Holmgren, L. R. (2005), 'Do drug samples influence resident prescribing behavior? A randomized trial', *American Journal of Medicine* 118 (8):881–4. Lo, B., and Field, M. J. (2009), *Conflict of Interest in Medical Research, Education, and Practice*, Institute of Medicine (US) Committee on Conflict of Interest in Medical Research, Education, and Practice, Washington DC: National Academies Press. Spurling, G. K., et al. (2010), 'Information from pharmaceutical companies and the quality, quantity, and cost of physicians' prescribing: a systematic review', *PLoS Medicine* 7 (10):e1000352.

22 Of course, where people feel that psychiatric drugs have genuinely helped them, it is right to respect their experiences. To repeat the words of influential psychiatrist Professor Joanna Moncrieff, the use of some psychiatric drugs in some situations is warranted, especially if for the most severely distressed and if used for the shortest possible duration. But of course that is not where we are today, far from it, as a quarter of the UK adult population was prescribed a psychiatric drug last year, and the average duration of use has doubled in 10 years (despite long-term use being associated with a whole host of harms).

23 NHS Mental Health Taskforce Strategy (2020), 'The Five Year Forward View for Mental Health', https://www.england.nhs.uk/wp-content/uploads/2016/02/Mental-Health-Taskforce-FYFV-final.pdf (accessed Sept. 2020).

24 This increase may be partly explained by a rise in the number of people consulting mental health services overall. Nonetheless, rising suicides is not an outcome you'd want to see in a service whose raison d'être is to improve mental health. See: Nuffield Trust (2020), 'Suicide in mental health service users', https://www.nuffieldtrust.org.uk/resource/suicide-in-mental-health-service-users (accessed Sept. 2020).

25 Turner, J., et al. (2015), 'The History of Mental Health Services in Modern England: Practitioner Memories and the Direction of Future Research', *Medical History* 59 (4):599–624, doi:10.1017/mdh.2015.48.

26 Syme, Kristen L., and Hagen, Edward H. (2019), 'Mental

health is biological health: Why tackling "diseases of the mind" is an imperative for biological anthropology in the 21st century', https://doi.org/10.1002/ajpa.23965.

27 The mean SMR (standard mortality ratio) between persons with serious mental illness and the general population was 2.2 in the pre-1970s studies and 3.0 in the post-1970s studies, representing an increase of 37 per cent. See: Lee, Ellen E. et al. (2018), 'A Widening Longevity Gap between People with Schizophrenia and General Population: A Literature Review and Call for Action', *Schizophrenia Research* 196:9–13. This trend can be seen in other highly medicalised mental health settings. Australia is a telling example, where the gap in life expectancy has widened since the early 1980s – from 13.5 to 15.9 years for males and from 10.4 to 12.0 years for females between 1985 and 2005. See: Lawrence, D., et al. (2013), 'The gap in life expectancy from preventable physical illness in psychiatric patients in Western Australia: retrospective analysis of population based registers', *BMJ* 346, https://doi.org/10.1136/bmj.f2539. In the UK, we see the same. For people discharged with schizophrenia, the ratio was 1.6 in 1999 and 2.2 in 2006 (P<0.001 for trend). For bipolar disorder, the ratios were 1.3 in 1999 and 1.9 in 2006 (P=0.06 for trend). See: Hoang, U., et al. (2011), 'Mortality after hospital discharge for people with schizophrenia or bipolar disorder: retrospective study of linked English hospital episode statistics, 1999-2006',

BMJ 343:d5422, doi: 10.1136/bmj. d5422. In the UK, key drivers in decline in overall mortality in 2014–15 were respiratory diseases, circulatory diseases, Alzheimer's disease, nervous system diseases and mental disorders. See the *BMJ*: https://www.bmj.com/content/362/bmj.k2562.

28 De Mooij, Liselotte D., et al., 'Dying Too Soon: Excess Mortality in Severe Mental Illness', *Frontiers in Psychiatry*, 6 December 2019, https://doi.org/10.3389/fpsyt.2019.00855. NHS Digital (2020), 'Mental Health Bulletin: Annual report from MHMDS returns – England, 2011–12, further analysis and organisation-level data', https://digital.nhs.uk/data-and-information/publications/statistical/mental-health-bulletin/mental-health-bulletin-annual-report-from-mhmds-returns-england-2011-12-further-analysis-and-organisation-level-data (accessed Sept. 2020).

29 Please consult this interesting article, from which I am partly paraphrasing: Khullar, Dhruv, 'The Largest Health Disparity We Don't Talk About: Americans with serious mental illnesses die 15 to 30 years earlier than those without', *New York Times*, 30 May 2018, https://www.nytimes.com/2018/05/30/upshot/mental-illness-health-disparity-longevity.html (accessed Sept. 2020).

30 Kendrick, T. (2015), 'Long-term antidepressant treatment: Time for a review?', *Prescriber* 26 (19):7–8.

31 Gafoor, R., et al. (2018), 'Antidepressant utilisation and incidence of weight gain during 10

years' follow-up: Population based cohort study', *BMJ* 361:k195.

32 Viguera, A. C. (1998), 'Discontinuing antidepressant treatment in major depression', *Harvard Review of Psychiatry* 5:293–305.

33 Richardson, K., et al. (2018), 'Anticholinergic drugs and risk of dementia: Case-control study', *BMJ* 361:k1315.

34 Fava, G. A., et al. (2015), 'Withdrawal symptoms after selective serotonin reuptake inhibitor discontinuation: a systematic review', *Psychotherapy and Psychosomatics* 84:72–81. Blier, P., and Tremblay, P. (2006), 'Physiologic mechanisms underlying the antidepressant discontinuation syndrome', *J. Clin. Psychiatry* 67, Suppl. 4:8–13.

35 Higgins, Agnes, et al. (2010), 'Antidepressant-associated sexual dysfunction: impact, effects, and treatment', *Drug, Healthcare, and Patient Safety* 2:141–50.

36 Maslej, M. M., et al. (2017), 'The mortality and myocardial effects of antidepressants are moderated by preexisting cardiovascular disease: A meta-analysis', *Psychotherapy and Psychosomatics* 86:268–82.

37 Angermeyer, M., Matschinger, H. (2005), 'Causal beliefs and attitudes to people with schizophrenia: trend analysis based on data from two population surveys in Germany', *British Journal of Psychiatry* 186:331–4.

38 Kempa, Joshua J., et al. (2020), 'Effects of a chemical imbalance causal explanation on individuals' perceptions of their depressive symptoms', *Behaviour Research and Therapy* 56:47–52.

39 Schroder, Hans S. (2020), 'Stressors and chemical imbalances: Beliefs about the causes of depression in an acute psychiatric treatment sample', *Journal of Affective Disorders* 276:537–45.

40 Kvaalea, Erlend P., et al. (2013), 'The "side effects" of medicalization: A meta-analytic review of how biogenetic explanations affect stigma', *Clinical Psychology Review* 33 (6):782–94.

41 Larkings, J. S., and Brown, P. M. (2018), 'Do biogenetic causal beliefs reduce mental illness stigma in people with mental illness and in mental health professionals? A systematic review', *International Journal of Mental Health Nursing* 27:928–41.

42 Berardelli, I., et al. (2019), 'The Role of Demoralization and Hopelessness in Suicide Risk in Schizophrenia: A Review of the Literature', *Medicina* (Kaunas, Lithuania) 55(5):200, https://doi.org/10.3390/medicina55050200.

43 See: Timimi, S. (2011), 'Campaign to Abolish Psychiatric Diagnostic Systems such as ICD and DSM', http://www.criticalpsychiatry.co.uk/index.php?option=com_content&view=article&id=233:campaign-to-abolish-psychiatric-diagnostic-systems-such-as-icd-and-dsm-timimi-s&catid=34:members-publications&Itemid=56.

44 A good summary of this research is discussed in E. Watters (2010), 'The Americanization of Mental Illness', *New York Times*, https://www.nytimes.com/2010/01/

10/magazine/10psyche-t.html (accessed Dec. 2020).

45 Corrigan, P. W., and Watson, A. C. (2002), 'Understanding the impact of stigma on people with mental illness', *World Psychiatry* 1(1): 16–20.

46 Kvaalea, Erlend P., et al. (2013), 'Biogenetic explanations and stigma: A meta-analytic review of associations among laypeople', *Social Science & Medicine* 96:95–103, https://doi.org/10.1016/j.socscimed.2013.07.017. Mehta, S. and Farina, A. (1997), 'Is being "sick" really better? Effect of the disease view of mental disorder on stigma', *Journal of Social and Clinical Psychology* 16:405–19, 10.1521/jscp.1997.16.4.405.

47 Kvaalea, Erlend P., et al. (2013), 'The "side effects" of medicalization:

A meta-analytic review of how biogenetic explanations affect stigma', *Clinical Psychology Review* 33 (6):782–94.

48 Paradoxically then, the many anti-stigma campaigns stating that mental health problems are no different from physical health problems (framing emotional distress in medical terms of 'disease' and 'disorder') may have simply reaffirmed public fear that emotional suffering may point to long-term biological 'illness' over which sufferers have little control – messages that research shows *increases* stigma. The irony is that these campaigns, by applying this logic, will have unknowingly helped bring about the opposite of what they intended.

Chapter One: An Economic Prelude

1 Thatcher, M. (1981), Interview for *Sunday Times*, Margaret Thatcher Foundation, https://www.margaretthatcher.org/document/104475 (accessed 10 Nov. 2018).

2 Marglin, Stephen A., and Schor, Juliet B. (2011), *The Golden Age of Capitalism: Reinterpreting the Postwar Experience*, Oxford: Oxford University Press.

3 Kotz, D. M. (2017), *The Rise and Fall of Neoliberal Capitalism*, Boston: Harvard University Press.

4 Thatcher, M. (1985), Speech to Joint Houses of Congress, Margaret Thatcher Foundation, https://www.margaretthatcher.org/document/105968 (accessed Dec. 2018).

5 In this view he departed strongly from Hegel. While Hegel saw suffering as an essential part of the historical process, which would lead to an ultimate state of godly transcendence, for the more utilitarian Marx, it would lead to social revolution serving the full human unfurling. See: Green, R.M., and Palpant, N. J. (eds.) (2014), *Suffering and Bioethics*, Oxford: Oxford University Press, p.76.

6 We see this thinking permeating those on the economic right (in the works of Friedrich Hayek and Milton Friedman), as well as the

left (Jürgen Habermas, Theodor Adorno and Erich Fromm).

7 For a particularly useful introduction to key works in this area, see: Keith, H., and Hann, C. (2011), *Economic Anthropology*, London: Polity Press.

8 However, for many analysts, including myself, it is clear that such calculated intent was very much at the heart of the pharmaceutical industry's promotion of psychiatric drugs.

Chapter Two: The New Culture of Proliferating Debt and Drugs

1 PWC (2020), 'COVID-19: UK Economic Update', https://www.pwc.co.uk/premium/covid-19/uk-economic-update-covid-19.pdf (accessed Aug. 2020).

2 Bank of England (2020), 'Money and Credit – April 2020', https://www.bankofengland.co.uk/statistics/money-and-credit/2020/april-2020 (accessed Aug. 2020).

3 TUC (2020), 'Record household debt levels show why workers need a new deal', https://www.tuc.org.uk/blogs/record-household-debt-levels-show-why-workers-need-new-deal (accessed Dec. 2020).

4 Almenberg, Johan, et al. (2018), 'Attitudes towards debt and debt behaviour', https://voxeu.org/article/our-changing-attitudes-towards-household-debt (accessed Dec. 2020).

5 Brewer, J. (2017), 'Applicants to UK arts and design university courses decline by over 14,000 this year. It's Nice That', https://www.itsnicethat.com/news/ucas-art-and-design-university-applications-decline-210717 (accessed June 2018).

6 Harrow M. (2007), 'Factors involved in outcome and recovery in schizophrenia patients not on antipsychotic medication', *Journal*

of Nervous and Mental Disease 195:406–14.

7 For discussion on this point see Whitaker's defence: Whitaker, R. (2016), 'The Evidence-Based Mind of Psychiatry on Display', https://www.madinamerica.com/2016/05/the-evidence-based-mind-of-psychiatry-on-display/ (accessed Oct. 2020).

8 In the UK, for example, mental health disability has doubled since the late 1990s.

9 Data presented by R. Whitaker to the All-Party Parliamentary Group for Prescribed Drug Dependence (Houses of Parliament, Sept. 2016).

10 Harding, C. M., et al. (1987), 'The Vermont Longitudinal Study of Persons With Severe Mental Illness, I: Methodology, Study Sample, and Overall Status 32 Years Later', *American Journal of Psychiatry* 144:6.

11 Whitaker, R. (2012), 'E. Fuller Torrey's Review of Anatomy of an Epidemic: What Does It Reveal About the Rationale for Forced Treatment?', https://www.madinamerica.com/2012/05/e-fuller-torreys-review-of-anatomy-of-an-epidemic-what-does-it-reveal-about-the-rationale-for-forced-treatment/ (accessed Jan. 2020).

12 Another study, undertaken by the California Department of Mental Hygiene in 1961, looked at the effect of the antipsychotic Thorazine after it was introduced to hospitals in the mid 1950s. Of the 1,413 patients who were hospitalised for a first episode of schizophrenia, they found that it was the medicated patients who ended up staying in hospital for longer: of those who were drug-free, a full 88 per cent were discharged within 18 months of their admission, compared to only 74 per cent of those on Thorazine.

13 Van Scheyen, J. D. (1973), 'Recurrent vital depressions', *Psychiatria, Neurologia, Neurochirurgia* 76:93–112.

14 D. Goldberg (1998), 'The effects of detection and treatment of major depression in primary care', *British Journal of General Practice* 48:1840–44.

15 Hengartner, M. P., et al. (2019), 'Antidepressant Use During Acute Inpatient Care Is Associated With an Increased Risk of Psychiatric Rehospitalisation Over a 12-Month Follow-Up After Discharge', *Frontiers in Psychiatry* 10:79, doi: 10.3389/fpsyt.2019.00079.

16 Hyman, S. (1996), 'Initiation and adaptation: A paradigm for understanding psychotropic drug action', *American Journal of Psychiatry* 153:151–61.

17 Andrews, P. W., et al. (2011), 'Blue again: perturbational effects of antidepressants suggest monoaminergic homeostasis in major depression', *Frontiers in Psychology* 2:159.

18 Bockting, C. (2008), 'Continuation and maintenance use of antidepressants in recurrent depression', *Psychotherapy and Psychosomatics* 77:17–26.

19 Patten, S. (2004), 'The Impact of antidepressant treatment on population health', *Population Health Metrics* 2:9.

20 Jablensky, A., et al. (1992), 'Schizophrenia: manifestations, incidence and course in different cultures. A World Health Organization ten-country study', *Psychological Medicine Monograph Supplement 20*, Cambridge: Cambridge University Press.

21 Coryell, W. (1995), 'Characteristics and significance of untreated major depressive disorder', *American Journal of Psychiatry* 152:1124–29.

22 Hegarty, J. D., et al. (1994), 'One hundred years of schizophrenia: a meta-analysis of the outcome literature', *American Journal of Psychiatry* 151(10):1409–16.

23 With respect to one review, Whitaker said: 'The day the book was published, there was a review – by a Harvard physician – that compared me to an AIDs denier, claiming that nobody could seriously dispute the fact that psychiatric drugs had improved the lives of so many.'

24 Wunderink, L., et al. (2013), 'Recovery in Remitted First-Episode Psychosis at 7 Years of Follow-up of an Early Dose Reduction/Discontinuation or Maintenance Treatment Strategy: Long-term Follow-up of a 2-Year Randomized Clinical Trial', *Journal*

of the American Medical Association Psychiatry.

25 Insel, T. (2013), 'Post by former NIMH director Thomas Insel: Antipsychotics: Taking the Long View', https://www.nimh.nih.gov/about/directors/thomas-insel/blog/2013/antipsychotics-taking-the-long-view.shtml (accessed Jan. 2020).

26 Vittengl, J. R. (2017), 'Poorer long-term outcomes among persons with major depressive disorder treated with medication', *Psychotherapy and Psychosomatics* 86:302–4.

27 Ho, B. C. et al. (2011), 'Long-term antipsychotic treatment and brain volumes: a longitudinal study of first-episode schizophrenia', *Archives of General Psychiatry* 68(2):128–37.

28 Dreifus, C. (2008), 'Using Imaging to Look at Changes in the Brain', http://www.nytimes.com/2008/09/16/health/research/16conv.html?scp=1&sq=Nancy per cent20Andreasen&st=cse (accessed Jan. 2020).

29 Voineskos, A. N., et al. (2020), 'Effects of antipsychotic medication on brain structure in patients with major depressive disorder and psychotic features: Neuroimaging findings in the context of a randomized placebo-controlled clinical trial', *Journal of the American Medical Association Psychiatry*, doi: 10.1001/jamapsychiatry.2020.0036.

30 Warren, J. B. (2020), 'The trouble with antidepressants: why the evidence overplays benefits and underplays risks – an essay by John B. Warren', *BMJ* 370:m3200.

31 Jakobsen, J. C., et al. (2020), 'Should antidepressants be used for major depressive disorder?' *BMJ Evidence-Based Medicine* 25:130.

32 Cipriani, A., et al. (2018), 'Comparative efficacy and acceptability of 21 antidepressant drugs for the acute treatment of adults with major depressive disorder: a systematic review and network meta-analysis', *The Lancet*.

33 Kirsch, I. (2009), *The Emperor's New Drugs: exploding the antidepressant myth*, London: Bodley Head, p.54.

34 Timimi, S., et al. (2018), 'Network meta-analysis of antidepressants', *The Lancet*, doi.org/10.1016/S0140-6736(18)31784-7.

35 Putting it in technical terms, the difference was a mere 1.6 on the HAM-D scale – which measures the severity of depression – far below the 3.0 difference needed to be classed as 'clinically significant'. But even these very minor differences between placebos and antidepressants, we argued, could potentially be explained away, since most people experience side effects when taking an antidepressant (unlike when taking a placebo). This helps them work out during a clinical trial that they are on the antidepressant, which boosts their expectation of recovery and in turn the placebo effect. In short, side effects boost placebo effects, accounting for why an antidepressant may appear slightly more effective than a placebo when the two are compared in the treatment of severe depression.

36 Pigott, H. E., et al. (2010), 'Efficacy and effectiveness of antidepressants: current status

of research', *Psychotherapy and Psychosomatics* 79:267–79.

37 Longden, E., et al. (2018), 'Assessing the Impact and Effectiveness of Hearing Voices Network Self-Help Groups', *Community Mental Health Journal* 54:184–188.

38 Calton, Tim, et al. (2008), 'A Systematic Review of the Soteria Paradigm for the Treatment of People Diagnosed With Schizophrenia', *Schizophrenia Bulletin* 34 (1):181–92.

39 Open Dialogue approaches are now being piloted in a few NHS sites in the UK, while the Hearing Voices network in particular is growing in influence and impact.

40 Kendrick, T. (2015), 'Long-term antidepressant treatment: Time for a review?', *Prescriber* 26 (19):7–8.

41 Eveleigh, R., et al. (2018), 'Withdrawal of unnecessary antidepressant medication: a randomised controlled trial in primary care', *BJGP Open* 1 (4):bjgpopen17X101265, doi.org/10.3399/bjgpopen17X101265.

42 In 2018, Prof. John Read and I challenged this myth in a systematic review published in the journal *Addictive Behaviours*, which we later summarised in the *British Medical Journal*. When we published our research, it gained wide media coverage, creating substantial public and professional controversy, with rebuttals and counter-rebuttals going back and forth. Eventually, other research supportive of our position was published in *The Lancet*, and from that a professional consensus began to build. This ultimately led to the Royal College of Psychiatrists and NICE changing their national guidance, in line with the conclusions of our research.

43 McHugh, R. K., et al. (2013), 'Patient preference for psychological vs pharmacologic treatment of psychiatric disorders: a meta-analytic review', *Journal of Clinical Psychiatry* 74 (6):595–602, PMID: 23842011.

44 Mind (2013), 'We still need to talk: a report on access to talking therapies', https://www.mind.org.uk/media/494424/we-still-need-to-talk_report.pdf (accessed Mar. 2018).

Chapter Three: The New Dissatisfactions of Modern Work

1 Grint, K. (2005), *The Sociology of Work* (3rd edn), London: Polity Press.

2 During the 1990s, the average British household was working 7 hours longer each week (ibid., p.330). Also, hours worked in the UK and USA have risen since the 2000s. See: *The Economist* (2019), 'Why do some countries work longer hours than others?', https://www.economist.com/graphic-detail/2018/12/28/why-do-some-countries-work-longer-hours-than-others.

3 The average job tenure in the 1970s was 10 years. See: Green F., et al. (2000), 'Job insecurity

and the difficulty of regaining employment: an empirical study of unemployment expectations', *Oxford Bulletin of Economics and Statistics* 62:855–83.

4 Around 20 per cent of us now move jobs in any given year. See: Andersen, T., *Job Mobility in the European Union: Optimising its Social and Economic Benefits*, European Commission. Danish Technological Institute, final report, Copenhagen, Denmark. 2008. Macaulay, C. (2003), *Job Mobility and Job Tenure in the UK*, London: Office for National Statistics, http://www.statistics. gov.uk/articles/labour-market-trends/jobmobility-nov03.pdf (accessed June 2014).

5 Full Fact (2019), 'Has the gig economy doubled in size in three years?' https://fullfact. org/economy/has-gig-economy-doubled/ (accessed July 2020).

6 See: National Centre for Social Research (2007), *Travel to Work—Personal Travel Factsheet*, 'Commuting times increase substantially, to 54 minutes per day return (or 78 min if you work in London)', http://webarchive. nationalarchives.gov.uk/+/http:/ www.dft.gov.uk/pgr/statistics/ datatablespublications/personal/ factsheets/traveltowork.pdf (accessed Aug. 2015). Today more than 3 million Brits commute over 2 hours per day. See: TUC (2015), 'Number of Commuters Spending more than two Hours Travelling to and from Work up by 72 per cent in Last Decade', https://www.tuc. org.uk/workplace- issues/work-life-balance/number-commuters-

spending-more-two-hours-travel ling-and-work-72 (accessed Nov. 2015).

7 Jacobs, K., (2018), 'Is psychometric testing still fit for purpose?', *People Management*, https://www. peoplemanagement.co.uk/long-reads/articles/psychometric-testing-fit-purpose (accessed July 2020).

8 Kantrowitz, T. M. (2014), 'Global Assessment Trends', https:// www.cebglobal.com/content/ dam/cebglobal/us/EN/regions/ uk/tm/pdfs/Report/gatr-2014. pdf (accessed Jan. 2019). Also see: Society for Industrial and Organizational Psychology (2020), 'Personality Test', https://www. siop.org/workplace/employment per cent20testing/usingoftests.aspx (accessed July 2020).

9 Burns, Gary N., et al. (2017), 'Putting applicant faking effects on personality tests into context', *Journal of Managerial Psychology* 32 (6):460–8.

10 Frayne, D. (2015), *The Refusal of Work: rethinking post-work theory and practice*, Chicago: University of Chicago Press.

11 For instance, a CIPD report conducted in 2013 showed that, on average, the percentage of those reporting job satisfaction in the UK was 40 per cent, with the lowest figures found in the public sector (25 per cent) and in large business (30 per cent). See: Chartered Institute of Personnel and Development (2013), 'Employee Outlook', http://www.cipd.co.uk/binaries/ employee-outlook_2013-autumn. pdf (accessed Oct. 2017).

12 Chartered Institute of Personnel and Development (2018), 'UK Working Lives: in search of job quality', https://www.cipd.co.uk/Images/uk-working-lives-summary_tcm18-40233.pdf (accessed Dec. 2018).

13 Dahlgreen, W. (2013), '37 per cent of British workers Think Their Jobs are Meaningless', YouGov, https://yougov.co.uk/news/2015/08/12/british-jobs-meaningless/ (accessed Nov. 2018).

14 While changes in rates of satisfaction and engagement fluctuate from year from year, historically job satisfaction and engagement has been trending downwards since the 1970s. In the US, those who were very satisfied with their jobs fell by 8 per cent between the mid 1970s and the mid 1990s – see: Blanchflower, D. G., and Oswald, A. J. (1999), 'Well-Being, Insecurity and the Decline of American Job Satisfaction', http://www.dartmouth.edu/ ˜ blnchflr/papers/Job Sat.pdf (accessed June 2014) – with a similar trend in the UK. See: Kular, S., et al. (2008), 'Employee engagement: A literature review', Working Paper Series No. 19, Kingston Business School, http://eprints.kingston.ac.uk/4192/1/19wempen.pdf, (accessed Jan. 2014). Other studies have put the decline in job satisfaction higher; the Conference Board's survey showed it has decreased from 61.1 per cent in the mid 1980s (1987) to 42.6 per cent by 2010, thus dropping a full 19 per cent over 25 years. See: Ray, R. L. (2013), 'Job Satisfaction: 2013 Edition', Conference Board, https://hcexchange.conferenceboard.org/publications/publicationdetail.cfm?publicatio nid = 2522 (accessed Dec. 2017).

15 Office of National Statistics *UK Productivity Introduction*, https://www.ons.gov.uk/employmentandlabourmarket/peopleinwork/labourproductivity/articles/ukproductivityintroduction/octobertodecember 2017 (accessed Dec 2017).

16 Whitmore, M., et al. (2018), 'Promising Practices for Health and Wellbeing at Work', Rand Europe, https://www.rand.org/pubs/research_reports/RR2409.html (accessed Oct. 2017).

17 Some of the data and analysis in this chapter on MHFA, ACAS and CMHA is derived from my article: Davies, J., (2016), 'Back to balance: labour therapeutics and the depoliticisation of workplace distress', *Palgrave Communications* 2 (1):16027.

18 Mental Health First Aid England (MHFAE), 2015, http://mhfaengland.org/ (accessed June 2018).

19 Ibid.

20 Whitmore, M., et al. (2018), 'Promising Practices for Health and Wellbeing at Work', Rand Europe, https://www.rand.org/pubs/research_reports/RR2409.html (accessed Oct. 2017).

21 CMHA (2011), 'Workplace mental health PSA', https://www.youtube.com/watch?v=x-hacuOiUYw (accessed Feb. 2020).

22 See: CMHA (2017), 'Work Life Balance – make it your business', https://cmha.ca/resources/work-

life-balance-make-it-your-business (accessed June 2018).

23 See: ACAS (2012), 'Promoting Positive Mental Health at Work', http://www.acas.org.uk/media/pdf/j/i/Promoting_positive_mental_health_at_work_JAN_2012.pdf (accessed Jan. 2018).

24 American Psychiatric Association (2013), *Diagnostic and Statistical Manual of Mental Disorders*, 5th edn, Washington DC: APA.

25 ACAS (2018), 'Working for Everyone', http://www.acas.org.uk/

index.aspx?articleid=1900 (accessed Nov. 2018).

26 Wightwick, A. (2018), '500 Lecturers at Cardiff University Sign Open Letter Saying Their Workload is Unmanageable', WalesOnline, https://www.walesonline.co.uk/news/education/500-lecturers-cardiff-university-sign-14946705 (accessed Jan. 2019).

27 The paragraph is paraphrased from Davies, J. (2016), 'Back to Balance: labour therapeutics and the depoliticisation of workplace distress', *Palgrave Commununications* 2:27.

Chapter Four: The New Back-to-Work Psychological Therapies

1 Layard, Richard (2005), 'Mental health: Britain's biggest social problem?', Paper presented at the No.10 Strategy Unit Seminar on Mental Health, 20 January 2005.

2 There is a debate to be had as to whether it is fair to omit from these stats the people who never turned up to therapy at all. On the one hand, you cannot blame a service for the poor recovery of those it never treated; on the other hand, many of those, between the time of referral and treatment, may have improved, hence their reason for not attending.

3 Griffiths, Steve, and Steen, Scott (2013), 'Improving Access to Psychological Therapies (IAPT) Programme: Setting Key Performance Indicators in a More Robust Context: A New Perspective', *Journal of Psychological Therapies in Primary Care* 2:133–41.

4 Whiteford, H., et al. (2012), 'Estimating remission from untreated major depression: a systematic review and meta-analysis', *Psychological Medicine* 43(8):1–17.

5 A very small minority of IAPT services do follow-up surveys after treatment. In 2018, only 1.5 per cent of all referrals finishing a course of treatment were contacted for a six-month follow-up. The results are not published. Academic research into rates of relapse after treatment suggest the story is far from encouraging.

6 British Psychological Society (2017), 'New Savoy survey shows increasing mental health problems in NHS psychotherapists', https://www.bps.org.uk/news-and-policy/new-savoy-survey-shows-increasing-mental-health-problems-nhs-

psychotherapists (accessed Jan. 2020).

7 Murray, Marylou Anna, et al. (2017), 'GPs have levels of mental health comparable to the rest of the nation. GPs' mental wellbeing and psychological resources: a cross-sectional survey', *British Journal of General Practice* 67 (661):e547–e554.

8 Plant, R. (2012), *The Neo-Liberal State*, Oxford: Oxford University Press, pp.11–14.

9 Frayne, D. (2019), *The Work Cure: Critical Essays on Work and Wellness*, Monmouth: PCCS Books.

10 What counts as success for IAPT is located in the costs being saved via its back-to-work emphasis, not in whether the lives of people using the service are demonstrably improved; improvements that can be easily statistically massaged anyway. For IAPT, it is everywhere implied that individual needs are secondary to the needs of the wider economy; even though, if we look carefully at the service's cost-benefit analysis, it is struggling to reach the cost-effectiveness it initially promised. Even by its own measures, it is failing.

Chapter Five: The New Causes of Unemployment

1 Zabar's barrister informed me that Zabar was found guilty on just one count, of conspiring with his manageress to make a false script for an employee of the agency. She instructed him to complete this script, and he was paid nothing for doing so. Furthermore, while he knew that the script was false, he did not expect it to be submitted as a claim. However, it was later signed off by a senior manager as genuine. That manager conducted no proper scrutiny of the claim, while Zabar's own manager knew the claim was ineligible. Zabar received absolutely no training for his work.

2 In technical terms, Zabar was sentenced to 12 months' imprisonment suspended for two years. This was reduced on appeal by the Court of Appeal to six

months' imprisonment suspended for two years.

3 Sutcliffe-Braithwaite, F. (2013), 'Margaret Thatcher, individualism and the welfare state. History and Policy', http://www. historyandpolicy.org/opinion-articles/articles/margaret-thatcher-individualism-and-the-welfare-state (accessed Jan. 2020).

4 These examples in this section are taken from an excellent editorial in the *Red Pepper* e-magazine: Clark, W. (2013), 'Workfare: a policy on the brink', https://www.redpepper. org.uk/-workfare-a-policy-on-the-brink/ (accessed Dec, 2019).

5 This case study was told to me by Dr Lynne Friedli, who gathered many such stories for her research on psycho-compulsion.

6 Webster, D. (2013), 'Briefings on the DWP's JSA/ESA (and UC from 22 Feb. 2017) sanctions statistics

release', Child Poverty Action Group.

7 Webster, D. (2017), 'Inquiry into Benefit Sanctions Policy Belying the Oakley Review. Evidence submitted to the House of Commons Work and Pensions Committee'.

8 Ryan, F. (2019), 'Welfare Reforms are Pushing the Mentally Ill over the Edge', *Guardian*, https://www.theguardian.com/commentisfree/2019/jan/24/welfare-reform-mentally-ill-injustice (accessed July 2019).

9 Bulman, May, and Polianskaya, Alina (2017), 'Attempted suicides by disability benefit claimants more than double after introduction of fit-to-work assessment', *Independent*, https://www.independent.co.uk/news/uk/home-news/disability-benefit-claimants-attempted-suicides-fit-to-work-assessment-i-daniel-blake-job-centre-dwp-a8119286.html (accessed Dec. 2019).

10 ESRC (2018), Welfare Conditionality Project, http://www.welfareconditionality.ac.uk/wp-content/uploads/2018/06/40475_Welfare-Conditionality_Report_complete-v3.pdf (accessed Feb. 2020).

11 While Friedli and Stearn actively sought claimant testimonies of all kinds, the only ones that appeared forthcoming were those expressing negative views; something they began to feel captured the mood more broadly.

12 In what follows below, I paraphrase and directly quote from Izzy Koksal's important exposé in *Open Democracy*: Koksal, I. (2012), '"Positive Thinking" for the unemployed – my adventure at A4e', https://www.opendemocracy.net/en/opendemocracyuk/positive-thinking-for-unemployed-my-adventures-at-a4e/ (accessed Nov. 2019).

13 Quoted in: Friedli, L., and Stearn, R. (2015), 'Positive affect as coercive strategy: conditionality, activation and the role of psychology in UK government workfare programmes', *Medical Humanities* 41:40–7.

14 Quoted in ibid.

15 Ibid.

16 Department for Work and Pensions (2003), *'Dirty Old Town'. Employment and Regeneration in Salford. A Joint Study by Disadvantaged Groups and the Labour Market Division to Understand the Differences in Worklessness Between Areas*, London: Department for Work and Pensions.

17 Shildrick, T., et al. (2012), 'Are "cultures of worklessness" passed down the generations?', https://www.jrf.org.uk/report/are-cultures-worklessness-passed-down-generations (accessed Nov. 2019).

18 Dewson, S., et al. (2007), *Evaluation of the Working Neighbourhoods Pilot: Final Report*, Leeds: Department for Work and Pensions.

Chapter Six: Education and the Rise of New Managerialism

1 Department of Education (2011), 'Support and Aspiration: a new approach to special educational needs and disability', http://www.educationengland.org.uk/documents/pdfs/2011-green-paper-sen.pdf (accessed June 2018).

2 For antidepressant figures see: Bachmann, Christian J. (2016), 'Trends and patterns of antidepressant use in children and adolescents from five western countries, 2005–2012', *European Neuropsychopharmacology* 26 (3):411–19. ADHD prescriptions increased from around 4,000 a year in 1996 to around 35,000 by 2006. See: Beau-Lejdstrom, R., et al. (2016), 'Latest trends in ADHD drug prescribing patterns in children in the UK: prevalence, incidence and persistence', *BMJ Open* 6:e010508. As the decade rolled on, the prescribing figures continued to increase: rising a full 200,000 between 2005 and 2009 alone (from 14.9 per cent of all children in 2005 to 17.8 per cent by 2009). This meant a rise from 1.1 to 1.3 million (i.e, 200,000) in 4 years. Calculations are approximate and were based on analysis of: Department of Health (2009), 'Schools, Pupils and their Characteristics', https://www.gov.uk/government/uploads/system/uploads/attachment_data/file/219260/sfr10-2012.pdf (accessed Jan. 2020).

3 Department of Education (2011), 'Support and Aspiration: a new approach to special educational needs and disability', http://www.educationengland.org.uk/documents/pdfs/2011-green-paper-sen.pdf (accessed Jan. 2018).

4 Snowdon, K. (2019), 'Proportion of pupils with SEND continues to rise, and 4 more findings', *Schools Week*, https://schoolsweek.co.uk/send-pupil-proportion-rise-dfe/ (accessed Dec 2019).

5 When the Education Policy Institute assessed in 2019 how widespread off-rolling was, they found that around 7.5 per cent of all pupils were removed from school rolls without any explanation. They were unable to determine what proportion of these were off-rolled, although the implication was that it might well be high. See Hutchinson, J., and Crenna-Jennings, W. (2019), 'Unexplained Pupil Exits from Schools: a growing problem?', https://epi.org.uk/wp-content/uploads/2019/04/EPI_Unexplained-pupil-exits_2019.pdf (accessed Dec. 2019).

6 Adam, R. (2019), 'One in four teachers say pupils are being forced out to boost school rankings', *Guardian*, https://www.theguardian.com/education/2019/may/10/one-in-four-teachers-in-england-say-they-have-witnessed-off-rolling (accessed Nov. 2019).

7 Adams, R. (2016), 'Schools Under Scrutiny in Crackdown on League Table Gaming', *Guardian*, https://www.theguardian.com/education/2016/apr/08/gcse-league-table-gaming-schools-crackdown (accessed July 2019).

8 E.g. in Strathern, Marilyn (2000), *Audit Cultures: Anthropological Studies in Accountability, Ethics and the Academy*, London: Routledge.

9 Belfield, Chris, et al. (2018), *Annual Report on Education Spending in England*, Institute for Fiscal Studies, https://www.ifs.org.uk/publications/13306 (accessed Oct. 2018).

10 Skinner, Barbara, et al. (2019), 'Managerialism and teacher professional identity: impact on well-being among teachers in the UK', *Educational Review*, doi:10.1080/00131911.2018.1556205.

11 As one representative teacher put it: 'There's a great deal of pressure on people to perform to targets and there seems to be a loss of spontaneity that teachers used to have ... So it's all conforming to the syllabus and the rigour of that syllabus rather than responding to the children and pupils that you've got in your care. It's talk about statistics rather than the children.' (Ibid.)

12 Ofsted (2019), 'Summary and recommendations: teacher well-being research report', https://www.gov.uk/government/publications/teacher-well-being-at-work-in-schools-and-further-education-providers/summary-and-recommendations-teacher-well-being-research-report (accessed Jan. 2020).

13 I first met Timimi in 2012, when interviewing him for my previous book, *Cracked*. At that time I learnt that his mild and peaceable demeanour masks an incisive intelligence, unsparing in its commitment to call out where and when our interventions cause harm. We stayed in contact and had collaborated on a few projects. Despite this, we rarely got an opportunity to meet offline, so it was refreshing to be talking and walking along the majestic Göta river with a psychiatrist I deeply admired.

14 Mental Health First Aid England (2018), 'A Whole Organisation Approach to Young People's Mental Health', https://mhfaengland.org/mhfa-centre/resources/for-schools/Youth-MHFA-Brochure-digital_wp.pdf (accessed Jan. 2019).

15 Pelosi, Anthony (2008), 'Is early intervention in the major psychiatric disorders justified?', *BMJ* 337:a710.

16 Timimi, Z., and Timimi, S. (2020), 'Psychiatrisation of school children: Secondary school teachers' beliefs and practices on mental health and illness', in Fixsen, A., and Harbusch, M. (eds), *Troubled Persons Industries – The Expansion of Psychiatric Categories beyond Psychiatry*, Routledge, accepted for publication.

17 Newland, Oliver (2019), 'Child mental health referrals up 26 per cent in five years, says report', *5 Live Investigates*, https://www.bbc.co.uk/news/health-45748562 (accessed July 2020).

18 Challen, Amy, et al. (2012), *UK Resilience Programme Evaluation: Final Report*, Department of Education, https://assets.publishing.service.gov.uk/government/uploads/system/uploads/attachment_data/file/

1824I9/DFE-RR097.pdf (accessed Sept. 2019).

19 The only resilience training scheme that has been robustly studied to date, the UK government's Resilience Programme (UKRP), showed poor results. While there was some minor short-term benefit on depression scores, absence rates and academic attainment, these impacts were short-lived. There was also no impact on behaviour scores, whether measured by pupil self-reports or by teacher reports, or on life satisfaction scores. (Ibid.)

20 See: Govorov, Elena, et al. (2020), 'How Schools Affect Student Well-Being: A Cross-Cultural Approach in 35 OECD Countries', *Frontiers in Psychology*, 25 March 2020. And: OECD (2009), 'Comparative child well-being across the OECD', https://www.oecd.org/social/family/43570328.pdf (accessed July 2020).

21 I am quoting and paraphrasing here from: Gregory, L. (2017), 'The price of prizes and the cost of competition in our schools – and the story of the willow weave dragonflies', https://weneedtotalkabout childrensmentalhealth.wordpress.com/2018/08/21/the-price-of-prizes-and-the-cost-of-competition-

in-our-schools-and-the-story-of-the-willow-weave-dragonflies/ (accessed June 2019).

22 OECD (2009), 'Comparative child well-being across the OECD, https://www.oecd.org/social/family/43570328.pdf (accessed July 2020).

23 NHS Digital (2017), 'Mental Health of Children and Young People in England', https://digital.nhs.uk/data-and-information/publications/statistical/mental-health-of-children-and-young-people-in-england (accessed Jan. 2020).

24 'I think tackling these things will be more possible in Wales than in England,' said Gregory, 'as there is a different government in Wales' – one led by deeper socially democratic principles. 'In Wales they are a little more critical of the pressures we are putting our kids under', which may explain why the Welsh government has abolished SATs tests for pupils aged 7 and 11. Welsh schools are not entirely free of testing, however. They have yearly national tests instead of SATs. A major difference is that schools are not graded and judged on the basis of these national tests results, unlike with SATs. They are just used to help teachers assess child development.

Chapter Seven: Deregulating the So-Called Chemical Cure

1 Gorman, Joseph B. (1971), *Kefauver: A Political Biography*, New York: Oxford University Press.

2 Avron, J. (2011), 'Learning about the Safety of Drugs – A Half-Century of

Evolution', *New England Journal of Medicine* 365:2151–3.

3 Cohn, J. (2003), 'Politics, Profits and Pharma', *Frontline*, http://www.pbs.org/wgbh/pages/frontline/

shows/prescription/politics/
(accessed Jan. 2020).

4 Margaret Thatcher Foundation,
Archive, 'Conservatism: Lawson
minute to MT ("Visit of Milton
Friedman") [brief for MT's
forthcoming meeting with
Friedman]' 22 Feb. 1980, https:/
/www.margaretthatcher.org/
document/117157 (accessed Jan.
2020).

5 *The Daily Hatch* (2013), 'Milton
Friedman's *Free to Choose*. "Who
protects the consumer?"', https:/
/thedailyhatch.org/2013/08/12/
milton-friedmans-free-to-choose-
who-protects-the-consumer-
transcript-and-video-60-minutes/
(accessed Jan. 2020).

6 Rather than the industry being just
a lobbying group, it now ostensibly
became part of the state: 'what
had been merely interest groups
crossed the political threshold and
became part of the extended state',
while the number of medicines
being approved for consumption
more than doubled compared
to 1970s levels. See: Gaffney, A.
(2014), 'How Many Drugs has FDA
Approved in its Entire History?
New Paper Explains', *Regulatory
Focus*, http://www.raps.org/
Regulatory-Focus/News/2014/
10/03/20488/How-Many-Drugs-
has-FDA-Approved-in-its-Entire-
History-New-Paper-Explains/
(accessed May 2018).

7 Corley, T. A. B. (2003), 'The British
pharmaceutical industry since 1851',
in Richmond, L., et al. (eds.), *The
Pharmaceutical Industry: a guide
to historical records*, Aldershot:
Ashgate, pp.14–32.

8 Davis, C., and Abraham, J.
(2013), *Unhealthy Pharmaceutical
Regulation: Innovation, Politics and
Promissory Science*, Basingstoke:
Palgrave Macmillan.

9 Patients4NHS (2019), 'Private
companies' involvement in the
NHS', http://www.patients4nhs.
org.uk/private-companies-
involvement-in-the-nhs/
(accessed Feb. 2020).

10 E.g. the Department of Health, the
Department of Trade and Industry
and the National Institute for
Clinical Excellence.

11 Health Select Committee (2004–5),
*The Influence of the Pharmaceutical
Industry: Fourth Report of Session*,
https://publications.parliament.uk/
pa/cm200405/cmselect/cmhealth/
42/42.pdf (accessed June 2018).

12 Turner, E. H. et al. (2008),
'Selective publication of
antidepressant trials and its
influence on apparent efficacy',
New England Journal of Medicine,
17:252–60.

13 Kirsch, I. (2009), *The Emperor's
New Drugs: exploding the
antidepressant myth*, London: Bodley
Head.

14 https://www.psychiatrist.com/
JCP/article/Pages/switching-the-
antidepressant-after-nonresponse.
aspx.

15 One counter-argument is that our
medical guidelines (under NICE)
would surely prevent this in the
UK. These guidelines are fairly
strict and indicate which drugs
have the best evidence base and
safety profile. While this may be
true, assuming that NICE itself is
privy to all the data and that doctors
abide by the guidelines, which we

know is debatable (consider, for example, that most people taking benzodiazepines in the UK have been prescribed them long term, despite NICE stating they should not be prescribed for longer than 4 weeks), any drugs can be prescribed off-label, thus circumventing what official guidelines dictate.

16 Goldacre, B. (2014), 'Drug Firms Hiding Negative Data are Unfit to Experiment on People', *Guardian*, http://www.guardian.co.uk/commentisfree/2010/aug/14/drug-companies-bury-negative-research (accessed Dec. 2011).

17 Timimi, S. (2018), 'Starting Young: children cultured into Becoming Psycho-Pharmaceutical Consumers', in Davies, J., *The Sedated Society: the causes and harms of our psychiatric drug epidemic*, London: Palgrave.

18 Davis, C., and Abraham, J. (2013), *Unhealthy Pharmaceutical Regulation: Innovation, Politics and Promissory Science*, Basingstoke: Palgrave Macmillan.

19 The MHRA would no doubt respond that its 'yellow card scheme' counters the problem of only requesting short-term trials. This scheme enables doctors to report any adverse drug effects to the MHRA. Critics point out that doctors have a patchy record in completing the cards, and that their receipt rarely translates into new drug policy. In short, yellow cards are an inadequate replacement for long-term clinical trials, even if, when used effectively, they garner important information.

20 For more information see: Department for Business, Innovation & Skills (2014), 'Review of the pharmaceutical manufacturing and production sector', https://www.gov.uk/government/uploads/system/uploads/attachment_data/file/316202/bis-14-855-review-pharmaceutical-manufacturing-and-production.pdf (accessed Jan. 2020). Also see: Abraham J., and Ballinger, R. (2011), 'The Neoliberal Regulatory State, Industry Interests, and the Ideological Penetration of Scientific Knowledge: Deconstructing the Redefinition of Carcinogens', in *Pharmaceuticals, Science, Technology, & Human Values*, https://doi.org/10.1177/0162243911424914. Finally, the duration of time taken to assess a drug for public use has dropped substantially since deregulation (from 154 days in the 1980s to just 44 days a decade later). While defenders say rapid drug approval is good for business (after all, a drug's patent starts running out once it is submitted for regulatory review), critics point out that assessments are now shorter not because processes have improved but because industry lobbying has been successful. Essentially, the shortening has come at the expense of more thorough regulation, and less thorough regulation has come at the expense of patients' health.

21 Lynn, M. (2020), 'It's time to scrap wealth-destroying taxes and empower Britain's army of entrepreneurs', *Telegraph*, https://www.telegraph.co.uk/business/2020/11/14/dominic-cummings-exit-should-open-bold-era-rishinomics/ (accessed Nov. 2020).

22 Gibson, L. (2005), 'UK government fails to tackle weaknesses in drug industry', *BMJ* 331(7516):534.

23 The best we have right now is an annual review, conducted by people appointed by the MHRA, many of whom, incidentally, have financial conflicts of interest with the pharmaceutical industry. Reading the reports (each of which comprise around two pages of 'all is good' statements) is frustrating to say the least.

24 As one previous member of the Health Select Committee commented to me in confidence: 'I simply did not have the same regard for him [Kevin] as I did for his successor.'

25 Gibson, L. (2005), 'UK government fails to tackle weaknesses in drug industry', *BMJ* 331(7516):534.

26 As Hinchliffe said, 'It would have been different under Jeremy Corbyn, had he been the leader, but not under Tony Blair. It was all light touch in regulation ... Governments need the pharmaceutical industry and so they can't upset it too much.'

27 Adams, B. (2019), 'UK looks to shake up trial, medicines regulations amid Brexit', *FierceBioTec*, https://www. fiercebiotech.com/biotech/

u-k-looks-to-shake-up-trial-medicines-regulation-rules-amid-brexit (accessed Dec. 2019). 'The *Guardian* view on Boris Johnson's NHS plan: trading patient data', *Guardian* editorial, 8 December 2019, https://www.theguardian. com/commentisfree/2019/dec/ 08/the-guardian-view-on-boris-johnsons-nhs-plan-trading-patient-data (accessed July 2020).

28 Williams, K. (2016), 'How the car industry trumped banking for sociopathic corporate behaviour', *Guardian*, https://www. theguardian.com/commentisfree/ 2016/apr/29/car-industry-banking-emissions-scandal-vw (accessed Jan. 2020).

29 Chazan, G. (2014), 'Energy Providers Face Prosecution Over Price Fixing', *Financial Times*, https://www.ft.com/ content/ab44af16-1cbb-11e4-88c3-00144feabdc0 (accessed Jan. 2020).

30 Millstone, E., and Lang, T. (2008), 'Risking regulatory capture at the UK's Food Standards Agency?', *The Lancet* 372(9633):95–97.

31 Davis, C., and Abraham, J. (2013), *Unhealthy Pharmaceutical Regulation: Innovation, Politics and Promissory Science*, Basingstoke: Palgrave Macmillan.

Chapter Eight: Materialism No More

1 William Davies calls this 'productive dissatisfaction' – an idea to which I am indebted. See: Davies, W. (2016), *The Happiness Industry*, London: Verso Books.

2 Such as Fritz Pearls, Aaron Beck, Rollo May, Abraham Maslow and Carl Rogers.

3 I discuss this in more detail in my earlier academic book, from which I am paraphrasing: Davies, J. (2012),

The Importance of Suffering: the value and meaning of emotional discontent, London: Routledge.

4 Fromm, E. (2013), *To Have or To Be*, London: Bloomsbury Academic.

5 Fromm, E. (1993), *The Art of Being*, London: Routledge.

6 Ibid., p.76.

7 Piff, Paul K., et al. (2012), 'Higher social class predicts increased unethical behaviour', *PNAS* 109(11): 4086 4091, https://doi.org/10.1073/pnas.1118373109.

8 Kasser, T. (2003), *The High Price of Materialism*, Boston: MIT Press.

9 Ibid., p.18.

10 Ibid., p.56.

11 Ibid., p.57.

12 Ibid., p.50.

13 Ibid., p.57.

14 Ibid., p.31.

15 Ibid., p.31.

16 Ibid., p.72.

17 Ibid., p.1.

18 Kasser, T. (2018), 'Materialism and living well', in E. Diener, et al. (eds), *Well-Being*, Salt Lake City, UT: DEF Publishers, doi:nobascholar.com.

19 Kasser, T. (2003), *The High Price of Materialism*, Boston: MIT Press, p.17.

20 Dittmar, H., et al. (2014), 'The Relationship Between Materialism and Personal Well-Being: A Meta-Analysis', *Personality Processes and Individual Differences* 107(5), 879–924, doi: 10.1037/a0037409.

21 I'll explore this further in the final chapter, when we look at the damaging effects of income inequality.

22 Steidtmann, Dana, et al. (2012), 'Patient Treatment Preference as a Predictor of Response and Attrition in Treatment for Chronic Depression', *Depression and Anxiety* 29(10):896–905.

23 Khalsa, S. R., et al. (2011), 'Beliefs about the causes of depression and treatment preferences', *Journal of Clinical Psychology* 67(6):539–49, doi: 10.1002/jclp.20785.

24 Pilgrim, D., and Rogers, A. E. (2005), 'Psychiatrists as social engineers: a study of an anti-stigma campaign', *Social Science & Medicine* 61(12):2546–56.

25 Goldstein, Benjamin, and Rosselli, Francine (2003), 'Etiological paradigms of depression: The relationship between perceived causes, empowerment, treatment preferences, and stigma', *Journal of Mental Health* 12:6, 551–63, doi: 10.1080/0963823031000162791 9.

26 Quote taken from: Fraser, G. (2015), 'Giles Fraser: my hopes for the Occupy St Paul's drama that puts me on the stage', *Guardian*, https://www.theguardian.com/stage/2015/may/24/giles-fraser-occupy-london-st-pauls-protest-drama-temple-donmar (accessed Sept. 2019).

Chapter Nine: Dehumanising Productivity

1 Keynes understood the 15-hour week as a result of progress. However, he also cautioned that using leisure appropriately was an art to be cultivated. Managed in the wrong way, it could become an

affliction – it was how it was used that determined how it should be defined. In this view, he mirrored Erich Fromm, who also argued that people could fly from freedom into a host of pathological and unhealthy activities, as argued in his book *The Fear of Freedom.*

2 This idea can be most clearly inferred from his book *The General Theory*, where he discusses the bourgeois savers or hoarders, a group he despised his whole life and whom he felt were partly responsible for the Great Depression. He valued more the investors, who keep a dynamic economy alive, in particular if their investments have a strong social conscience. See: Rothbard, M. N. (2010), *Keynes the Man*, Auburn: Ludwig von Mises Institute.

3 I infer these positions principally from Keynes's autobiographical essay 'My Early Beliefs', where he states the primary beliefs that shaped his life. Significantly influenced by the philosopher G. E. Moore, and speaking of his 'religion', as he called it, he said: 'with wealth, power, popularity or success [my religion] had no concern whatever, they were thoroughly despised'. For Keynes, the prime objects in life 'were love, the creation and enjoyment of aesthetic experience and the pursuit of knowledge'. See: Keynes, J. M. ([1933] 1972), *Essays in Biography*, Vol.10, London: Macmillan. As the economist Piero V. Mini described him: 'Keynes was a Renaissance man with the self-consciousness of an existentialist. He had the breadth of interests, the curiosity

and the genius of the former, together with the depth of passion and restlessness of the latter. Action and introspection, financial activity and literature, history and logic, statistics and psychology, business and book-collecting, the political arena and the theatre ... there were few spheres of human activity or reflection from which he was cut off. And from all of them he derived insights that at the right moment gave rise to observations of startling originality.' See: Mini, Piero V. (1991), *Keynes, Bloomsbury and the General Theory*, London: Palgrave Macmillan.

4 It was led by psychologists such as Carl Rogers, Carl Jung, Abraham Maslow, Otto Rank, Erich Fromm and Clark Moustakas (to mention a few).

5 Petrarch in his *secretum meum* argued that we possess vast intellectual and creative potential, which we must use to the full. God had bestowed these attributes to be used in his glory, so to the extent we applied them, we would approximate to his divinity and thus partake in his glory. In 1486, Pico's *Oration on the Dignity of Man* argued that all God's creatures existed upon a chain that led to heaven, and humans enjoyed a high position on this chain. In order to ascend its highest levels, we must develop and exercise our intellectual and contemplative capacities. Our ability to manifest our development in cultural and intellectual works was what conferred our status and dignity. Paraphrased from: Davies, J. (2011), *The Importance of Suffering: the value and meaning of emotional*

discontent, London: Routledge, p.182.

6 Spinoza, in his *Ethics* of 1677, believed that all living beings contained a *conatus* – the tendency inherent in all things to increase their power and strive for perfection. The *conatus* directed our acts along routes developing our highest capacities. However, we would become frustrated and destructive when our *conatus* was impeded. Paraphrased from: Davies, J. (2011), *The Importance of Suffering: the value and meaning of emotional discontent*, London: Routledge, p.182. Adam Smith believed that any government intervention inhibiting the development and expression of our 'God-given talents' would interfere with the processes by which the betterment of society and the individual was achieved. State over-involvement took from our hands our right to develop our moral and economic lives in ways furthering our capacity for creativity and initiative. Nations could only flourish when their citizens were free to follow their own initiative and talents. Paraphrased from: Davies, J. (2011), *The Importance of Suffering: the value and meaning of emotional discontent*, London: Routledge, p.182.

7 As Copleston says of Mill's ideas: '[Mill] ... insists that the principle of utility demands that every man should be free to develop his powers according to his own will and judgement, provided that he does not do so in a way which interferes with the exercise of a similar freedom by others. It is not in the common interest that all should be moulded or expected to conform to the same pattern. On the contrary, society is enriched in proportion as individuals develop themselves freely. [Mill says]: "The free development of individuality is one of the principal ingredients of human happiness, and quite the chief ingredient of individual and social progress." Hence the need for liberty.' Copleston quoted in: Davies, J. (2011), *The Importance of Suffering: the value and meaning of emotional discontent*, London: Routledge, p.182. Humboldt, in his *Limits of State Action*, wrote: 'The end of man ... is the highest and most harmonious development of his powers to a complete and consistent whole.' He believed that 'the object on which every human being must ceaselessly direct his efforts, and on which especially those who design to influence their fellow men must ever keep their eyes, is the individuality of power and development.' Humboldt quoted in: Davies, J. (2011), *The Importance of Suffering: the value and meaning of emotional discontent*, London: Routledge, p.182.

8 Keynes's admiration for self-betterment was most acutely seen in his admiration for the idea of philosopher kings – a state of leadership embodying the highest human integrity.

9 Marx discussed the concept of 'species-essence', which capitalism failed to realise by the alienation it caused – being 'alienated', in other words, meant being estranged from certain vital parts of our human nature. Only a different

social system could enable us to re-engage with these parts so that we could once more be fully human. The system allowing our full human realisation he termed 'communism'. Only living under this new system would human beings be able to fully exercise their human nature and individuality. Paraphrased from: Davies, J. (2011), *The Importance of Suffering: the value and meaning of emotional discontent*, London: Routledge, pp.182–3.

10 Of course, the irony here is that the UK has been in a slump of productivity for years, while the Germans and Scandinavians, who have a more social version of the market, have far higher productivity levels.

11 APA (1980), *Diagnostic and Statistical Manual of Mental Disorders*, 3rd edn, Washington DC: American Psychiatric Association, p.xxii.

12 Ibid., 12.

13 Mayes, R. and Horwitz A. (2005), DSM-III and the revolution in the classification of mental illness. *Journal of the History of the Behavioral Sciences* 41(3):249-67.

14 See: Greenberg, P. E., et al. (1993), 'The economic burdens of depression in 1990', *Journal of Clinical Psychiatry* 54:405–18. Crott, R. G., and Gilis, P. (1998), 'Economic comparisons of the pharmacotherapy of depression: An overview', *Acta Psychiatrica Scandinavia* 97:241–52.

15 Krause, R. (2005), 'Depression, antidepressants and an examination of epidemiological changes', *Journal of Radical Psychology* 4(1).

16 This new narrative soon began to change how we did things on the ground. During the mid 1980s, for example, workplace 'employee assistant programmes' would flourish, expanding their remit to cover workplace mental distress, largely through making mental health referrals. See: Attridge, M., et al. (2009), 'History and growth of the EAP field', *EASNA Research Notes* 1(1):1–4.

Chapter Ten: You Only Have Yourself to Blame

1 See: Davies, J., et al. (2018), *Antidepressant Withdrawal: A Survey of Patients' Experience* (an APPG for PDD report).

2 Diagnoses for me were therefore unhelpful medical descriptions, telling me more about how many doctors view human experience than about what matters: the stories, struggles, needs and hopes of the people seeking help. Indeed, as there are no objective tests (no blood, saliva or urine tests or any other kind of physical examination) that can verify any diagnosis (and this is because, unlike in general medicine, no biological causes or markers for any mental disorders have been discovered), none had been given any objective evidence that their sufferings constituted a pathological medical condition. This approach, while held as the gold standard in mental health

services, would in truth lead to little other than the illusion of understanding for doctors, and stigma and self-stigma for patients, while the medications themselves, although helpful for some of the more severely distressed in the short term, were in the long term holding people back. Furthermore, their effects ended up confusing us all: what experience was drug-induced and what the product of the person or the condition? After some time, nobody would really know any more, patient, psychologist or doctor.

3 This evidence explains not only why placebos (i.e. sugar pills) work as well as antidepressants for most people (they work because they are administered through a doctor/ patient relationship), but also why it is the quality of relationship developed between professional and patient (irrespective of the intervention being deployed) that best predicts how well a person will recover.

4 From the 1960s onwards, research into what has been called 'equivalence' had a seminal affect on psychotherapy. This research showed that when different psychological therapies are compared, they all broadly perform equally well, or equivalently, assuming the same amount of contact time between patient and therapist. What appeared to shape outcomes was less the mode of therapy deployed than the quality of the relationship developed between therapist and client, a theory that has been broadly asserted ever since. I have written more about

this here: Davies, J. (2019), 'Lessons from the Anthropological Field: reflecting on where culture and psychotherapy meet', in Martin, K., *Psychotherapy and the Work of Culture*, London: Routledge.

5 Kendrick, Tony, et al. (2009), 'Management of depression in UK general practice in relation to scores on depression severity questionnaires: analysis of medical record data', *BMJ* 338:b750.

6 Ilyas, S., and Moncrieff, J. (2012), 'Trends in prescriptions and costs of drugs for mental disorders in England, 1998–2010', *British Journal of Psychiatry* 200(5):393–8, doi:10.1192/bjp.bp.111.104257.

7 PHQ-9 and GAD-7 are less frequently used in primary care today, although they are used throughout IAPT services and as online diagnostic tools on the NHS.

8 Jacque Peretti, *Billion Dollar Deals and How They Changed Your World: Health*, BBC2, 2017.

9 I refer here in particular to Frederic Hayek, in whose *Road to Serfdom* he equates social democracy with communism.

10 Indeed, Friedman's most popular book captures this idea: Friedman, M. (1980), *Free to Choose*, New York: Pelican Books.

11 When Friedman met Thatcher in Downing Street soon after she was elected prime minster, he was concerned that her message had recently slackened. She needed to keep emphasising the link between new capitalism and freedom. As Nigel Lawson put it to Thatcher at the time: Friedman 'privately fears that the government are concentrating too much on the

mechanical means and ignoring the moral ends'. In other words, use the rhetoric of freedom to take the moral ground. See published memo from Lawson to Thatcher, http:/ /fc95d419f4478b3b6e5f3f71d0f e2b653c4f00f32175760e96e7. r87.cf1.rackcdn.com/E6DD 924ED1284679BC1A6 7C63ABA99E0.pdf (accessed July 2018).

12 The information and quotes for this anecdote are derived from an excellent article by Philip Maughan, which I directly paraphrase: Maughan, P. (2013), 'Mental health and Mrs Thatcher: "All due to a lack of personal drive, effort and will" – A discussion over dinner', *New Statesman*, https://www. newstatesman.com/lifestyle/2013/ 05/mental-health-and-mrs-thatcher-all-due-lack-personal-drive-effort-and-will (accessed Jan. 2020).

13 The interview appeared in *Woman's Own*. Source: Thatcher Archive,

THCR 5/2/262, https://www. margaretthatcher.org/document/ 106689 (accessed Jan. 2020).

14 Field, Frank (2009), 'Thatcher wasn't perfect, but she helped bring shipping jobs to Birkenhead', https://www.politicshome.com/ thehouse/article/thatcher-wasnt-perfect-but-she-helped-bring-shipping-jobs-to-birkenhead (accessed Nov. 2020).

15 Public Health England (2019), Prescribed Medicines Review: *Report*, https://www.gov.uk/ government/publications/ prescribed-medicines-review-report.

16 See: Kleinman, A. (1997), *Social suffering*, Oakland: University of California Press. Das, V., Kleinman, A., Lock, M., Ramphele, M. and Reynolds, P., et al. (eds.) (2001), *Remaking a world: violence, social suffering and recovery*, Oakland: University of California Press.

Chapter Eleven: The Social Determinants of Distress

1 The Equality Trust (2020), 'The scale of economic inequality in the UK', https://www.equalitytrust.org. uk/scale-economic-inequality-uk (accessed Aug. 2020).

2 Class: The Centre for Labour and Social Studies (2017), 'The Facts – Inequality', http://classonline.org. uk/blog/item/the-facts-inequality.

3 Full Fact (2018), 'Does the UK have the Poorest Regions in Northern Europe?', https://fullfact.org/ economy/does-uk-have-poorest-regions-northern-europe/.

4 Ibid.

5 Cribb, J. (2018), 'Income inequality in the UK', Institute for Fiscal Studies (IFS), https://www.ifs.org. uk/docs/ER_JC_2013.pdf.

6 The Equality Trust (2019), 'The Scale of Economic Inequality in the UK', https://www.equalitytrust.org. uk/scale-economic-inequality-uk.

7 Whichever way you look at it, taxation policy in the era of new capitalism has avowedly favoured the rich over the poor, even when you take receipt of state benefits

into account. According to the Office of National Statistics, net income inequality is decreased by the benefit system (from XII to x4), at least of those in receipt of benefits. See: ONS (2019), 'Effects of taxes and benefits on UK household income: financial year ending 2019', https://www.ons.gov.uk/peoplepopulationandcommunity/personalandhouseholdfinances/incomeandwealth/bulletins/theeffectsoftaxesandbenefitsonhouseholdincome/financialyearending2019 (accessed Aug. 2020).

8 Wilkinson, Richard, and Pickett, Kate, The Equality Trust, http://www.equalitytrust.org.uk/why/evidence/physical-health (accessed Jan. 2021).

9 As the debates are too extensive to cover here, any interested reader can consult them online at The Equality Trust: https://www.equalitytrust.org.uk/.

10 Wilkinson, Richard, and Pickett, Kate, The Equality Trust, http://www.equalitytrust.org.uk/why/evidence/physical-health (accessed Jan. 2021).

11 Layte, Richard, and Whelan, Christopher T. (2014), 'Who Feels Inferior? A Test of the Status Anxiety Hypothesis of Social Inequalities in Health', *European Sociological Review* 30(4)525–35, https://doi.org/10.1093/esr/jcu057.

12 Wilkinson, R., and Pickett, K. (2018), *The Inner Level: How More Equal Societies Reduce Stress, Restore Sanity and Improve Everyone's Well-Being.* London: Allen Lane, p.5.

13 Bowles, S., and Jayadev, A. (2014), 'The Great Divide: one nation under guard', *New York Times*, https://opinionator.blogs.nytimes.com/2014/02/15/one-nation-under-guard/.

14 An excellent resource to consider, which complies much of this research, is the Power Threat Meaning Framework, see: Johnstone, L., & and Boyle, M., with Cromby, J., et al., Dillon, J., Harper, D., Kinderman, P., Longden, E., Pilgrim, D. & Read, J. (2018), *The Power Threat Meaning Framework: Towards the identification of patterns in emotional distress, unusual experiences and troubled or troubling behaviour, as an alternative to functional psychiatric diagnosis.* Leicester: British Psychological Society.

15 Marmot, M. (2020), 'Michael Marmot: Post COVID-19, we must build back fairer', BMJ Opinion, December 15, 2020 https://blogs.bmj.com/bmj/2020/12/15/michael-marmot-post-covid-19-we-must-build-back-fairer/?utm_source=twitter&utm_medium=social&utm_term=hootsuite&utm_content=sme&utm_campaign=usage.

16 The two reports from which I paraphrase, quote and summarise are: Pūras, D. (2017), Statement by Mr Dainius Pūras, Special Rapporteur, on the right of everyone to the enjoyment of the highest attainable standard of physical and mental health at the 35th session of the Human Rights Council, https://www.ohchr.org/en/

NewsEvents/Pages/DisplayNews. aspx?NewsID=22052&LangID=E (accessed Feb. 2020); and Pūras, D. (2019), Right of everyone to the enjoyment of the highest attainable standard of physical and mental health, Human Rights Council, United Nations https://www. un.org/en/ga/search/view_doc. asp?symbol=A/HRC/41/34 (accessed Feb. 2020).

17 As Pūras also admitted, the biomedical model itself can be useful for a minority of patients when used properly. 'If a patient starts to behave in an unusual way and you then find that he has a brain tumour', said Pūras 'then you apply the biomedical model – you identify the pathology and then tackle it. But in mental health this only works in about one of every 10,000 cases, despite psychiatry saying it applies across the board.'

18 See: Davies, J. (2013), *Cracked: why psychiatry is doing more harm than good*, London: Icon Books.

Conclusion

1 The groups and organisations are many. Those that embody – in full or in part – the aforementioned principles include:
The Association for Humanistic Psychology Practitioners
Drop the Disorder
Hearing Voices Network
Psychologists for Social Change
Recovery in the Bin
Soteria Network
Open Dialogue UK
National Survivors User Network
Mindful Occupation
Council for Evidence-based Psychiatry
Mad in the UK
Critical Psychiatry Network
Mental Health Europe
Critical Mental Health Nursing Network
The Free Psychotherapy Network
The Alliance for Counselling and Psychotherapy
The United Kingdom Council for Psychotherapy
The British Association of Counselling and Psychotherapy
The British Psychological Society
The Association of Clinical Psychologists

2 Saad-Filho, A. (2020), 'From COVID-19 to the End of Neoliberalism', *Critical Sociology*, https://doi.org/10.1177/0896920520929966 (accessed 29 May 2020).

3 Mutikani, Lucia, 'What to know about the report on America's COVID-hit GDP', World Economic Forum, https://www.weforum. org/agenda/2020/07/covid-19-coronavirus-usa-united-states-economy-gdp-decline/ (accessed Oct. 2020). BBC News, https:// www.bbc.co.uk/news/business-53918568 (accessed 26 Aug. 2020).

4 Comas-Herrera, Adelina (2020), 'Mortality associated with COVID-19 outbreaks in care homes: early international evidence', ILTCPN, 2020, https://ltccovid.org/

2020/04/12/mortality-associated-with-covid-19-outbreaks-in-care-homes-early-international-evidence/ (accessed Oct. 2020).

5 Van Lancker, Wim, and Parolin, Zachary (2020), 'COVID-19, school closures, and child poverty: a social crisis in the making', *Lancet Public Health*, https://doi.org/10.1016/S2468-2667(20)30084-0.

6 BBC News Online (2020), 'Coronavirus: higher death rate in poorer areas, ONS figures suggest', https://www.bbc.co.uk/news/uk-52506979 (accessed Jan. 2021).

7 Weale, Sally (2020), 'Four in 10 pupils have had little contact with teachers during lockdown', *Guardian*, https://www.theguardian.com/education/2020/jun/15/2m-children-in-uk-have-done-almost-no-school-work-in-lockdown (accessed Sept. 2020).

8 Saad-Filho, A. (2020), 'From COVID-19 to the End of Neoliberalism', *Critical Sociology*, https://doi.org/10.1177/0896920520929966.

9 Sheridan, Danielle (2020), 'Companies accused of furlough fraud after data found two thirds of workers carried on working', *Telegraph*, https://www.telegraph.co.uk/news/2020/08/23/companies-accused-furlough-fraud-data-found-two-thirds-workers/ (accessed Sept. 2020).

10 Campbell, Denis (2020), 'UK lockdown causing "serious mental illness in first-time patients"', *Guardian*, https://www.theguardian.com/society/2020/may/16/uk-lockdown-causing-serious-mental-illness-in-first-time-patients (accessed Sept. 2020).

11 Office for National Statistics (2020), 'Coronavirus and depression in adults, Great Britain: June 2020', https://www.ons.gov.uk/peoplepopulationandcommunity/wellbeing/articles/coronavirusanddepressioninadultsgreatbritain/june2020 (accessed Sept. 2020).

12 Fujiwara, Daniel (2020), 'The Wellbeing Costs of COVID-19 in the UK. An Independent Research Report by Simetrica-Jacobs and the London School of Economics and Political Science', https://www.jacobs.com/sites/default/files/2020-05/jacobs-wellbeing-costs-of-covid-19-uk.pdf (accessed Oct. 2020).

13 NHS (2020), 'BSA Medicines Used in Mental Health, England 2015/16 to 2019/20', https://nhsbsa-opendata.s3-eu-west-2.amazonaws.com/mh-annual-narrative-final.html (accessed Sept. 2020).

14 Pierce, Mathias (2020), 'Mental health before and during the COVID-19 pandemic: a longitudinal probability sample survey of the UK population', *Lancet Psychiatry* 7(10):10883–92.

15 Public Health England (2020), 'Guidance for the public on the mental health and wellbeing aspects of coronavirus (COVID-19)', https://www.gov.uk/government/publications/covid-19-guidance-for-the-public-on-mental-health-and-wellbeing/guidance-for-the-public-on-the-mental-health-and-wellbeing-aspects-of-coronavirus-covid-19 (accessed Oct. 2020).

16 The Collective Psychology Project (2020), 'Collective Resilience: How we've protected our mental health during COVID-19', https:/

/www.collectivepsychology.org/
wpcontent/uploads/2020/09/
Collective-Resilience.pdf (accessed
Oct. 2020).

17 Social & Human Capital Coalition
(2020), 'Only 9 per cent of Britons
Want Life to Return to "Normal"
Once Lockdown Is Over', https://
social-human-capital.org/only-9-
of-britons-want-life-to-return-to-
normal-once-lockdown-is-over/
(accessed Oct. 2020).

18 UCL (2020), 'Third of people report
enjoying lockdown', https://www.
ucl.ac.uk/epidemiology-health-care/
news/2020/jul/third-people-report-
enjoying-lockdown (accessed Oct.
2020).

19 Harrabin, Roger, 'Climate change:
Could the coronavirus crisis spur
a green recovery?', BBC Online,
https://www.bbc.co.uk/news/
science-environment-52488134
(accessed Oct. 2020).

20 Lenton, Timothy (2019), 'Climate
tipping points – too risky to bet
against', *Nature*, https://www.
nature.com/articles/d41586-019-
03595-0 (accessed Oct. 2020).

21 In this conviction I follow many
good evidence-based reasons. In
particular, see the compelling
arguments set down in David M.
Kotz's excellent book, *The Rise and
Fall of Neoliberal Capitalism*, Boston:
Harvard University Press.

INDEX